The Story of
The Lygon Arms

Alison R. Ridley and Curtis F. Garfield
Illustrated by Robert Roy Evans

The Story of The Lygon Arms

Printed and bound in Great Britain by Burgess,
Thames View, Abingdon, Oxfordshire OX14 3LE.

Copyright © 1992 by Porcupine Enterprises, 1 Springhill
Cottages, Snowshill, Broadway, Worcestershire.
All rights reserved.

ISBN 0-9621976-1-0

In memory of the Russell family,
who inspired an abiding love
of The Lygon Arms and its traditions.

The authors gratefully acknowledge the ongoing support of Managing Director Kirk Ritchie and the staff of The Lygon Arms.

Credits

Archives Historian	Susan Campbell
Diagrams	William J. Bylund
Designer	John Rumery
Editor	Virginia R. Ellis, M.A., Oxon.
Editorial Consultant	A. de Bonneval
Historical Consultants	Canon Ronald Appleton, M.A., Oxon.
	Charles Wrong, M.A., Oxon.
Maps	Peter A. Price
Proof Readers	T. Frederick, Nicholas Scarf
Special Assignments	Roderick Bryant, James Ellis

****

Pen and ink drawings by Gordon Russell included by special arrangement with Trevor Chinn, Archivist, Gordon Russell Trust.

Permissions

The following material has been included by permission:

The Broadway Parish Register, (1532-1710), courtesy of Nicholas Harrison, Archivist, Worcester County Record Office.

Inventory of estate of Phillip Hodges, innkeeper, White Hart Inn, 1680, courtesy of Nicholas Harrison.

1903 Inventory of The Lygon Arms by permission of Trevor Chinn, Archivist, Gordon Russell Trust.

"The Monks of Pershore" by Margaret Bramford, from *The Book of Pershore*, by Philip Barrett.

The 1675 Map by John Ogilby, cosmographer to King Charles II, photographed courtesy of Robert and Sarah Steen, the White Hart Royal, Moreton-in-Marsh.

TABLE OF CONTENTS

Acknowledgements..vii
Introduction..xi
Prologue:
    Twenty Farms and
    Twelve White Harts xiii

Whyte and Sambache Era:
15th and 16th Centuries

I.   "Whyte of Bradway"..3
II.   "Five Silver Spoons"...17
III. "By Champaine Ground...14 Longe Myles"......................33
IV. "Your Highness Is Come Unto Cotswold" 39
V.   "These High, Wild Hills and Rough, Uneven Ways"........43

Treavis Era:
17th Century

VI. "My House or Inn...
     Called the Whyte Harte" 55
VII. "The King with All his Army"..67
VIII. "A Crowning Mercy" - Aftermath.....................................79
IX. "At The Signe of the Whyte Harte" 89

Cormell and Torrington Era:
18th Century

X.   "A Common Inn, Situate in Broadway..." 97
XI.   "A Most Comfortable Cleanly House...
     the White Hart.." 107

Lygon and Drury Era:
19th Century

XII. Spring Hill Manors and "the Lygon's Arms"..................115
XIII. "One of the Finest Hunting Districts in the
Kingdom"..129

The Russell Era:
20th Century

XIV. "Ha'pennies Make Pennies and Pennies Make Pounds" 141
XV. "A Family Business"...155
XVI. "The Fortunate Proprietor"..165

Epilogue:
    The Savoy Hotels: Towards the 21st Century................171

End Notes..175
Appendices..187
Opinions About the Architecture....................................199
Diagrams of Rooms...139, 208, 209
Bibliography..211
Index 215

Full-page illustrations:
The Abbot of Pershore in his Broadway pastures xii
"Whyte of Bradway" and wool merchants 2
Fair on the feast of St. John the Baptist, 24th June, 1535............16
Elizabethan rider above Broadway 42
Ursula Treavis in the Inglenook kitchen 54
King Charles I and his cavalry..66
Viscount Torrington at the White Hart Inn, 1787 106
The Lygon Family of Spring Hill, mid-1820's 114
Charles Drury's era: coach and travellers 128
Sydney Russell and Henry Ford, 1928 140

Acknowledgements

The Story of The Lygon Arms has come into being with the help of a great many people. During all past centuries, armies have campaigned through the Cotswold hills. To create this narrative we enlisted a small army of our own: experts in various fields who have soldiered with us for the past three years, undertaking seemingly impossible missions without hesitation. We try below to acknowledge as many of these colleagues as possible.

Our special thanks to Kirk Ritchie, Managing Director of The Lygon Arms, who first endorsed the idea of this history and encouraged us to proceed. His single-minded conviction and unwavering support are responsible for the creation of this book. For his faith in us we are grateful, but any errors of omission or commission in the text are ours alone.

We are also grateful to Barry Hancox and the entire staff of The Lygon Arms, who made available to us on a continuing basis, the rich resources of the inn and graciously endured our frequent intrusions and ceaseless questions.

We are greatly indebted to Sydney Bolton Russell and his oldest son, Gordon, who published, in 1914, a small book entitled *The Story of an Old English Hostelry*, researched and illustrated by Gordon Russell. This chronicle provided valuable background and suggested new paths to explore. The first glimmerings of this present history began some years ago in conversations with Sir Gordon and Lady Russell at Kingcombe and are acknowledged here as a primary debt of gratitude.

We are enormously grateful to Douglas J. Barrington, who steered The Lygon Arms from the end of World War II into the modern era. He courteously shared with us his special knowledge of previous decades, made available to us his personal scrapbooks—a heritage from the Russell family—and collaborated with patience and understanding.

Two distinguished scholars, Canon Ronald Appleton and historian Charles Wrong, generously contributed historical advice. Their tolerance and good humour were as unwavering as their criticisms were just. Canon Appleton, former Vicar of Winchcombe, undertook a number of unusual quests in archives and libraries; his knowledge of the ecclesiastical history of Worcestershire in the early centuries was indispensable, as was his wise, sustaining counsel. Charles Wrong reviewed the entire manuscript in its final stages; his penetrating scholarship, his detailed knowledge of the history of England, and his stylistic cogency have been crucial to the completion of this endeavour.

Our warmest thanks to Susan Campbell, Archives historian, Worcester County Record Office, who has not only provided meticulous archival research but has collaborated with an interest and enthusiasm beyond the call of duty. Her knowledge of the sources of local history is extraordinary, as is her unerring instinct for uncovering nuggets of hitherto buried historical treasure.

A. de Bonneval, herself the author of several institutional histories, gave us important editorial assistance and coped with special research assignments. We welcomed her bracing wit during periods of tribulation as well as her subtle expertise. The scrupulous and unremitting attention to details provided by Nicholas Scarf in the final production weeks has been invaluable. Unwavering support was also given by Colonel and Mrs. F.A. Scott, whose devotion to The Lygon Arms began more than forty years ago.

Numerous individuals in archives and libraries gave us timely assistance. We are indebted to the entire staff of the Worcester County Record Offices at Spetchley Road and St. Helens; particular thanks go to Nicholas Harrison, Archivist, who devoted many hours to transcribing and interpreting the Broadway Parish Register of 1532, concerning the repair of the churchyard wall, and the will and inventory of Thomas White, 8th August, 1556.

We are especially grateful to Colin Harris, Principal Library Assistant, Department of Western Manuscripts, Bodleian Library, Oxford, who came to our rescue in several crises; Rachel Roberts, Archivist, and Rachel Heath, Archives Assistant, Birmingham Library Services; Mairi Macdonald, Deputy Archivist, Shakespeare Birthplace Trust; the staff of the Gloucester County Record Office; and Trevor Chinn, Archivist, Gordon Russell Trust. We also acknowledge the help of Librarians Sheila Duggan and Gillian Brown of the Broadway Library, both of whom have helped us in unusual and time-consuming ways; Librarian Cathy Evans and the staff of the Evesham Library, in particular Neil Alderson, Pauline Prew and Joan Robertshaw; and the continuing assistance of Susan Hand, Sally Linden, and Claire Loranz of the Research Division of the Clapp Library, Wellesley College, Wellesley, Massachusetts.

We acknowledge the generous help of Canon David St. Z. Welander of Gloucester Cathedral and of Dr. Roger Mortimer, Archivist, Westminster Abbey, both of whom supplied missing pieces of the puzzle. We owe a particular debt of gratitude to Dr. James Ellis, who not only reviewed the material on William Shakespeare and offered invaluable suggestions, but also provided other expert and wide-ranging editorial advice. We are profoundly grateful to Sir Alexander Glen, who illuminated a previously obscure part of Oliver Cromwell's movements in the autumn of 1651 by recalling a conversation that took place during an Arctic expedition in 1935.

Other specialised assistance was provided by solicitors Dorothy Montouris and Angela Woodruff, who transcribed complex legal documents from various centuries; Merian J. Evans, who unearthed a series of Lygon family letters in the Phillipps-Robinson Collection at the Bodleian Library; and architectural historians Nicholas Moore, Richard Morriss, and Bruce Watson, who gave us their views about the inn's complicated architecture. We are also grateful to Trevor Chinn for his crucial and timely assistance and to William Bylund for his patient help.

Colourful details were supplied by several local residents whose varied knowledge of Broadway and the surrounding area have been of the utmost help. We particularly salute Valentine and Gertrude Freeman, who gave unstintingly of their time and memories, and who read the manuscript in various stages of incompletion, offering wise suggestions. We are also grateful to Jack and Olive Hodge, who shared with us anecdotes about Sydney Russell's years of residence at the Tower Close in Snowshill; Stuart Lloyd Drury, for recollections of his family; Jean Lindner for memories of her grandfather, Dr. Rees Price; Ronald Wagner for many stories about The Lygon Arms; and the Sandbach families of Laverton and Cutsdean for memorabilia about the Sambache (Sandbach) family in earlier times. We also thank Dr. Colin Houghton for his initial encouragement.

We acknowledge the dedication of the entire staff of Burgess, in particular we thank Howard Carter, Susan Gale and Stephen Neville. We are also grateful to our colleague, John Rumery, whose design of the book combined talent and supreme patience. Various other individuals have provided timely help. These include Heather Chester, Jane Collard, Maggie Cullen, Pamela Edwards, Sally Hooper, Lena Jordan, Captain G. E. Locker, Jean and Arthur Mills, Gail Ryder, Derek and Marie Seymour, Ann Stanley and Bill and Marie Watson.

Unusual and irreplaceable assistance was given by Roderick Bryant, who grappled successfully with numerous difficult assignments over more than three years. His unique local insights, his puckish good humour and his determination to see the job through have buttressed the authors in all weathers, both literary and climatic.

We are supremely grateful to Virgina R. Ellis, Emma B. Kennedy Professor of English at Mount Holyoke College, South Hadley, Massachusetts, who has been indispensable to the creation of this book from its earliest stages. Her keen scholarship and discerning literary judgement were a constant encouragement throughout, as were her skills as editor in the final months. Her contribution to this history is beyond measure.

Finally, we salute the long-lasting influence of the late A.B. Rodger. His rigorous schooling and buoyant enthusiasm first encouraged us to explore the obscure coppices of past centuries, not as a dry and dusty path, but as a treasure hunt full of wonder and delight. Without the sustaining memory of his discipline and imagination this book would not exist.

Trackway, and Camp and City lost,
Salt Marsh where now is corn
Old Wars, old Peace, old Arts that cease,
And so was England born.

—Rudyard Kipling

INTRODUCTION

The story of The Lygon Arms spans more than four centuries, at least twenty innkeepers, and many reigning monarchs of England. It is one of the world's most famous hostelries, in the heart of England's green and pleasant land. Pack horses from the wool trade have stopped here, King Charles I's cavalry, and the North Cotswold Hunt. Stage-coaches, carriages, Model T's, aeroplanes and Jaguars have brought guests to its doors. It has been a resting place for royalty, a retreat for travelling noblemen, a refuge for weary soldiers, a haven for artists and literary people, and a gathering-place for statesmen. It has witnessed great and small events in the lives of great and ordinary people from all walks of life and several continents.

A churchman's farm, a hospitable manor house, a small inn for wool merchants, a growing hostelry, the best among English country inns and now a world famous hotel—it has been all these. From the White Hart and the White Swan, emblems of medieval kings, to the "Lygon's Arms" for generals who fought at the Battle of Waterloo, this ancient house has grown and flourished.

Its story combines strong tradition with proven history. The early years are conjecture, but closely-reasoned conjecture, based on what evidence remains. From the tenth to the fourteenth centuries we are dealing in probabilities only. Saxon King Eadgar, Abbot Foldbrith of Pershore, Richard II and his white hart livery, the Merchant Staplers on their way to the coast— these figures are dimly perceived, just visible. By the mid-fifteenth century we arrive on firmer ground when Whyte of Bradway first appears on the scene.

From then on the Lygon's story becomes clearer: as facts emerge the road is plainly marked. The procession of innholders, their families and customers, mingle with local and national events to mirror the life of the inn and the nation. The progresses of Queen Elizabeth I, the armies of the great Civil War, the loss of the American colonies, the long struggle with Napoleon, the reign of Queen Victoria and the two World Wars—all these have touched the Lygon, directly and indirectly.

We have attempted to trace the faint outline of earlier times, fragments of tradition and folklore, as well as the evidence uncovered by long searching of legal records, because we believe that people who visit the Lygon today will want to know as much as possible about this old yet modern Inn. History, as Trevelyan has pointed out, is not just dry-as-dust facts but the "fair field full of folk". This is uniquely true of the Lygon. We hope that visitors may, with us, revere and rejoice in "this our ancient house".

972-1399 A.D.

Prologue

Twenty Farms and Twelve White Harts

Long before there was a Lygon Arms, or a White Hart Inn, or even a village of Broadway, sheep grazed on Broadway downs. If it were not for the sheep, there might never have been a village here in this cup of the hills, and certainly no need for an inn. But there were sheep, and consequently there is a story to tell.

Bones found in ancient barrows show that there were sheep on the upland pastures of Broadway as long ago as the Iron Age. Later, the Romans prized the Cotswold wool so highly they sent it back to Rome. "The wool of Britain is spun so fine," said Alexandrinus, "that it is in a manner comparable to the spider's thread."[1]

Even the small sheep that the Romans brought with them were so well nourished on the forage enriched by Cotswold limestone that they grew thick and heavy fleeces. Later, at the height of the wool trade, thousands of sheep would graze here and their "golden fleece" would become the backbone of England's economy for generations.

These same rich pastures of Bradanwege (Broadway) were later farmed by the Saxons. They were specifically mentioned in one of the earliest records of the division of land in Worcestershire, the Charter of King Eadgar in 972 A.D. At the ancient royal capital of Winchester, before a "glittering gathering of all the mighty men of the kingdom,"[2] the young king signed the document that founded the Abbey of Pershore and forged the first links that led to Broadway's prosperity and the beginnings of The Lygon Arms as we know it today.

King Eadgar's Charter shows the exact number of manors in each village awarded to the newly-founded royal convent. Longton or Langatune, is at the top of the list with thirty manors, and Broadway or Bradanwege is next with twenty. In a total of forty-three villages named, most have ten, seven, five or fewer manors as the total farmed.[3] Thus, sheep farming was well established in Broadway before 1000 A.D.

The oldest Abbey records indicate that between 972 and 1086 these twenty Broadway sheep farms were operating "in demesne for the Abbot's table."[4] Abbot Foldbrith, the first abbot (984-988), and his successors came periodically to oversee these flourishing farms. In very early times the monks probably lodged in an old settlement near what is now St. Eadburgha's Church. Whether or not there was, at the same time, salt mutton on a trestle table in a farmhouse located near the site of today's Lygon Arms cannot be proved. It is certainly possible. Such a vast flock would have required a large number of workers and a lodging place near the church could not have housed them all.

Exactly when the Church was built is not known. Princess Eadburgha was King Eadgar's aunt and the grand-daughter of King Alfred the Great (871-901). There is a tradition that when Eadburgha was a child she was offered the choice between some bright jewels and a book of the gospels; without hesitation, she chose the scriptures. From that day she lived a life of piety, eventually becoming a prominent member of the Convent of Winchester. She was renowned for good works in her lifetime, and after her death miracles were reported.

Oddo, an eleventh century Mercian overlord, paid one hundred pounds, a great price for that time, to move some of her bones to the Abbey of Pershore. He spent most of his life atoning for the sins of two of his ancestors, both notorious despoilers of church lands, and one so evil he is said to have been "eaten alive by vermin." Oddo was a great benefactor of Pershore Abbey and devoted to Eadburgha. It is therefore possible that Eadburgha was canonized* and that the first Broadway church was built some time between her death in 960 and Oddo's own death in 1056.[5]

The official construction date is between 1122 and 1200 A.D., but it could have been somewhat earlier. There is an unusual record in the 1086 Domesday survey for the village of Bretforton,[6] less than five miles from

---

* We do not know exactly when Eadburgha became a saint. In the early days of Christianity before 1171 A.D., it was customary for people to become saints in their own country by popular accord and soon after they died. Eadburgha was a much-loved Anglo-Saxon princess and after her bones were moved to Pershore, legends about her would have grown. Historian Rees Price believes the church dedication to be an original Anglo-Saxon one. He cites Thomas Habington, who, in turn, quotes William of Malmesbury: "Here in Pershore rest some of the bones of happy Eadburgh, which are instantly cclebrated with reverence, which she hath merited with the glory of miracles, more often shown in this place than in any other."

Broadway: "there are oxen for one plough but they draw stone to the church."* Thirty years before Domesday, when Oddo had become a respected monk at Pershore Abbey, oxen may well have hauled stones to build his memorial to Eadburgha before he died. The great abbey bells voiced the faith of Saint and overlord through succeeding centuries, as they still sound today.

Ten years after Oddo's death William the Conqueror swept across the Channel from Normandy and took over the realm, but the Broadway sheep farms continued to prosper. Although the Saxon King Edward the Confessor, Eadgar's grandson, had given away a vast area of the Pershore lands to Westminster Abbey in 1065, by the time of the Domesday survey in 1086 when William had "deep speech with his wise men" in Gloucester to begin the accounting of his lands, the Broadway manors remained under Pershore control.[7]

The object of the Domesday survey was to describe in precise detail quantities of land, or hides, paying geld, or tax, to the King. A hide was that quantity of land capable of supporting one family and being worked by one plough team, roughly 120 acres in modern terms.[8] The Latin document says, in part:

> The Land of Saint Mary of Persore...held and still holds the manor of Persore itself.... This same church holds Bradeweia. [Broadway] There are thirty hides paying geld [tax]. In demesne are three ploughs and a priest and forty-two villeins [villagers] with twenty ploughs; there are eight serfs [slaves]. Total in King Edward's time was worth twelve pounds, ten shillings; it is now worth fourteen pounds, ten shillings....[9]

Some of these valuable lands were seized by Urse (The Bear) d'Abitot, a powerful and rapacious Norman nobleman who was Sheriff of Worcestershire for forty years and had a reputation for acquiring land "by fair means and foul."[10] His descendants, however, remembered him

---

* "Ibi sunt boves ad i carucam sed petram trahunt ad aecclesiam."
The official who made this note seems to be disapproving of the job assigned to the oxen and to think they should be doing something more strenuous and less devout, hence the use of the word "sed."
This "aecclesiam" referred to by the Norman official may have been the Bretforton village church or it may have been Evesham Abbey, which, under the leadership of Walter of Cerasia and his successors, was extensively rebuilt soon after the Norman Conquest. All nearby villages would have been required to assist in this large effort. However, since Bretforton is one of the few villages so specifically noted in the survey, the possibility exists that these oxen were drawing stones to build or rebuild the local chapel rather than the Abbey and that they might have been similarly employed in Broadway at about the same time. The old stone font, still to be seen in St. Eadburgha's Church, may be pre-Norman.

with enough respect to include his bear in the cognizance of the Earls of Warwick. It is this bear that is one of the supporters of the Lygon coat of arms today.

Despite Urse's greed, the abbots did not lack for lands in their demesne. Pershore Abbey tracts were scattered all over Worcestershire and were substantial enough to support at least fifty monks in Pershore as well as a steady stream of pilgrims and Plantagenet kings. Since these lands were located in outlying corners of the county, Abbot Foldbrith and his successors spent much of their time walking the roads to oversee their widespread holdings. Monastic life was by no means all prayer and meditation:

> Labouring in vineyards, tending wheat and lentils
> Herding sheep and oxen
> Gathering herbs and samples.
> On foot to Broadway, Malvern, Mathon,
> Evesham Stow and Oxford;
> Scything, sowing, gathering, mowing, homewards to the cloister.*[11]

"On foot to Broadway" would have meant a frequent tramp of some fifteen miles. At the end of the day if there was no room at the abbot's house, weary monks would have had to repair to another nearby farm after consuming their food and ale.** During the busy lambing, shearing, and slaughtering seasons, this overflow of monks and shepherds would have been especially large, so it is likely that there was, near the village green and present Lygon Arms, a churchman's manse which not only sheltered the abbot's extra retinue, but may gradually have evolved into a resting place for other holy men on their way to Winchcombe or Pershore.

The abbot and his monks appear to have lived rather well. The first tax record—The Lay Subsidy Roll for the year 1280—shows the Abbot's assessment as five marks,[12] by far the highest in Broadway, so by the mid-thirteenth century at the latest, he was firmly established in the village and kept a comfortable amount of goods and chattels in his house.

One reason the abbot kept a supply of the best food and wine on hand

---

* *The Monks of Pershore*, Margaret Bramford, 1977.
**While wine was drunk only on feast days, ale was a staple of the monks' diet, as was a great quantity of fish. There is an undocumented but persistent legend in Broadway that the Abbots of Pershore brought fish from their pools, fifteen miles distant, to a monastery located where the Fish Inn now stands at the top of Fish Hill. There the holy men are said to have stored the fish in the cool crevices of the nearby quarry. It is more likely that this was the origin of the name "Fish" than the alternative belief that it derives from the irregular twisting of the road up the hill. If there was a monastery where the Fish Inn is now, the abbots had places to stay at both ends of Broadway on their way to Stow and Oxford.

Prologue xvii

in Pershore, gathered from such estates as Bradanwege [Broadway], was the frequency of royal visits. King John was the first of several Plantagenet kings to stay at Pershore Abbey. In August 1204, he commanded the Sheriff of Gloucester to send a large number of casks of wine to the monks. King Edward I visited the Abbey in 1281 when William de Lege was Abbot, stayed for eight days and came again in 1294.[13] The King or some of his retainers may have visited Broadway on one of these occasions; silver Edward I coins were found by workmen when The Lygon Arms was being refurbished in the early 1900's.[14]

These Plantagenet kings may be responsible for the deep-rooted tradition that long ago The Lygon Arms was called the White Hart Inn. The white hart was first used as a royal emblem by King Richard the Lion Heart as part of his seal ring in the late twelfth century. His successors, Edward II and Edward III, visited Pershore Abbey in the early fourteenth century, and Edward III is said to have been responsible for the white harts still to be seen in Gloucester Cathedral. The white hart became even more prominent in the reign of King Richard II, Edward III's grandson, as his personal emblem.

King Henry III came to Pershore Abbey several times and in 1251, the "thirty-fifth year of our reign," singled out Broadway as an appropriate site for a market and fair. His decree "firmly commands" that there shall be "a market in Broadway each week of the month on Friday and one fair each year lasting for three days after the Feast of the Nativity of St. John the Baptist." (24th June)[15]

Fairs had to be granted by the king and would have been allowed only in centres of commerce that served large numbers of people and were far enough apart not to interfere with one another. They were highly competitive events, strictly regulated to produce income for vendors and a tariff for the king. Business was so brisk and crowds so vast that a court of the dusty feet, "pedis pulverisati curia," was held on the fair-ground itself to settle disputes on the spot. The largest fairs lasted for several days, some for weeks, selling principally "corn, ironmongery, leather and wool."[16]

By the time this annual fair was established, Broadway was already a flourishing wool village. The Tax Roll for 1280 reveals that the village supported a blacksmith, a carter, a woodman, a quarryman, a tanner, a pigman, cask and wheel makers, and several shepherds. Broadway also required two mills, and the two millers, Hugh and Simon, paid taxes of three shillings and sixteen pence respectively.[17] The mills that paid this tax were located on the stream that flowed and still flows behind St.

Eadburgha's Church towards Mill Hay. This stream not only provided the power for these mills but supplied water for the abbot to wash his sheep at the time of shearing each spring.

Since the Broadway flock was the largest one overseen by the Abbey, the shearing took place there and was presided over by the Abbot and Prior in person. There is a strong tradition that the abbots of Pershore not only used Broadway as their headquarters to oversee flocks and shepherds as seasons required, but that they stayed in the village for their health during the warm months of the year. The Abbot's Grange near the village green, and the Prior's Manse at the corner of the road to Willersey, are both believed to have been built about 1327.

One local historian has made a strong case for a Medieval village shaped much as Broadway is today, in the form of an "L." He points out that the Abbot's Grange is equidistant from St. Eadburgha's at one end of the village and the Prior's Manse at the other and that these three places would have been focal points of daily life. The green, where the Abbot's courts as well as the jollifications of holy days took place, was in the angle of the "L" as it is today. A short distance behind it was the Abbot's private chapel, located where St. Michael's Church now stands.[18]

The land between these major landmarks would have been inhabited by shepherds and other farmers. This strengthens the likelihood that there was a small inn near where The Lygon Arms now stands, midway between the two religious houses, the Grange and the Manse, able to deal with travellers from either direction.

Moreover, the monks were not allowed to put up every wayfarer. They could house the "very rich and the very poor...noblemen of high rank, royal messengers and pilgrims," but most travellers had to find other accommodation.[19] Since Cotswold wool was highly prized in European markets, and since Broadway was surrounded by some of the best sheep pastures in England, from very early times the village was regularly visited by merchants buying wool and sheepskins. Tired men and horses needed food and a dry place to sleep.

As time went by, an increasing variety of travellers used the roads. Cotswold byways would not have differed greatly from those in southern England traversed not only by Chaucer's religious pilgrims—the Monk, the Prioress, the Friar—but by other professionals, high and low—the Franklin, the Squire and the Miller. There were also pedlars, wandering entertainers—jugglers, pipers and minstrels— itinerant friars, and the ever-present thieves and robbers, often well-organised to spot and rob a group of pack horses and men who might carry a rich prize.[20] But the largest group of law-abiding travellers, apart from the monks, was the merchants, thus portrayed by Chaucer:

> Next all in motley garb a Merchant came
> With a forked beard. High on his horse he sat,
> Upon his head a Flanders beaver hat;
> His boots were buckled fair and fettishly
> He spoke his words with great solemnity,
> And great sagacity in all ways showed;
> No man could tell of any debt he owed...

The poet's words are telling. These merchants sat their horses proudly and dressed well so that potential customers would not suspect that they were worried by large debts as they waited for profits from sales of raw wool on the Continent. These sales could take months, but meanwhile the wool merchant must continue to "ride about in Cotteswolde" with no sign of concern.

The wool traders were part of a complicated network by which England supplied wool, and in later years cloth, to Flanders and the rest of Europe. Their buying and selling kept them constantly on the move. Of all the major exports—wool and wool fells, cheese, butter, tin, and coal—wool topped the list for many generations. The woolsack, the symbolic seat of England's Chancellor in Westminster Hall, was the symbol of the true wealth of both king and commoner.[21]

As the merchants journeyed through the Cotswolds during the summer clip and the Martinmas slaughter, one hostelry in Broadway may have caught their attention. Slightly more than four hundred years after Chaucer's travellers, Lord Byng, visiting the White Hart Inn, (later The Lygon Arms), stated that it "bears all the marks of having been a manor house or manorial inn." Therefore, if the building was first an additional summer residence for the Abbot of Pershore and his retinue, a hundred years later it could have evolved into a convenient place for ordinary merchants to stay.

This inn did not have luxurious accommodation. Guest ate their meals sitting according to rank at long trestle tables. Loaves, joints of mutton and other meats, pasties, nut brown ale and wine were the order of the day. Common travellers slept together in one large room on long, sack-like mattresses stuffed with straw, an exercise that was not without hazard.[22] A manual for travellers of the time gives a bit of sage advice from a veteran of the roads:

> William, undress and wash your legs, then dry them with a cloth and rub them well for the fleas that they may not light on your legs, for there is a peck of them lying in the dust under the rushes. Hi! The fleas bite me so! And do me great harm for I have scratched my shoulders until the blood flows...[23]

Bills for food and lodging were paid separately and were largely a matter of luck. Two travellers in the year 1331 itemized their daily costs for a journey on horseback from Oxford to Durham:

Bread	4 pence	Candles	1/4 pence
Beer	2 pence	Fuel	2 pence
Wine	1 1/2 pence	Beds	2 pence
Meat	5 1/2 pence	Fodder for horses	10 pence[24]
Pottage (soup)	1/4 pence		

Since this party of travellers was from Merton College, accompanied by servants, the travel expenses of a relatively well-off merchant and his packmen were probably similar. Wayfarers complained constantly about prices. In 1350, King Edward III passed a statute to force "hostelers and herbergers" to sell food at a reasonable rate. He intervened again in 1354, to stop "the great and outrageous cost of victuals kept up in all the realm by innkeepers and other retailers of victuals to the great detriment of the people travelling through the realm." [25]

Unfortunately, the king's concern for travellers did not extend to the roads, which were in deplorable condition throughout the Middle Ages, especially in the country districts. The King tried to suggest that their upkeep and repair was a pious and meritorious work so that the Church would take on the expense. In this he showed a subtle cunning. The abbots and their monks, those "vast landed husbandmen," as the king well knew, had their own very secular reasons to keep roads and highways in repair. Consequently, the abbots of Pershore, anxious to sell their wool, would have made sure that the trackways to their sheep farms on the hills near Broadway were in good condition.[26] But the church no longer owned or controlled all the lodging places. The townsmen of the wool villages recognised the need to provide the merchants, who were the lifeblood of their newly-acquired prosperity, with more comfortable places to stay in their spring and autumn travels to the wool collecting centres.

One historian has suggested that a veritable "chain of White Hart Inns" started in different parts of England during the latter part of the fourteenth century or that existing hospitable farmhouses or inns were renamed in honour of the young King Richard II. These inns, he contends, were built by the towns and corporations in response to the growing demands of the merchants:

> To the reigning king alone they looked for any future marks of favour. Hence these inns almost invariably bear the badge of the reigning king. When Richard II was deposed, the White Hart often gave way to the White Swan of Henry IV...Barons and Earls might dispute and make war on one another as to who was the sovereign *in law*; the concern of the towns was with the king *in fact*.[27]

This is a general argument for White Hart inns all over the country, but when it is coupled with other evidence it becomes especially applicable to Broadway. In the year 1377, at the outset of his reign, the personal popularity of King Richard II was immense. Eleven years old when he ascended the throne, he came in on a wave of hope and rejoicing. Whatever lay in store later in his reign, he began as a popular ruler, welcomed and celebrated by his people. Spirits lightened and there was a general feeling that this young man would be just and merciful.[28] The king's youth was, in itself, his greatest asset.*

In the year 1378, young King Richard held a Parliament in the city of Gloucester. He ceremonially visited the great cathedral where his martyred great-grandfather, Edward II, was buried. "Round the great pillars next to Edward's tomb, are painted many figures of stags which uphold the report that at his funeral he was drawn by stags from Berkeley Castle to Gloucester."[29] Richard II is supposed to have completed the work of adorning this tomb when he held his Parliament in the cathedral precincts. "Twelve White Harts chained and gorged with a ducal coronet"[30] are still visible in Gloucester Cathedral today, as is King Richard's "Parliament room" nearby.**

---

*Richard II took over when a deep melancholy pervaded the land. His grandfather, King Edward III, was senile when he died and many of the accomplishments of his fifty years of rule had been forgotten. The Black Prince, hero of the battles of Crécy and Poitiers, had died young. War with France was again a real possibility, and the people were still suffering from the after-effects of the Black Death.
**Until recently, the broom plant, Plantagenista, another royal badge, was also visible on stained glass windows in Gloucester Cathedral. These old windows were moved, but both these badges, the white hart and the Plantagenet broom plant, are still to be seen on Richard II's effigy in Westminster Abbey. More information about the legend of the white hart and its connection with Richard II appears in Appendix A.

News of the young King's visit to Gloucester would have spread throughout the countryside, and Broadway villagers might have celebrated by naming their inn for the boy. There is a tradition that the White Hart Inn in Gloucester dates from the King's visit. Therefore it is probable that the association of Richard II's White Hart emblem with other Cotswold inns started at the same time.*

When rebellions broke out late in the century, King Richard's use of the White Hart as the livery for his personal bodyguard increased. One of its last appearances was also the most dramatic. In September 1397 King Richard summoned Parliament to meet at Westminster Hall, his favoured meeting place, which he had recently rebuilt with oak rafters. Wary of treachery, the King also summoned his "Cheshire archers," four hundred strong, to protect him in London. This bodyguard, in scarlet and white livery with the royal hart prominent, mounted guard in Westminster. They were "not only placed ready to shoot but at one point drew their bows to the ear...."[31]

This was to be King Richard's last parliament. Two years later his cousin, Henry Bolingbroke, took the field against him. Richard was deposed, imprisoned, and murdered in the Tower of London. Henry IV became king in 1400. Seventy-eight years were to pass before "Whyte of Bradway" becomes an official part of this story in a contemporary letter about the wool business. Whether or not the Whyte** family were already established innkeepers in Broadway in the reign of King Richard or earlier is a matter for conjecture, as is the possibility that the inn was called the White Hart at that time. In the early 1400's it may have been re-named the White Swan for King Henry IV, or even a combination of the Hart and the Swan for King Henry V, who used both emblems. Precise evidence shows that by 1620 the inn *was* called the Swan; by 1641 it was once more the White Hart and by 1840 it had at long last become The Lygon Arms.

---

*There are also White Hart inns in Winchcombe and Moreton-in-Marsh of more recent known origin. These may, however, like their Broadway counterpart, date back to older inns on or near the same sites.
**In a 1327 Lay Subsidy Roll a Willielmo le Whyte was living and working in Bradway and assessed for twelve pence. His profession we can only surmise.

I

1450-1536
"Whyte of Bradway"

> "I thank God and ever shall
> It is the shepe hath paid for all..."
> John Barton, wool merchant.

It is not an accident that the oldest wool market in Chipping Campden* where the wool merchants gathered in the fifteenth century, is less than a quarter of a mile from the old stone Church of St. James, grey-gold in Cotswold light. This was an age when men did business fast and furiously while they were on this earth, but set aside a portion of their worldly profits to endow and beautify their churches to lay up for themselves treasure in heaven. William Grevel in Campden, John Fortey and William Midwinter in Northleach, and others like them all over the land lie at peace, their feet on carved woolpacks, their brasses showing what their sheep looked like, their solid presence in the musty air of the church bridging a gap of more than five hundred years.

As they rode from Campden to Broadway and back in the course of business in that century these merchants would have looked forward to resting at an inn in Broadway near where the Lygon Arms stands today, midway between the Abbot's houses, the Grange and the Manse.

The Abbots of Pershore were still the major sheep farmers of the time. An old Abbey business record states that "at Broadway there was a wide stretch of upland pasture sufficient to graze a large flock of Pershore sheep. In 1415 and 1416 the shepherd started with a flock of 713 sheep and by the end of the year had 602 as well as 653 moved from flocks at Leigh and Pershore plus 120 young ewes." That, even in those days, was an enormous flock.

In addition to most of the land comprising the "Manor of Broadway," the abbot's holdings stretched as far as Chipping Campden and Bourton.[1] In all this vast acreage the abbot owned a number of country houses, or villas, but his place as major landowner was gradually being

---

*Where the Woolstaplers Hall now stands.

challenged by new yeoman farmers. Lawsuits over lands became more frequent in this century, as the Wars of the Roses and the resulting disorder made it easier for an ambitious layman to seize land and hold it.

Ever since the Black Death, (a devastating series of plagues starting in 1348) had wiped out a third of the population of England there had been a labour shortage, which meant that those who worked on the land, especially sheep farmers, had an advantage over landowners. A thrifty peasant could save enough money to buy both his freedom and his neighbour's holdings.[2]

In Broadway these small independent farmers would have resented the control of the abbots and the vast extent of the Abbey's holdings, and as long term lessors would have contested it.* In the year 1458 two lay people, John and Elizabeth Stanley, with their friend Robert Molyneux, challenged Abbot Edmund of Pershore about the control of a large piece of sheep pasture between Broadway and Chipping Campden. Since the land in question exceeded 1,000 acres, it was no wonder that the Abbot protested that they had unjustly "cut him off from his holdings and his villa in Bradway...." King Henry VI ordered that "twelve legal freemen" be chosen and that a trial be held. The list of jurors included names of families later associated with the Lygon Arms– Sambache, Corbett, and Lygon, all "armigers," or knights entitled to coats of arms.

The Stanleys were represented by their bailiff, the Abbot by a certain Thomas Pachet and two other royal officials. The jury, either surprisingly impartial or heavily intimidated, found for Abbot Edmund, and the Stanleys were instructed to "go quietly away" and to pay Abbot Edmund forty shillings damages.[3] The Abbot had long-standing tradition on his side, since the ownership of the land in dispute went back to Abbot Gervase, who was appointed in 1204.

Although the Stanleys lost their case, this lawsuit, (one of the few where records survive), shows clearly that some of the Abbey's tenants were no longer content with mere tenant status.** These yeoman farmers, in Broadway as in other parts of England, had a new sense of self-respect and the discipline to go with it. Men whose grandfathers had

---

* Such lawsuits were tried in a Manor Court or Court Leet with a jury system in which tenant farmers actually became judges of the actions of the lord or abbot. Sometimes the King backed one side, sometimes the other.
**No maps still exist, but the lines between outright ownership and a long-term lease (for fifty years or more) were becoming blurred. It is possible that such long-term lessors may have been locally regarded as owners and the boundaries of their lands identified by the use of their names.

fought with the Black Prince at Crécy in 1346, and who themselves might have served King Henry V at Agincourt in 1415, would not be bullied by an Abbot or a lord. The "stout yeomen whose limbs were made in England," an effective fighting force in time of war, were in their home pastures, a new breed that was growing in strength. The country was still overwhelmingly rural and small farmers were gaining ground, both on Cotswold and in the halls at Westminster.

At the same time, the wealthy merchants were consolidating their power in London. They refused to become embroiled in the continuing strife between the rival families of Lancaster and York and compelled the armies of both factions to respect their financial power.[4] At the top of this mercantile aristocracy were the Merchants of the Staple. This organization had evolved because the king was quick to seize on the importance of the export tax on wool to swell his coffers. He granted a monopoly to the Merchant Staplers so that he could go to them for loans whenever he needed instant cash, using the export tax as collateral.

From then on, the Staple had the king in a vice. He was always in need of money for the day to day affairs of state at home and frequently for foreign wars. As long as wool remained England's largest export and biggest source of profit, the merchant staplers, with their monopoly of the wool trade, remained the most influential group in the realm, simply by the power of the purse.[5]

Simultaneously, a strong bond had developed between the merchant staplers and the sheep farmers. Mutual advantage was the common factor. The king was in constant need of money and the merchants could not exert power over him unless they could provide funds swiftly; the wool magnates, in turn, were dependent on the sheep farmer for this flow of ready money. So the nub of the matter was the sheep.[6] Cotswold wool was considered among the best in England in the fifteenth century,* and Broadway was near the centres of wool trading. Thus sheep and their wool drew men of all kinds to the Cotswolds, and, in ever-increasing numbers, to Broadway. Farmers, merchant middlemen and merchant sta-

---

*Authorities disagree on whether Cotswold wool was first or second in quality. Trevelyan states unequivocally that it was "the best"; Eileen Power, in several careful studies, puts it second to Hereford and the `Lemster ore,' or golden fleece of the counties nearer the Welsh border. It was certainly of very high quality through several centuries and much prized by dealers and royalty alike. In the year 1425 when the export of wool was temporarily forbidden, the King of Portugal appealed to Henry VI for 60 sacks of Cotswold wool to make cloth of gold for himself in Florence. King Edward IV, in 1468, gave John, the King of Aragon a gift of 20 Cotswold ewes and four rams.

plers alike congregated there several times a year to talk and bargain, buy and sell. In the midst of this group of affluent businessmen was a certain "Whyte of Bradway."[7]

This Whyte may have been the father of Thomas Whyte (White),* the first recorded resident of the premises that later became the Lygon Arms; this building is listed as the White Hart in the year 1532. The older Whyte and his busy life as a wool merchant in the Cotswolds and elsewhere offer compelling clues about the Whyte family in Broadway and how they eventually became landlords of the oldest village inn.

Whyte seems to have been well known among his wool trading colleagues because he is referred to simply by his own name and that of his village. His name has come down to us in a letter Thomas Betson, a merchant Stapler, wrote on 31st July, 1478 to his master's wife, Dame Elizabeth Stonor:

> ...Good Madam, I beseche you to speke unto my mayster, to the intent that I myght have the money here as shortly as can be. I muste pay to John Tate six pounds for the fells that I have shipped now, and to Whyte of Bradway I muste pay four pounds and I muste pay to the porters and others for costs ten shillings. And so God save my soul I have it not. I will not be so barc agayn of money a good whyle, with God's grace. It was the best dett I saw in his booke, so God helpe me, and perforce I tooke it over unto me for payment and I hold me pleased withal...Jhesu preserve you ever... Amen....[8]

A fine mixture of whimsicality, nervous apprehension over his "debt," a genuine cri-de-coeur for financial help, and religious zeal, all typical of the correspondence of that time.

Thomas Betson was a Merchant of the Staple and Whyte was, evidently, one of his major middlemen in dealings with wool growers or sheep farmers. John Tate was another major supplier and ranks with William Midwinter in importance.** Whyte cannot be far behind, since the amount owed to him is only two pounds less than Betson's debt to Tate. Whyte was on the selling end of the wool business; Betson was a buyer. Both would have been involved in the cycle of the seasons. This began with the selling and buying of "clip," or wool, after the shearing in May and June;

---

* The spelling of this name changed in the mid-sixteenth century.
**Historians' knowledge of the wool trade in England in the Middle Ages is based mostly on two important records, *The Stonor Letters and Papers, 1293-1483*, and *The Cely Papers 1475-1488*. These are discussed in more detail in Appendix B, as is the evolution of the Fellowship of the Staple under King Edward III.

it continued with the exchange of fells, or sheepskins, in November and the winter months, after the great autumn slaughter of sheep.

Both transactions, wool and fells, would have been followed by packing and sealing of "sarplers" or sacks in Northleach, and then transport on pack horses by the "ancient trackways over the Wiltshire and Hampshire downs, which had been used before the Roman conquest, and thence through Surrey and Kent to the Medway ports by the Pilgrims' Way...."[9]

There followed a sea voyage to Calais, sometimes beset by storms or pirates or both, then inspection at the port and the beginning of sales on the Continent. If the wool was not purchased in Calais it would go on to fairs in Bruges, Antwerp and other European cities. It might be after Christmas before the merchant was paid, and longer still before he had negotiated the foreign currencies back to England. Not all merchants could "sell a French crown" speedily, as Chaucer's merchant does. There were many rates of exchange, which could be both exasperating and disastrous for a merchant. William Midwinter, major supplier that he was, and presumably well off, complains continually that he is "bare, without money"[10] and wishes to be paid with all speed. Whyte may have suffered likewise.*

There were four major fair seasons in Europe at that time, the Cold Mart in the winter months, the Pask (Pasques) at Easter, the Synxen (St. John) fair in midsummer, and the St. Remys (Balms or Bammys) fair in the autumn (28th October).[11] Betson would have attended all but the midsummer one. Whyte, his counterpart in Broadway, would have gone to the annual fair on St. John the Baptist's day (24th June) in Broadway, which occurred just after the annual shearing and storing of the clip. He also ventured to other towns for the autumn fairs, because Whyte was not only a middleman, but a sheep farmer in his own right. He sold both wool and fells wherever he could get the best price.

Whyte's first name was possibly Thomas, as suggested by this record from Early Chancery Proceedings in the years 1476-1485: "One Thomas Whyte of Broadway, husbandman, brought an action of debt against Thomas Wynnam, a man of power and might dwelling in a foreign shire, in London for 12 sacks of Cotswold wool he had ordered and kept for six

---

*Richard Cely at one point writes distractedly to his brother: ``I must pay William Midwinter at Bartholomews tide twenty pounds and at All Hallows tide twenty pounds for the said fells, Sir, I pray you have these days in remembrance... my poor honesty lies thereupon and at my comings out of Cottysswolde..."

years."[12] This entry not only supports the probability that Whyte of Broadway was named Thomas, since the date is only a few years later than Betson's mention of Whyte in his letter to Dame Elizabeth, but also documents his considerable wealth. If Whyte, "husbandman" could afford to wait six years to be paid for 12 sacks of Cotswold wool at the going rate of roughly 120 shillings a sack, he must have been making a substantial annual income. Twelve sacks at this rate would have been worth about £72.*

The name Thomas Whyte crops up again in the Cely letters. Agent William Cely, writing to his "worshipful master, Richard Cely, merchant of the Staple at Calais at London in Martt Lane" on the fourteenth day of April in 1484, mentions a Thomas Whyte who had dined with him at his "ostes" [host's house] at his master's request. Richard Cely was trying to get to the bottom of some gossip about himself, his brother and a lady who had been inquiring about their respective incomes with a view to matrimony. Whyte is supposed to have known something about the matter. According to William: "touching the matter that your mastershypp wrote me of Thomas Whyte, certainly, Sir, I spoke with him and he dined at home with my host...he showed how the matter lay between another man and you. However, he said she had you more in favour than the other man...but Sir, you have his good will...."[13]

The faithful William not only discovered from Whyte that the lady in question had Richard Cely "more in favour than the other man," but told the brothers that he had calculated that their annual income was over £200 a year and, therefore they were in a good position to pursue any courtship if they wished to do so.[14] Since some of Richard Cely's romances were conducted in places like Northleach and Winchcombe,

---

*Wool was then, as it still is, weighed in tods. There were 28 pounds to each tod. In the year 1481 a tod was worth about 12 shillings and four pence in Northleach. (Gissing 12) An act was passed by Henry VII in 1494 that there should be only 294 pounds "To the sakke of wolle." (O.E.D.) This means each of Whyte's sacks contained about ten tods of wool or a value of 120 shillings each. Twelve sacks, therefore, would have been valued at 1,440 shillings or £72. This is, of course, an approximate figure, because the available dates for this computation range from 1476-85 to 1481 and 1494, but even making allowances for this rough estimate, if the combined annual income of Richard and George Cely was £200, Whyte of Bradway was a wealthy man by any standard of his time.

The weight of a tod (28 pounds) evolved from a medieval custom: a merchant carried with him three stones weighing 7, 4 and 3 pounds each for a total of 14. When a bargain was about to be struck each woolman would place his stones on one side of a scale. When seller and buyer were satisfied that the scale balanced, both sets of stones (28 pounds in all) would be placed on one side and wool would be piled on the other.

Thomas Whyte, from the same countryside, might well have been aware of gossip about him, his income, and a prospective bride.

There is no clear proof that "Whyte of Bradway," the Thomas Whyte of Broadway in the suit against Wynnam, and the Thomas Whyte who is William Cely's informant on romantic matters are all one and the same man. However, given the common denominator of the wool trade and Whyte's standing among wool traders, it is entirely possible.

By the time Whyte appears relaying gossip to William Cely in Calais in the year 1484, he may have been a Merchant of the Staple himself or have had other business at the port. John Tate, whom Betson mentions as one of his sources of wool in 1478 is mentioned by William Cely in 1482 as "leftenaunte" of the Staple in Calais. If Tate could rise so far in four years, Whyte certainly could have done so in six. The sheep had paid for all in more ways than one.

Shipment of fells and fleeces demanded a precise, carefully timed annual routine. Whyte would have spent much of each year in his own village making sure these autumn fells and spring fleeces reached Cely's boat or another in time for the European markets. To the greater world he was "Whyte of Bradway" but at home, in Bradway, he was undoubtedly a hard worker who got wet and muddy along with the rest of his shepherds. In his younger days he would have led a life of hard, unremitting work from dawn to dusk, with only Sundays and holy days for rest and recreation. He may have raced, wrestled, and competed in archery contests on feast days, along with other village youths, but for the most part he would have concentrated on his farm and his sheep.

The Church provided some of the few bits of colour and pageantry in an otherwise strictly disciplined life of outdoor labour. The year was measured in Church festivals—"Maye games" and "ravells" following Lent and Easter in the spring, the feast of St. John the Baptist in June, when the shearing took place, Lammas day in August when the harvest began. All-Hallows in November, and a fortnight of "holy days" between Christmas and Twelfth Night.[15] Whyte would have been involved in all these. He would have given his shepherds a generous sheep shearing feast in June, and he might himself have participated in the Nativity pageant in December.

Prosperous as it was, however, the wool trade was not free from risks for Whyte or any other dealer. The phrase "good cottyswold woll" or "fayr woll" recurs often in both the Stonor and Cely letters. This was not simply a phrase the merchants used for patting themselves proudly on the back as they journeyed to and fro. Good wool had a very distinct meaning in the trade of the time. It was the opposite of "bad wool," wool of poor quality, too old, improperly packed, or, occasionally, wool mixed with some other substance and packed in sarplers along with the rest of the load in the hopes that it would avoid detection. As the sacks of wool passed through the customs at Calais, every now and then a sarpler was opened at random by the officers to test it for quality.* Whyte had to make sure he could trust his packers not to try to make a quick, private profit by stealing an occasional sack and replacing it with "bad wool," which if discovered, would have had a disastrous long-term effect on his hard-won reputation.[16]

Whyte and other wool traders also faced competition from Italian Lombard bankers. These sleek, well-dressed men from the cities of Italy, rode about the Cotswolds, driving their own bargains with wool growers. They might buy all the available clip from Whyte's own sellers—the small Cotswold sheep farmers—before Whyte could better their offers. They then bypassed the Staple at Calais and took the wool straight to the Mediterranean markets in their own boats, making a tidy profit in the process. As Chaucer had earlier pointed out they could not be legally stopped: "in Cotteswolde they also ride about and bien [buy] what them liste [choose]." The Lombards did exactly as they pleased, lined their fur pockets and were a menace to Whyte and other English wool traders.

Possibly the greatest risk was transport by sea. Not all ships were as large as the *Margaret Cely*, which was about 200 tons. Smaller ships were at greater risk. Most successful merchants crossed and re-crossed the rough English Channel several times in a single year, and captains and crews did so even more often. All were accustomed to the dangers encountered at sea.**

There were storms which sometimes claimed whole cargoes, and fires, in which the wool burned below the hatches. The letters are full of

---

*There is at least one recorded case of a swindle: William Cely, the Cely agent, informs the brothers in the year 1487 that he averted a disaster barely in the nick of time by substituting one sack for another. As he saw that Sack #24 was about to be opened and knowing it to be bad wool, he had substituted #8, 'fayr wool,' and changed the labels before the official reached it. But he warns the brothers to be on guard because "great search is being made" to detect fraud and they will be in danger of discovery if Peter Balys' books are examined.
**Betson introduces us to master mariners Henry Wilkins, master of the *Christopher* of Rainham, John Lollington, master of the *Jhesu* of London, Robert Ewen sailing the *Thomas* of Newhite, all of whose "berds" had, no doubt, been "shake by many a tempest."

accounts of piracy, ships being chased by Scottish, French and other predators. Cely describes one, the *Robert Eryke*, chased by Scots between Calais and Dover. The crew "scaped narrow."[17]

Whyte, Betson, and the Celys probably knew each other and may even have stood on the same quay in uneasy comradeship, keeping watch for a cargo, and like Chaucer's merchant, praying that the seas might be kept free, no matter what the cost, between Holland, France and the English coast. There would have been inevitable, frequent interchange. William Cely wrote from London to his master, George, in Calais in 1481 that he had just sent 464 fells to George in the *Thomas* of Newhite. He identified the shipment as follows: "the said felles lyeth next to the mast lowest under the felles of Thomas Betson...." Whyte's fells may have travelled on the same boat further from the mast.[18]

Whyte was well acquainted with the risks of the wool trade and when he grew older and his wealth increased, he may have decided to put some of it into an investment in the future for himself and his family. As he watched the traffic that passed his door increase each year and saw the need for a larger place for merchants like Thomas Betson to stay, a shrewd man who was raising a family might well have taken the opportunity to enlarge his farmhouse.

This farmhouse, which was already providing housing on an informal basis several times a year for shepherds, pilgrims and merchants may have become a larger and more formal inn some time in the late 1400's. Whyte may have followed the contemporary custom of shaping a building or enlargement in the form of the first initial of the name of the reigning King, and constructed the expansion of his house in the shape of an "H" for King Henry VII.* The start of his reign in 1485 coincided with the height of Whyte's prosperity as a wool merchant and would have been a good time for Whyte to embark on a new venture. It was an H-shaped building when John Treavis added to it more than a hundred years later and this early outline can still be traced today. Such an H-

---

*King Henry VII may have passed through Broadway on July 1, 1495, on his way from Chipping Norton to Evesham, but whether he did or not, residents of the village would have been aware that the Wars of the Roses had come to an end and that a certain measure of security had been restored for honest workers after the battle of Bosworth. The man who now sat on the throne was a careful and prudent businessman who wanted his writ to run in peace and made sure of it by putting his faith in the men of each county. In 1497 King Henry appointed four commissioners and Justices of the Peace in Wigorn, or Worcestershire who were all local men. The partnership between the monarch and the Commons, which was the strength of the Tudors, had already begun. [Temperley, 415]

shaped building* does not preclude a "manorial inn" or churchman's hostelry, such as we have previously described, being located on the same site at a much earlier time. Moreover, there is physical evidence of such a building still visible in the Lygon Arms: a great wooden doorway with strap hinges possibly dating from the fifteenth century.**[19] It is possible that Thomas Whyte, wool merchant of Broadway was living there with his family and became an innkeeper as he grew older. He supplied ale to village residents, travelling merchants and may have entertained both Vicar John Botrey of Broadway and Abbot Robert Stanway from Pershore, who was more popular than his predecessor Edmund.

To this Abbot Stanway, or one of his more efficient scribes, we are indebted for a vital piece of evidence which directly pertains to the story of the Lygon Arms. In the year 1490 a conventual lease was drawn up between the Abbot of Pershore and two Broadway residents, Robert Handy and Robert Faulkes. This lease is battered and damaged by age, and parts of it are illegible, but enough remains to tell us that Handy and Faulkes were leasing a large area of land in the "Manor of Bradway in the Countie of Worcester aforesaid...houses, landes, medowes, and pasture...." This lease is for a period of thirty-one years. The annual rent is £30. [20]

For his thirty pounds Handy gets "all manner of pasture of sheep upon the hill" which...used to belong to the abbot and Convent of Pershore or their tenants, and all the houses of the Inner Court there. In addition he is to use "the close called Strayery Close for strayery to be put there (a pound for stray animals)"*** and "the close called Withyholde...at all times...to have and hold the same in the same manner as John Davyes of Aldermysnter lately hath occupied them and also as Robert Handy and Robert Faulkes or either of them hath had and occupied...."

The abbot at the time of the "ensealing" of this lease delivered to Robert Handy "four hundred sheep called wethers." During the term of the lease Handy is to have all the wool of these 400 sheep as well as the tithe wool. Handy must supply sufficient meat and drink and bedding to

---

*There is a marked similarity between the Lygon Arms and Claydon, the Verneys' home in Buckinghamshire, built about 1485. Claydon was also H-shaped when it was first built. [*Verney Memoirs* 1-7]
**Modern architects do not agree on the date of this old doorway.
***This "Strayery" or pound may have been located exactly where the village pound was for generations; it shows clearly on a map from the late 1800's [Gordon Russell Ltd. Archives]. This site is on the right-hand side of the road to Evesham on a small green, a few hundred yards beyond today's Lygon Arms..

the abbot's steward holding Court there and six men with him and "meat and litter for their horses, that is to say for a night and a day and other time during the said term...."

Handy promises for himself and his successors or assignees to repair and maintain a large number of buildings, including the two sheep houses there and the Whyte Halle and Woolhouse "and them Agayne wynds and rayne shall make defensible." He must also keep all hedges in proper order. The abbot and his successors agree to pay Handy 16 shillings a year and one of his shepherd's wages, and as much corn as the shepherd has previously had a year "as of old time." Handy is also to have 13 shillings and 4 pence a year for the keeping and custody of the hill and sufficient "loppe and shreding of treez and firebote (firewood) without wasting any...."[21]

This old document tells us several important things. First, the lease is renewable. Handy and Faulkes, as well as John Davyes, have leased these premises before and will probably do so again. There is precedent for the way business is conducted, "as of old time." Second, the abbot and his steward make frequent visits and expect to be put up at Handy's expense. Third, we can conclude that both Handy and Faulkes are experienced shepherds since they are entrusted by the abbot with a large flock of sheep and a vast quantity of land. Fourth, a "Whyte halle" is mentioned as one of various outbuildings for which Handy is responsible, next to the Woolhouse and the sheep houses. It included a "draughte" or privy, and was undoubtedly used as a gathering place for merchants considering the local wool. This building was probably named after Whyte of Bradway or his family, who had undoubtedly been in the wool business for some generations, as presumably had the Handy and Faulkes families. (In the following century, in 1535, boundaries to a lease of lands are similarly identified by the "Whyte furlong," and the "Whyte more," [open grazing land][22] which suggests that this Whyte Hall is also part of the Whyte family lease or holding). Fifth, the term of the lease is for thirty-one years or until the year 1522.

Ten years after this date, in 1532, each Broadway tenant who could afford it signed an agreement with the Vicar, Robert Byshop, to maintain in perpetuity a six-yard section of the churchyard wall. The names of Henry Handy and Richard Faulkes are listed consecutively in this agreement. Next to their names is that of Thomas White, who is identified as the proprietor of the White Hart Inn. These three, out of a total of forty, seem to have signed as a group, simultaneously. What could this signify?

In 1490 Robert Handy, Robert Faulkes,* and Whyte of Bradway were all in the business of raising sheep and selling wool. All three were operating on a large scale and were probably collaborating. They may have been neighbours, or at least have lived close to each other with adjoining pastures. It is probable that, forty-one years later, the men with the same names who are listed together are occupying identical premises and continuing the family businesses already established by 1491. People at that time did not move about as much as they do today, and their professions could not change as rapidly. Many of the family names on the agreement about the churchyard wall continue into a second and third generation, and there is good reason to assume that Handy, Faulkes, and White were following this traditional pattern, especially since it is probable that the older Whyte had just made substantial improvements to his house and hostelry.

Therefore, we can conclude that Henry Handy and Richard Faulkes are the sons of Robert Handy and Robert Faulkes and that Thomas White is the son of Whyte of Bradway. They will work together as a group in the upkeep of their adjacent measures of churchyard wall, pooling their efforts, just as they will carry on their fathers' businesses—sheep and innkeeping.

This identifiable succession from three sheep farmer fathers to their three sons, all friends and colleagues in both generations, makes more credible the possibility that by the late fifteenth century, old Whyte was running a hostelry in the same place as his successor, Thomas White, in 1532. The boundaries would not have been precisely as they are today and the amount of pasture and arable land would have been greater but the combined evidence of the 1532 record and the abbot's lease strongly suggests that there was a Whyte family inn operating on or near the present site of the Lygon Arms as early as 1490.

---

*Richard Faulkes's will, 27 March, 1548, shows that he was a sheep farmer who left his plough and other farm equipment to his son Myles, his "dun mare and a Pair of Shepe" to his daughter, Margaret, and his other sheep, his harvest and remaining possessions to his wife, Habel.

Oldest Broadway Parish Register 1532 – 1710.

II

1532-1620
"Five Silver Spoons"

"Jog on, jog on, the foot-path way
And merrily hent the stile-a,
A merry heart goes all the day,
Your sad tires in a mile-a..."
The Winter's Tale

It was bright noonday on the twenty fourth day of June in the year of our Lord 1535 and the annual Bradway Fair was in full swing. The pedlar sang as he hopped over the stile and hurried down the hill. The sun shone on the booths lining both sides of the village green and on the brightly-dressed crowd who thronged there.

There were tinkers with bulky packs thrown over their shoulders, chapmen watering their horses in the stream, minstrels, tumblers, and beggars with sore legs. At the gate, officials wearing the livery of King Henry VIII collected payment from all who passed through. A large crowd of merchants sold iron pots, leather coats, hats, and coloured ribbons. The field, crowded with people from the whole countryside, smelt of gaiety and sweat. It was the fair of St. John the Baptist and of Eadburgha, the people's patron Saint.

The wool merchants congregated in a corner of the green to exchange gossip. On a bench near the wall of the abbot's house, old Whyte sat holding court, freely giving his opinion on the quality of the clip just completed to anyone who would listen. He was now well into old age and no longer the powerful merchant of the Staple he once was—although he was still respected by the younger traders. They nodded politely and went about their business.

Old Whyte dozed in the sun, smiled and remembered. He had been there since early morning and had already finished a few tankards of ale. He had been coming to this fair for as long as he could recall. When he was a boy he had saved all year so he could buy a few sweetmeats at the June revel. He could remember Venetian merchants selling spices and sugar, and he could smell in his mind the pungent scent of nutmeg, quince and ginger. He could hear the harness bells of the pack horses as they were loaded with the bulky woolsacks for the trip to Northleach and then over the old pony tracks to the sea. As a young man he had bargained with the rich merchant staplers who had came to buy his wool and the clip he had bought from his neighbours after the spring shearing. Even the ale seemed to taste better then, especially if he had haggled for hours with a fussy man like Thomas Betson.

Whyte reflected with pride that the inn, which he had started informally when there were too many merchants and other travellers for the abbot and his bailiff to accommodate, would be a busy place tonight. His son Thomas ran it now, and had done so for the past ten years. Old Whyte was glad he had given it to Thomas and his wife Joan, as a wedding present. It was halfway between the abbot's house and the prior's, and a good stopping place for travellers. He had helped Thomas enlarge it and a good job they had made of it—feather beds, good meat and wine, and always fish for saints' days and in Lent.

Tom had kept up the sheep farming and there were still flocks of Whyte sheep grazing on the downs above the church, and shepherds to tend them; but now there were also orchards of fine pears for perry wine and apples for cider, as well as plums and other fruits for jams, jellies, and wines, carefully made by Joan Whyte, his daughter-in-law.

The wool business had fallen off since Whyte's youth. Exporting wool through the Staple at Calais to markets in the Netherlands was only a shadow of the business it had been when Whyte was a young man. He was known as "Whyte of Bradway" then and bargained with some of the most important members of the Fellowship of the Staple. Master Thomas Betson, representative of the Stonors, and Richard Cely, oldest son of a family so wealthy they sent wool and fells to Calais in their own ships, had been frequent visitors to his home to bid for his clip. But that was a long time ago.

Whyte had turned many an honest penny in the days of King Richard and King Henry VII. Careful fellow, Henry. Taxed all the villages for household expenses and saved money, but he had kept England out of war and brought order back. The new king, Hal, he didn't know about. He had left poor Queen Catherine and married Mistress Anne Boleyn. His wife and the other women didn't like it—daughters when sons were wanted and still-born children were a familiar story in country villages, and village women had little sympathy with the King just because he wanted a son. Married to Queen Catherine for twenty-five years, he had been.

Whyte saw his grandsons on their way to the shooting at the butts, got to his feet and hobbled to the other side of the field. Gathered to watch the archery were his other grandsons and their mother, Joan. A good woman, Joan. She made excellent plum jam and Tom was proud of the way she kept his inn. The boys were pushing and shoving to get a better view, and he wondered where his grand-daughter, Elizabeth, could be. Ah, there she was, sitting by a hawthorn bush with young Will Sambache—smiling and laughing like the courting couple they were. Well, come to think of it, it was nearly time. Elizabeth was pretty, like her mother, and would be fifteen years old at Martinmas. Whyte mused that young Sambache's family had plenty of land and money to spare. Will spent a lot of time at the inn, helping Tom with the ploughing and the harvest and lending a hand in the kitchen if business became brisk. An excuse to hang around Elizabeth, he shouldn't wonder.

A shout went up. Young Rob Handy had won first prize with Richard Whyte second. Good for the boy not to win every year, he supposed grudgingly. Handy's father, Henry, was one of Tom's shepherds, dividing time between the abbot's land and Tom's own holdings. Whyte noticed Vicar Byshop, walking past with finely-dressed Squire Ralph Sheldon, over from Abberton to give out the prizes with his six-year-old daughter, little Mistress Anne.

There was a noise and a strumming of instruments, and the crowd shifted and blocked the old man's view. The dancers had arrived, all in white with red ribbons, and the jugglers; already all the young ones were running to get ready for the dancing that would take up the rest of the afternoon. Suddenly he felt tired and sleepy.

Just then he noticed that his daughter-in-law, Joan, and Elizabeth were getting ready to leave to prepare the feast which was to come later. He blinked and thought it might be a good idea to go with them and have a sleep at the inn—it was growing too hot. Elizabeth and Will held out their hands to him and smiled. The old man got up and limped over to go with them, thinking that God had been good to him and his family.

After the Fair of St. John the Baptist the crowd at the inn would have been large and varied. Landlord Thomas White, by the year 1535, had established a reputation for hospitality that attracted a noisy group of local regulars as well as visitors. In an age when class divisions were taken for granted and easily accepted, the inn would have been a gathering point for the yeoman farmer, the magistrate, the Justice of the Peace, the labourer who could afford a pint, pilgrims, scholars from Oxford, and many others. White, Handy, Faulkes, Darston, and Vicar Byshop would all have met and mingled in the hostelry, and a boisterous influx of merrymakers from the Fair would have swelled the celebrating crowd on this Feast of St. John in June, 1535.

Wine from Gascony, Burgundy and Spain, as well as English ales, would have flowed. Popular drinks brewed from local hops and malt were the heady "huffe cap, mad dog, angel's food, dragon's milk, stride wide and lift leg."[1] Old Whyte, already tipsy from ale in the sun, would have been in bed long before sunset, but young Thomas White, his wife Joan, their sons, and daughter, Elizabeth, would have been up late serving guests and clearing away, probably with the help of aspiring suitor Will Sambache.

By June of 1535 Thomas White was running the inn which later became the White Hart; three years before this, in the year 1532, he is listed in the oldest Broadway Parish Register as being at the White Hart premises. He and his father may have been innkeepers some time before this date. Young Thomas was one of forty inhabitants of the town who had sufficient income to sign an agreement with Vicar Robert Byshop of St. Eadburgha's to build and maintain the churchyard wall. These parishioners assumed this responsibility for themselves and their successors, or future occupiers of their premises, in perpetuity. The document reads:

> It was agreed by Sr. Robert Byshop then Vicar of Broadway and his parishioners that the churchyard shall be repaired and fenced after this manner following: Viz: That the said Sr. Robert and his successors from henceforth shall repair or make ye Great Gate in ye old Churchyard and every one of those following and their successors a perch of six yards long beginning at ye Great Gate and so proceeding eastward.[2]

This important record was found in 1710 on a piece of "old velum" in the chapel coffer. It covers three centuries and lists not only White but John Treavis in 1633 and Francis Phipps in 1710 as successive proprietors of the White Hart. The original, unfortunately, has long since vanished, but luckily for historians, a copy was made early in the twentieth century by Mr. Rees Price. This record appears to be accurate, since the listings for Treavis and Phipps agree with other information about these two innkeepers from wills and deeds. (See copy of "old velum," p.15)

As previously discussed, this first recorded innkeeper is probably the son of "Whyte of Bradway." Baptismal and marriage records reveal that the White family was well established in Broadway and nearby villages at this time.[3] The almost universal custom of naming the oldest son after the father strongly suggests that innkeeper Thomas was the son of the wool merchant and was, born some time between 1485 and 1500.

What do we know about Thomas White? A few vital facts emerge from his will, dated 8 August, 1556. He was a devout man, married to a "Joan," with children and grandchildren that he dearly loved. He left bequests not only to his wife, his son-in-law and his daughter, but also to three grandchildren. He was prosperous, but since his will and inventory do not specifically allude to the inn, he had apparently given up innkeeping by the time of his death, probably due to illness. It appears that some time before 1556, White ceded the inn to his son-in-law William Sambache and his daughter Elizabeth, who had married in 1545. His own words bring him vividly to life:

> I Thomas White of Bradwey in the diocese of Worcester being sick and diseased in my body but whole in mind and of perfect remembrance do make my testament and last will in form and manner following.
>
> First I bequeath my soul to almighty God and to our Lady Saint Mary and to all the holy company of heaven, my body to be buried in the parish church yard of Bradwey beforesaid.
>
> Item I bequeath to every of the three children of my daughter Elizabeth Sambache one feather bed, the which feather beds are in the parlour that hath the chimney.
>
> Item I bequeath to William Sambache my son-in-law five butts and three tops all of oak lying together under the (seame) [same].
>
> Item I bequeath to William, my [first] daughter's oldest son five silver spoons.
>
> The rest of my goods unbequeathed movable and unmovable (my debts paid, my funeral expenses deducted), I bequeath to Joan my wife whom I make the whole executrix of this my testament and last will.[4]

This document is witnessed by his wife "Joane" and the Vicar, William Dickins. Only a prosperous man would have had feather beds to leave, since most ordinary people still slept on straw or rush pallets. Only a prosperous man could afford to leave five silver spoons to a grandson, and only the well-to-do had been able to build chimneys into the wall. Moreover, the inventory of Thomas White's estate indicates a large house with several chambers, a quantity of plate, and a "Wool Chamber."[5] This confirms that he was carrying on the family wool business as well as running the inn. In addition, the White family, Thomas and his father, were apparently owners of such vast sheep pastures that their name was used to identify boundaries in other land transactions of the period. Most notably, the lease made by the Abbey of Pershore with Anthony Darston [Daston] in 1535 specified "another shephousse about the White furlong..." and "pastures, fields...part of White more...."[6]

So Thomas White, his inn, and his wool business had prospered. Elizabeth may have been his only child, or at least his only child to produce grandchildren, since no other grandchildren are mentioned.* Elizabeth White Sambache had three children at the time of her father's death in 1556. One of the younger sons was probably named Anthony, listed as a "sonne of Wm. Sambache gent." in a Parish Register of 1550.[7]

Elizabeth White Sambache's oldest son William, who, as a child, inherited the five silver spoons, married on 8th May, 1578, in the parish of Shrawley, Jane Severn, whose family was entitled to a coat-of-arms.[8] In April 1579, they had a son, John, the first of twenty-six children.**

There is a clear line of innkeepers from Thomas White in 1532 to John Treavis in 1620 including Whites, Sambaches and their in-laws. William and Elizabeth White Sambache and their children presumably ran the White Hart Inn between White's death in 1556 and their old age, at which point their son, young William, and his wife Jane took over, probably about 1580. The second couple continued to run the inn until 1620, when a deed records that on 29th November of that year, John Treavis bought the inn from "William Sambache the Elder" (the boy who inherited the spoons in 1556) and his son, Walter.***[9]

What sort of an inn were the Whites and Sambaches running in the last half of the century, and what sort of house were they living in? It is

---

:*There are a number of records of the White family of this era. No less than seven Thomas Whites were married or christened in the 1500's in Broadway, Halesowen, Elmley Castle, Castlemorton, Pershore and Bretforton. Especially interesting is the Thomas White christened in Bretforton 16 January 1538, who may be a son or a nephew of the 1532 innholder.

**As far as can be determined, only two of these children died in infancy.

***Although we know that from Thomas White's death in 1556 until its purchase by John Treavis in 1620, the inn remained in the possession of two generations of the Sambache family, it is uncertain what it was called during a short part of this period. When John Treavis bought the property in 1620 the deed refers to it as "the Swan," but when he died in 1641, twenty-one years later, his will once more names it as the "White Hart" in his substantial bequest to his wife, Ursula and oldest son Thomas. For some brief part of this time it seems to have been known "by the sign of the Swan", but for purposes of clarity, we refer to it throughout these early centuries as the White Hart Inn.

probable that either White or his son-in-law made some additions to the original fifteenth-century building, probably of half-timbered construction, but possibly of stone as well.* Additional fireplaces and chimneys may also have been added.**

The family, as in the previous generation and for some centuries to come, were running a farm as well as an inn. The men and boys laboured in the fields, ploughing, sowing, and harvesting as demanded by the season. They grew oats and wheat as well as barley for making beer and the house included a brewhouse as well as a wine cellar. They grazed cattle as well as sheep, assisted their Master Shepherd, and cared for the orchards.

The women too were busy. A "Booke of Husbandrye" of the time itemises the prescribed duties of a housewife: "pray on getting out of bed, clean the house, dress the dishboard, milk the cows, suckle the calves, dress the children, cook the meals, bake and brew, send corn to the Mill, make butter and cheese, tend the swine and collect the eggs...."[10] Although servants may have helped Mrs. White and Mrs. Sambache with this routine, the innkeeper's wife and daughters did not have much leisure time.

It was the duty of one of the daughters to watch the younger children and make sure they did not escape to some wood or coppice to snare a rabbit, fish in the stream or savour the joy of poaching a bird from the Abbot's preserve. Partridges are frequently mentioned in menus of the day, and were undoubtedly a welcome relief from salt meat during much of the year.

Cattle, sheep, and swine were killed and salted at Martinmas (mid-November) since it was difficult to feed animals through the winter months, and the cooler temperatures helped prevent the meat from spoiling. "From Christmas to May, weak cattle decay..." said an agricultural

---

*John Leland several times mentions "houses all builded of timber" in Midland counties near Broadway, but the well-to-do were beginning to use stone for building in the sixteenth century.

**Parson William Harrison, who kept a journal in the mid 1500's, notes: "within the remembrance of men living...in their young days (the kings Harry) there were not above two or three chimneys if so many, in uplandish towns (villages), religious houses and manor places of their lords always excepted, but each one made his fire against a reredoss in the hall where he dined and dressed his meat." It appears that White may have had one, but only one, by the time of his death in 1556, since he identified his bequest of the feather beds by the parlour "that hath the chimney," which implies that the other parlours did not have chimneys at that date.

rhyme of the time.*[11] Vegetables to helped vary the winter diet as well. A contemporary writer tells us that even "poor commons" of this time were growing "melons and cucumbers" and root vegetables such as "parsnips, turnips and carrots"[12] that could be stored through the cold months in a root cellar. Cider and perry, pressed from the apples and pears of the Vale of Evesham, would be drunk throughout the year. In addition to beef, mutton and bacon from the last swine killing and chicken and goose were sometimes served. "Geese they eat in two seasons, when they are fatted upon the stubble after harvest and when they are green about Whitsuntide."[13]

Venison pasty was eaten occasionally and pottage or soup, made of cabbage, was a staple, as were bacon and rabbits or conies: "the flesh whereof is fat, tender and more delicate than ...in other parts...."**

Jane Sambache's kitchen provided good bread. The family ate barley and rye bread upon occasion, but more often bread made with wheat flour. Parson William Harrison's journal casts light on the sorts of food consumed during much of this century:

> The bread throughout our land is made of such grain as the soil yieldeth, nevertheless the gentility commonly provide themselves sufficiently of wheat for their own tables, while their household and poor neighbours in some shires are forced to content themselves with rye or barley, yea, and in time of dearth, many with bread made out of beans, peas or oats and some acorns among....[14]

William and Jane Sambache could have afforded wheat bread. Harrison tells us that even in a rude cottage of timber and clay the diet was "large" and that "these English have their houses made of sticks and dirt but they fare commonly as well as the King..." This was said of the average small husbandman living in a cottage. Thomas White and later his son-in-law Will Sambache, were not "poor husbandmen." They were prosperous yeoman farmers, a class that, by the middle of the sixteenth century had

---

*Due to this slaughter of beasts in the autumn, meat had to be salted and stored. Consequently, cooks used all manner of spices for flavouring and cooking it. Pepper was used to season "tainted meat" at other times of year and great fortunes could sometimes be made by importing it.
**A 1551 menu for a nearby county shows what was eaten by twenty servants when the master and mistress were not in residence: "For dinner three pieces of boiled beef, one piece of roast meat, a coney and a partridge...for supper five joints of mutton and another coney...in Lent, fish only..."

gained in power and influence. Bishop Hugh Latimer's famous definition is the most specific:

> My father was a yeoman, and had no lands of his own, only he had a farm of three or four pound a year at the uttermost and hereupon he tilled so much as kept half a dozen men. He had walk for a hundred sheep and my mother milked thirty kine. He was able and did find the king a harness with himself and his horse—I can remember that I buckled his harness when he went unto Blackneath field..."[15]

Thus, the yeoman farmer was a tiller of soil and grazer of sheep in time of peace, but in military emergency a soldier for the King and an increasingly powerful political force, whether he was merely a husbandman with a few acres and a small number of animals or a wealthy farmer like Anthony Daston, whose lands adjoined Thomas White's and who had enough influence and power to be Sheriff of Worcestershire for forty years.

In the Cotswolds sheep were still the chief source of wealth, but sheep farming had become more controversial. A big farmer like Daston continued to make a profit. But in many parts of England and to some extent in the Cotswolds, the lack of tillage ruined the small farmer. A man with only a few animals who grew his own food might lose his land and become one of the thousands of homeless beggars who roamed sixteenth-century England.

Wool was so profitable that some landlords gradually evicted their tenants in order to graze more sheep to produce the "golden fleece," or raised rents so that tenants could not afford to renew their leases:

> Where a farm for twenty pounds was set,
> Under thirty they would not it let...[16]

Thomas More in his *Utopia*, maintained satirically:

> the wool growers leave no ground for tillage, they enclose all into pastures. . . they throw down houses....yea, and certain abbots, holy men no doubt...enclose their land for pasture, pluck down towns and leave nothing standing but only the church to be made into a sheephouse . . . [17]

Abbots William Compton and John Stoneywell, who bore office in Pershore in the mid-sixteenth century, did not make leases for a mere twenty or thirty pounds. Instead they leased to men like Daston who paid sixty-four pounds for vast acres in 1535, or to Ralph Sheldon of Abberton who paid eighty-five pounds a year in 1538. The abbots wisely left most of the administrative problems to these tenants—Sheldon,

Daston and one Walter Welche.[18] But there is a record of at least one fierce quarrel between Abbot John Stoneywell and several of his Broadway tenants which may have been partially caused by general concern about enclosure. It was led by Bailiff Christopher Westerdale of Broadway, who opposed the abbot.[19]

This dispute, which centred on the long-term lease of a vast parcel of abbey lands, would certainly have provoked lively discussion around the fire at the inn during the long winter evenings, especially since Daston, who gave employment to a large number of people, was one of the chief litigants. King Henry VIII himself became involved, since two of his courtiers insisted that they had a prior claim to the lands in question. No outcome to this controversy, which went on for more than a decade, is recorded. However, Daston still held the lease of his lands in 1558, and his wife, Anne Daston, became, after his death, one of the richest landowners in the whole countryside. It can be assumed, therefore, that Daston and his Broadway neighbours emerged as the winners.*

Such disagreements with powerful local churchmen like Stoneywell, even if they indirectly involved King Henry VIII, were based on purely economic grounds, the use of lands, rather than the vexatious question of who was the head of the Church—the Pope or the King. Whether a man's conscience compelled him to remain loyal to the Church of Rome or to accept the King's supremacy over matters spiritual as well as temporal** might have been discussed at the inn in hushed voices, but earning one's daily bread was still the first priority. In Broadway and the Cotswolds that meant having enough land to graze sheep as well as to till for food.

Although the export of wool had slowed by mid-century, this was offset by the fact that Worcestershire had become a centre for the production of cloth, at one time employing 8,000 people. White and his family became accustomed to entertaining the agents of the clothiers when they travelled to Broadway each June to bid for the summer clip.

The Clothiers and the Merchant Staplers had, in fact, become competi-

---

*The case of Abbot John Stoneywell v. Broadway tenants Anthony Daston, Ralph Sheldon and absentee lessors Walter Welche and Philip Hoby is detailed in Appendix C.
** There is one solitary record of criticism of King Henry VIII's church policies which some Vicar or Vicar's clerk was brave enough to set down in the Broadway Register for 1563. It inveighs against "That lustful beast who quareling with ye Pope....in his sinfull change of wives destroyed ye religious houses and gave away ye lands to such courtiers as flattered him in his robberies, lewdness and murders...."(Barnard, 208)

tors. Each blamed the other for forcing up the price of wool and for being avid for profits. In 1577 the clothiers of Worcester declared that the high price of wool was caused by "the greedy covetousness of the merchant staplers."[20] Parson Harrison castigated both groups and blamed them for economic conditions in general: "It is to be wished that the huge heap of them were somewhat restrained."[21]

There were statutes which allowed only clothiers or Merchants of the Staple to buy wool in large quantities, but individual middlemen, called broggers or forestallers, often bypassed the rules of the Staple and bought wool under the table at black market prices. They found willing sellers among the wool growers, but were fined if they were caught. Not everyone got away with it. The risks became alarmingly apparent in Broadway when Ralph Parsons of Cropthorne was twice charged with forestalling in 1553 and 1555, when Joseph Phelps of Bengeworth was convicted in 1568, and when Henry Inkbarrow of Evesham faced arrest a few years later.[22]

Eventually this problem reached the doors of the inn itself. Two of William Sambache's customers were accused of forestalling. William Brooke, alias Wover, was charged in 1565, and a Mr. Spencer (no first name given) in 1567.*[23] Spencer may have been arrested at or very near the inn since his family home, "Spencer Cottage," was exactly to the east of the hostelry and forms the right wing of the present-day Lygon Arms.

Some of the gossip at the inn would have focussed not only on local arrests for selling wool illegally at black market prices but also on those who had set up looms in their homes to avoid selling raw wool to the large clothiers in nearby towns, making more money by weaving their own cloth.**

---

*These five cases are the only ones recorded which specifically mention Broadway and nearby towns, but since the whole area was still a major source of raw wool, there were undoubtedly many other instances of illicit trading.
**Cloth making was lucrative, and, as it gradually superseded the sale of wool as the major business of Worcestershire, it also began to assume the lustre of romance. An Elizabethan ballad sang the praises of John of Winchcombe, one of the most famous clothiers of his day:
"Within one room being large and long,
There stood two hundred looms full strong
Two hundred men, the truth is so,
Wrought in this room all in a row.
By every one a pretty boy
Sat making quilts with mickle joy
And in another place hard by

Innkeepers White and Sambache may not have participated directly in this underhand dealing, but they doubtless took advantage of the opportunities for making a profit from the high price of wool and the competition to acquire it. Neither Mrs. White nor the two Mrs. Sambaches would have had time or inclination to join the legion of women described as spinning, carding, "walking," and performing all the other steps that were required to turn raw wool into cloth but certainly would have been aware that their neighbours, who were not running a prosperous inn, would have been doing so in nearby cottages.[24] As the century progressed, probably both Whites and Sambaches remembered with gratitude the first "Bradway" sheep farmer who had the foresight to ally the wool business with innkeeping and thereby enable them to avoid a net of risks and restrictions. Whether to buy wool or cloth, men still travelled the "Broad high Waye" into the village and as long as they did there was a good living to made at the family inn.

Possibly this inn would not have been on quite so grand a scale as the one described below by an Elizabethan traveller, but it would have been much more comfortable than the flea-ridden hostelry described in the Prologue:

> The world affords not such inns as England hath, either for food and cheap entertainment after the guests own pleasure or for humble attendance on passengers, yea even in very poor villages. For as soon as a passenger comes to an inn, the servants run to him, and one takes his horse and walks him till he be cold, then rubs him and gives him food, yet I must say that they are not much to be trusted to this last point without the eye of the master or his servant to oversee them.
> Another servant gives the passenger his private chamber and kindles his fire; the third pulls off his boots and makes them clean. Then the

> A hundred women merrily
> Were carding hard with joyful cheer
> Who singing sat with voices clear..."

No doubt the number of men employed by Winchcombe is slightly exaggerated, but this cloth maker from nearby Gloucestershire was a legendary hero of song and story as early as 1520, and is supposed to have become so rich he led an army of his own apprentices to Flodden field, 100 strong, and afterwards feasted the young King Hal (Henry VIII) at his own London house. He was better known as "Jack of Newbury" when he moved from Gloucestershire to Berkshire, and his portrait still adorns the wall of the museum in Winchcombe. It is worth noting that this clothier, like "Whyte of Bradway," is well-known and successful enough to take his name from whatever town he is based in, "John of Winchcomb" or "Jack of Newbury." He may, in fact, have been a companion of "Whyte of Bradway" in his travels throughout the countryside.

host or hostess visit him and find if he will eat with the host or at a common table with others, his meal will cost him sixpence or in some places but fourpence; yet this course is not honourable and not used by gentlemen. But if he will eat in his chamber, he commands what meat he will, yea the kitchen is open to him to command the meat to be dressed as he best likes. And when he sits down at table, the host or hostess will accompany him, or if they have many guests at least visit him taking it for courtesy to be bid sit down.

While he eats, if he have company especially, he will be offered music, which he may freely take or refuse. And if he be solitary the musicians will give him good day with music in the morning...A man cannot more freely command in his own house than he may do in his inn. And at parting, if he give some few pence to the chamberlain and ostler, they wish him a happy journey.[25]

The description of this inn suggests a quality of service that would require many servants. Either landlord Sambache employed at least an ostler (stable boy) and one or two women to help his wife, or his children were pressed into service. Servants could leak news about an inn's guests or at least sufficient gossip to make trouble.

Both William Harrison the parson and William Shakespeare the playwright agree on the quality of the inns—food, beer, wine, clean linen in the beds and on the table, tapestry on the walls and good conversation. But Shakespeare suggests the sinister purpose sometimes lurking behind the courtesy of mine host, an intended robbery when people carried quantities of gold and silver instead of cheque books and credit cards. Harrison tells us that this practice led: "to the utter undoing of many an honest yeoman as he journeyeth on his way." Shakespeare's Falstaff and his band of rogues, forewarned by innyard gossip that a wealthy traveller was on the move, lay in wait for a "franklin in the weald of Kent" who had "brought three hundred marks in gold," and pulled off a most lucrative robbery.[26]

This episode, touched off by a dishonest servant of the inn where the franklin was staying, highlights the dilemma of the sixteenth century innkeeper. The crying need of an inn for a sizeable workforce that was both cheap and trustworthy provided an ample motive for the very large family which William Sambache and his wife Jane produced. This "William the Elder" is the grandson of Thomas White, the son of Will and Elizabeth White Sambache, and the same young William who inherited the silver spoons from his grandfather Whyte. He, with his wife Jane Severn, had no less than twenty-six children. When he died in 1630, an old man of "four score and three years," even the Broadway Parish Register notes proudly that "William Sambache gent,...of the eldest famille, buried 16th April 1630, was the father of 26 children by Mrs. Jane Severn, sole wife...."[27]

Of the sons and daughters born to this couple, sons John, Anthony, Sheldon, Richard, Thomas and Walter, all noted as baptised between 1579 and 1606, would have been old enough to help with the ongoing work of the inn. So would daughters Christian, Frances, Jane, Ursula and Cicely. Other children born after 1611 would have been too young to do more than keep up the fires and feed the hens. But for a time at least there were enough children to spread the workload even when the older sons and daughters had married and gone off to homes and jobs of their own.

The era of White and Sambache innkeepers, from before 1556 until 1620, covered more than seventy years of one of the most eventful periods of English history. Thomas White and Joan, young Will Sambache and Elizabeth White, and later, William Sambache and his wife Jane Severn and their many children, encompassed the reigns of all the Tudor monarchs from King Henry VII to Elizabeth, as well as the first Stuart, King James I. Through these decades, the innkeepers, old and young, watched the road from Evesham and the rough track over the hill from Stow on-the-Wold and Campden to see what weary travellers were coming their way. But regardless of business fluctuations, in each successive generation, the five silver spoons were kept polished and remained in a conspicuous place of honour.

"Mediæval Doorway". Drawn by Gordon Russell.

Elizabethan Chimneys. Drawn by Gordon Russell c. 1913.

III

1535-1600
"By Champaine Ground...14 Longe Myles..."

Two indefatigable wayfarers, John Leland and Thomas Habington, were on the roads near the Sambache inn at opposite ends of the sixteenth century, and their carefully-kept journals give us a picture of what the countryside was like in the days of the Sambaches' tenure as innkeepers, although there is no conclusive proof that they were ever their guests.

John Leland, "a sad-faced man with hooked nose and drooping mouth," began to explore the counties of England to write for King Henry VIII a monument to "the old glory of your renowned Britain...that it may flourish through the world...." He travelled the countryside extensively for eight years after 1535 but only finished a few volumes before "he fell beside his wits...."[1] He is a unique source.

Thomas Habington, who was banished from court after being implicated in a minor role in the Babington conspiracy to assassinate Queen Elizabeth in 1587, was pardoned on condition that he spent the rest of his life at his country estates in Worcestershire. The fact that Habington was also Elizabeth's godson may have influenced the Queen to clemency. He traveled throughout the county from 1588 onwards while compiling his *Survey of Worcestershire*.

Leland, a graduate of both Cambridge and Oxford universities, was appointed Keeper of the King's Libraries by Henry VIII before 1530. His official charge was to find books in the monastic houses that would be suitable for the king's own library. King Henry had been educated in the new, liberal tradition of Erasmus and was, in his younger days, something of a scholar.

Leland recognised the danger of books being scattered to the four winds as the monasteries were dissolved and made vigorous efforts to get Thomas Cromwell to help him in his quest. He wrote to Cromwell that:

"it would be a great profitt to students and honour to this realm...to multiply books by printing and to restore us to such a truthe in histories as we have longe wanted."[2]

Although he was concentrating on visits to abbeys and monasteries, Leland notes many places near Broadway, for instance, Northleach, " a praty uplandish towne,"[3] or that "Cirencester...in Coteswolde...hath the most celebrate market in all that quarters on Monday."[4] He informs us that "Camden is a market towne in Glocesterhire"[5] and "the towne of Evesham is...large and well buildyd with tymbar....[6] from Evesham I passyd 6 or 7 miles all by champaine grownd* in the Vale of Evesham being all or most parte in Worcestar-shire to Stanway a mile to Dydbroke and a quarter of a mile beyond is Hayles...."

When Leland was travelling, bridges were rare, and therefore worthy of note. Most of the time it was necessary to ford a river and get wet in the process. Leland records an instance when he "passed over Wye river, which for lack of good knowledge in me of the ford did sore trouble my horse." Three bridges near Broadway impressed him. The one at Worcester he describes as "a royal piece of worke, highe and stronge, and hathe 6 great arches of stone...."[7] The bridge at Tewkesbury appears to have been less sturdy. Leland pauses to give a detailed picture of this structure built in the reign of King John in the early thirteenth century:

> He that was put in trueste to do it first made a stone bridge over the great pour of both the armes of Avon by north and weste; and after to spede [speed up the building] and spare mony, he made at the northe ende a wodde [wood] bridge of a greate length for sudden land waters, putting the residue of the mony to the making of the castel of Hanley....King John gave to the mayntenance of the bridge the whole tolle of the Wenday [Wednesday] and Saturday markets in the town, the which they yet possess, turnying it rather to theire owne profit than reparation of the bridge.[8]

Apparently work on the original bridge was scamped so that town officials could put money in their pockets. King John tried to do at least one good deed for the travelling merchants of his day, but even that seems to have backfired. In Stratford Leland tells us that the original old "poore bridge of tymbar and no causey [causeway] to come to it" had been replaced by Sir Hugh of Clopton in 1497. Sir Hugh, "having never

---

*"Champaine Ground: common, arable land...meadows...woods...chief forests and parks...." (*The Itinerary of John Leland*, 34)

wife nor children, convertid a great piece of his substance in good workes in Stratford, first making a sumptious new bridge and large of stone, where in the middle be six great arches for the maine streame of Avon and at each end certain small arches to bear the causway, and so to pass commodiously at such tymes as the river risith...."[9] This bridge is still in use.

Today we take our highways for granted, but in the fifteenth and sixteenth centuries the repair of roads was generally the responsibility of local residents and was seldom, if ever, done properly. There were frequent disputes about road repairs. William Sambache appears to have been personally involved in one such squabble in 1599, as the Quarter Sessions Rolls for 2nd October of that year record: "A writ to the Sheriff to distrain Anthony Dickins, Ralph Franklin and William Sambache, inhabitants of Broadway to answer for the ill repair of the Broad way, being the highway leading toward London."*

In his travels to destinations mentioned in his itinerary, such as Stow-on-the-Wold, Burford, Evesham, Winchcombe, Campden, Stanway, and other nearby villages, Leland must have passed through Broadway on more than one occasion. He makes few mentions of food and lodging, concentrating instead on mileage, scenery, soil conditions, local industries, and other points he considers of interest to the king.

The fact that Leland lodged and dined mostly in church quarters deprives modern historians of a look at life in the inns and roadside taverns of his day. He does tell us, however, that although he found many roads in the kingdom "very noiseome and tedious to travel in," the roads in the Cotswolds were at least tolerable for a rider, and some of them passed near the White Hart. A typical mileage entry reads:

From Evesham to Hailes 6 miles
                        Winchelscombe 7 miles
                        Pershore 5 miles
                        Worcestar 12 miles
From Campden to Chipping Norton 14 longe miles

---

*It is tempting to interpret "The Broad way" to mean the road running in front of today's Lygon Arms, but there is no proof that it was. The old road from Evesham to London ran through Childswickham and then through the west end to St. Eadburgha's Church where it turned left and followed what is now Connygree Lane in a circuitous route to the top of Broadway Hill.

Habington, on the other hand, makes frequent mention of Broadway (which he spells in several different ways) and was obviously there more than once. In one of his lesser-known entries, he describes the town:

> Bradewaye, thus aunciently wrytten, lyeth in Pearshore's hundred at the foote of Monte Wicessi, nowe called Broadewey hylles...and so seated at the edge of the vale of Eusham [Evesham] as it hathe partly the commodity of that ryche soyle and partly of the large pasture for sheepe which are about and above the brode waye and asent to those sayd hylles....[10]

Habington himself must have walked up Broadway hill or near it, because his description of the lie of the land is vivid: "included in the fertoile vale of Eushome and her fowle ways, wherein Oswald leadeth you up a faire rase on the Brodeway hylls called aunciently Wiccesse, reaching two miles beyond St. Edward's Stowe, but the parishes are so inclosed with Gloucestershire that you must needs leape from the one to the other for three miles...."[11]

Thomas Habington and his older brother William, who was executed for his involvement in the plot to kill the Queen, were friends of the Babington family. Since William Babington had obtained a lease of part of Broadway Manor from Queen Mary in 1558 and lived there for nearly twenty years, it is possible that Thomas Habington had visited Broadway as a young man before the plot. Certainly by middle-age Habington knew the history of Broadway well. He informs us:

> When the Abbey of Pershore was ruinated, and the...Monastery divided, the glory of this towne was fyrst distributed into two and now last into three partes, yet all tyll of late closed up in the family of Sheldon, for Mr. Baldwin Sheldon, a branch of this house purchased the manor of Brodwey which yet remayneth in his issue.[12]

Skipping over the controversial years between 1535 and 1558, he continues:

> Thys Manor of Bradewaye after Monasteryes weare dissolved fell to William Babington who aliened the entire Lordship to Rafe Sheldon and William Chyld and the heirs of the above named Rafe in 1575. William Babington sould also to Anne Daston, widowe, a messuage [house site] in Bradeway....[13]

Habington apparently visited Mistress Anne Daston, describing her as "the most bountifull gentlewoman for hospitality of her degree in England"[14] and referring sympathetically to her "long endurynge widowhood."[15] (Her second husband, Anthony Daston, died in 1572, and she lived on at Broadway's "Greate Farme" until 1619, when she died at the advanced age of ninety-one. She was a well-known and much loved Lady of the Manor.)

The entry that most closely relates Thomas Habington to William Sambache's inn at the foot of the street is as follows:

> Broadwaye, the Broad and High waye from the Shepherdes Coates [cottages], which on the mounted woldes shelter themsealfes under the hylles from the rage of stormes downe to the most fruytfull vale of Evesham, or rather of England, is a towne extended in a streete tedyous in leangthe, especially in the wynter...[16]

Only someone who had walked or ridden up the street from the lower to the upper end and back more than once could write a description so exact that any visitor to Broadway would recognise it today. This tells us that there was some kind of road up Fish Hill at least two hundred years before the turnpike was built. This route may, by the late 1500's, have been a swifter alternative than Connygree Lane, especially for travellers coming downhill to Broadway from Stow-on-the-Wold and Campden.

This route would have taken Habington directly past the White Hart, and there is no reason to suppose that he would not have stopped there. He must have had friends in the area, and might well have met them at the inn in the middle of a journey or afterwards. Since Habington rated the road as particularly tedious *in winter*, we can surmise that he found it less tiresome in the spring and summer months and consequently traversed it in more than one season.

The use of the word "street" suggests two other points: first, the road must have been fairly well marked and possibly cobbled, and second there were at least a few houses or cottages in the upper part of the town, near the present "Flea Bank" or sixteenth-century houses, two of which still have half-timbered walls showing. If Habington travelled this road, so probably did a great many others, all of them in need of a stopping point in journeys long or short.

"Group of 'Finds'" discovered during the restoration in the early 1900's. Drawn by Gordon Russell.

IV

"Your Highness Is Come Unto Cotswold...."

One day in July, 1575, the ancient bells of Worcester Cathedral rang out triumphantly. Members of the clothiers' and drapers' guilds donned their official robes of crimson and purple and displayed their banners; crowds of common people dressed in their best clothes and knelt in the streets as the city prepared a special welcome. Queen Elizabeth was honouring Worcester with a royal visit.

It was more than ninety miles from Whitehall, Greenwich, or Hampton Court to the White Hart Inn, but the royal influence would nevertheless have been felt at William Sambache's hearth and in the village of Broadway in the sixteenth century.* Royal progresses were deliberately planned to bring the sovereigns into contact with the people all over the kingdom, and Tudor monarchs travelled often. When the manufacture of cloth began to supersede the export of raw wool, an important source of royal income, the wool tax, fell dramatically. Consequently, the Cotswolds and their wool, and the problems of the clothiers in cities such as Worcester, were important enough to bring the Queen herself to this ancient city.

The Deputy Recorder of Worcester, William Bellue, very proud of his University M.A., knelt between the bailiffs to extend to Her Majesty the liberties of the city, and then embarked on a long and solemn speech. He emphasised Worcester's dependence on the cloth trade, citing seventh-century Mercian Lord Wolfarnis who "of his kinglie affection towards

---

*All the Tudor monarchs stayed in touch with their people. King Henry VII may have stopped in Broadway in the summer of 1495. King Henry VIII was closely involved in a Broadway land squabble between Abbot John Stoneywell and certain Broadway parishioners, King Henry's son, Edward VI, passed a statute in 1552 to "avoid the great prices and Excesses of Wines," which restricted the number of taverns and wine sellers in each town. Since Worcester was allowed only three, Broadway may have been limited to one inn at that date. Queen Mary I, in 1558, arranged for one of her favourites, the Catholic Sir William Babington, to lease the Manor of Broadway from Pershore Abbey, temporarily replacing Ralph Sheldon.

this towne abowete nyne hundred yeres past...by his charter granted and made Worcester a citie...about which tyme the inhabitants here first began their market of woole and trade of clothynge...," and went on to mention the "three hundred and fowrscore great loomes, whereby eight thowsand persons were well maintained in wealth and abilitie...."[1]

Mr. Bellue was more zealous for his city than accurate (perhaps because he received twenty pounds for his speech). He went on to point out with heart-rending pathos:

> But why remember we the tyme past with such commendacion of the floyrshing estate thereof? Whey do we shew your majesty things that late we are and now are not with that greef of mynde? [grief of mind] May we remember that Worcester (one of the ancient cities of your kingdom) was some time wealthy, beautiful and well inhabited?[2]

Why indeed? At about this time many of the wool growers in the country in small towns and villages were setting up looms and fulling mills of their own, and the clothier's trade, once the province of the cities, was spreading to country villages like Broadway, which were closer to the source of wool.

Bellue and the people of Worcester were hoping for some concessions for the future protection of their cloth trade. These they obtained some fifteen years later, when they were "rewarded for their trouble and their kneeling"[3] by a charter of incorporation for their weavers and clothiers in 1590.

After residing a week with the Bishop of Worcester, the Queen progressed to the village of Elmley Castle, where she was entertained by Broadway's Anne Daston, who went back to her old home for this purpose.[4] Elizabeth then proceeded to Sudeley Castle in Winchcombe, where she was greeted by people dressed as shepherds and shepherdesses to give emphasis to the chief business of the area. A man dressed in a white smock and carrying a crook of ram's horn bowed low and began to speak, reminding the Queen not of the importance of cloth making, but of the Cotswold wool that made it possible:

> Your highness is come unto Cotswold, an uneven country, but [a country of] people that carry their thoughts level with their fortune...the hills present nothing but cottages and nothing can we present to your Highness but this lock of wool, Cotswold her fruit and my poor gift to your Highness in which nothing is esteemed but the whiteness, Virginity's colour, nor to be expected but duty, shepherd's duty....[5]

The shepherd's words ring truer than the rhetorical eloquence of William Bellue, M.A. It is to be hoped that Her Majesty was suitably impressed.

As far as can be determined, Queen Elizabeth did not visit Broadway on this progress, but there is evidence suggesting that some of those who travelled with her in the royal train did stop at the White Hart, perhaps for a capon and a cup or two of claret. These bright, silent, witnesses are coins from the years 1573 to 1575 with the Queen's image stamped upon them, which were discovered in the rafters in some of the rooms during repairs and restoration by Sydney Russell in the 1920's.[6] Elizabeth had rescued her father's debased monetary system, and restored an "honest coinage" to the country, a few years before her summer progress to Worcestershire. Some of these new, silver coins found their way to the Sambache inn where they remained hidden for nearly three hundred years.

William and Elizabeth Sambache, by then middle-aged and celebrating their thirtieth wedding anniversary, would have been in the crowd that thronged to see the Queen at Sudeley. They might have been accompanied by Grandmother Joan White and some of their sons, possibly Will, the oldest, and Jane Severn from Shrawley, who were soon to be married.[7]

A bright summer afternoon, a popular queen who had kept the nation out of war and less haunted by the fears that had dominated the reigns of her father, her younger brother, and her older sister—it was a time of hope and prosperity. The Sambaches would have thrown their caps in the air and cheered with the others: "Long Live Good Queen Bess!"

"God Save the Queen" was a familiar cry the length and breadth of England in the years that followed that summer progress of 1575. Plotting for Mary Queen of Scots was ended by her execution in 1587, and the Spanish Armada was defeated the following year. The danger of invasion passed and people dared, for a brief space of time, to be hopeful.

Services in parish churches were conducted in the language of the people; prayers were said and psalms were sung in words that villagers understood. The Church of England services we know today are an inheritance from these Elizabethans, who were joyful, singing, uninhibited people. There was a new music and a new poetry at the Court in London, and in Broadway, at St. Eadburgha's, the Sambache family and their fellow villagers happily obeyed the command: "O be joyful in the lord, all ye lands: serve the lord with gladness, and come before his presence with a song."

V

"These High, Wild Hills and Rough, Uneven Ways"

> I know a bank where the wild thyme blows,
> Where oxlips and the nodding violet grows;
> Quite over-canopied with luscious woodbine,
> With sweet musk-roses and with eglantine...
> *A Midsummer Night's Dream*

The new music and the new poetry that were being sung and spoken at the Court in London came straight from Cotswold country, from the old heart of England. William Shakespeare knew the Cotswolds well and probably passed through Broadway on more than one occasion. Whether he visited the White Hart Inn cannot be proved conclusively, but there is strong circumstantial evidence that some time in the last years of his life, he journeyed to Broadway and stopped at the hostelry.

The case for Shakespeare in Broadway and at the White Hart Inn is, with one exception, not based on any startling new discoveries. We have merely examined with care the evidence previously gathered by several distinguished scholars and summarised where this assembly of facts could conceivably lead.

William Shakespeare had more than a casual knowledge of sheep and sheep farming and an investment in tithes and land that linked him to Broadway. He had a large circle of friends, colleagues and relatives by marriage in or near Broadway and various business reasons to keep in touch with these people. One of his family's oldest friends was Henry Strelly, who became Vicar of Broadway in 1610.

In the sixteenth century, Broadway was still a major centre for sheep farmers and anyone on the fringes of the wool trade would have reason to go there. Only eighteen miles to the north-east lay Stratford, where

Shakespeare's father, John, among various other pursuits, was a "considerable dealer in wool," buying, selling and appraising it. In 1592 John Shakespeare priced the goods of his neighbour Joseph Shaw, "Woll Dryer."[1] In a chancery suit in 1599 the elder Shakespeare sought to recover a debt of twenty-one pounds, plus ten pounds damages, for wool he had previously sold to one John Walford of Marlborough, Wiltshire, "payable on demand for twenty-one tods of wool."[2]

The details of such transactions were not lost on John's son, who shows a clear grasp of the sheep business in his great seasonal play, *The Winter's Tale*, written in 1611 when the playwright was spending more of his time at New Place in Stratford. In fact, in this play Shakespeare traces the sheep farmer's year from winter to autumn with piercing accuracy. In the lean winter months, hard on man and beast:

> You'll be so lean that blasts of January
> Would blow you through and through....

In March and April when the newborn lambs frolic and the weather is good:

> We were as twinn'd lambs, that did frisk i' the sun,
> And bleat the one at the other....

In the autumn there was the inevitable Martinmas slaughter:

> As fat as tame things, one good deed dying tongueless,
> Slaughters a thousand waiting upon that....

The sheep would have been fat and tame but they would, nonetheless, have been slaughtered, and in their thousands. This sounds like a boyhood memory and not a pleasant one.

The climax to *The Winter's Tale* is the great sheep-shearing feast in June for which the flustered shepherd is preparing as he tries to count his profits and goes off to buy provisions to feed his workers:

> Let me see, every 'leven wether tods, every tod yields pound and odd shilling, fifteen hundred shorn, what comes the wool to? *

> I cannot do't without counters. Let me see, what am I to buy for our

---

*Shakespeare seems to be accurate even to the cost of the wool, which, if the prices are accurate, has gone up only the "odd shilling" in the dozen years since his father's suit. John Shakespeare sued for twenty-one pounds as fair payment for twenty-one tods, plus ten pounds damages. William Shakespeare's shepherd rates each of his tods as worth "pound and odd shilling."

sheep shearing feast? My sister has made me four and twenty nosegays for the shearers...I must go buy spices for our sheep shearing...

This busy Master Shepherd has much in common with Robert Handy, Richard Faulkes, Thomas White and other wool men previously associated with the White Hart Inn. They had all hosted the customary sheep shearing feasts over generations and coped with the necessary planning and expense.

There are several other specific links between Broadway people and the Shakespeares of Stratford. First is the long and many-sided relationship between the playwright's parents, John and Mary Shakespeare, and later the playwright himself, with the Combe family of Stratford and Mickelton.

In the lawsuit against Walford, John and Mary Shakespeare had chosen John Combe, a wealthy Stratford business man and money lender, to examine their selected witnesses and to advise them in other legal matters.[3] John's uncle, William Combe, had been born in Broadway in 1551, (his mother was Katharine Sheldon Combe)[4] and although he later lived in Stratford he seems to have retained an affection for his birthplace, bequeathing ten pounds "to the poor of Broadway"[5] when he died in 1610. In 1602 the Combes, uncle and nephew, sold over one hundred acres of land to William Shakespeare for £320, "and all the Common pasture for Sheep, horses, kyne, or other Cattle in the fieldes of Olde Stretford aforesaid."[6]

Three years later Shakespeare made another investment which linked him with Broadway. On 24th July, 1605, he purchased from his friend and business colleague Ralph Hubaud, for the sum of four-hundred and forty pounds, "a moiety (one half) of tithes of corne, grayne, blade and heye" from lands located in Old Stratford, Welcombe, and Bishopton, as well as "tythes of wooll, lambe, and other small and privie tythes" in the parish of Stratford. Hubaud, a leading Stratford citizen, was married to Anne Daston, daughter of Anthony and Anne Daston of Broadway.*[8] Anne's mother, Anne Sheldon Savage Daston, outlived two husbands and lived at Broadway's Great Farm near Saint Eadburgha's church.

When Hubaud died in 1606, William Shakespeare owed him the not insignificant sum of £20.[9] Anne Daston Hubaud, sole executrix of her husband's affairs, went back to her own family in Broadway after

---

* Hubaud and Anne Daston were married at St. Eadburgha's 24th April, 1584.

Ralph's death. Might not Shakespeare have ridden over from Stratford to pay this large debt to his old friend's bereaved widow in person?

When Shakespeare had purchased his moiety of the Stratford tithes from Ralph Hubaud, the other half was in the possession of other Daston relatives—Thomas and Mary Combe.* When Thomas died in 1608 the tithes were jointly owned by his wife Mary and their oldest son William.[10]

It was this William Combe and his Uncle John who touched off the famous dispute when they tried to enclose a large portion of their open fields in Welcombe (near Stratford) in 1614. They proposed to turn arable land into pasture for sheep, thus putting many small farmers off the land and depriving them of employment. This attempt erupted into a major controversy in which tithe holders like Shakespeare were forced to consider whether their monetary investment as well as their reputations would be adversely affected.

The Welcombe case would have been common gossip throughout the countryside and would certainly have reached Broadway's Great Farm. There Mistress Daston's large estate was managed by two of the sons of her first marriage, William and Walter Savage and their families. By 1614 Walter Savage would undoubtedly have been glad of some assistance from his younger Stratford cousins, William and Thomas Combe, especially during haymaking and harvest. William's Welcombe enclosure would have been a topic of heated debate. William's younger brother, Thomas, to whom Shakespeare willed his sword, is thought to have been the playwright's godson.

Anne Savage Daston, sharp-witted and clear-eyed, undoubtedly knew both these young men well and gave them the benefit of her opinions as well as a good meal. What the Savages and Dastons thought of Shakespeare, who never opposed the enclosure,** and even profited well

---

*Thomas was the brother of the John Combe of Stratford mentioned above. His wife, Mary Savage Younge was the widowed daughter of Anthony Savage of Elmley Castle, the brother of Francis Savage, Mistress Daston's first husband. The sons of this marriage—Anthony, William and Walter Savage—were, therefore, second cousins to John Combe's nephews, William and Thomas.

** Contrary to popular rumour Shakespeare did not oppose the enclosure of Welcombe lands by old John and young William Combe. He retained his tithes throughout the Welcombe case and did well by them financially—earning sixty pounds a year. It was Shakespeare's friend, the Town Clerk of Stratford, Thomas Greene, who "could not bear [or endure] the enclosing of Welcombe..." and not the playwright. A leading Shakespearean scholar believes that Greene meant to write "barre" or "prevent", but is quite clear that the phrase is Greene's and not Shakespeare's.

from it in compensation from the Stratford Town Council—since sheep pastures paid less in tithes than fields of grain and hay—is not known.

Anne Sheldon Savage Daston is at the centre of the web of marriage and business which links Shakespeare to Broadway. She was a remarkable and durable figure who lived at Broadway's Great Farm throughout her long widowhood of forty-seven years, to be ninety-one years old at her death in 1619. After Francis Savage died she had married Anthony Daston. He died in 1572.

Left well off by both her husbands, indeed the richest landowner in Cotswold countryside, Anne Sheldon Savage Daston—still in her mid-forties when she was widowed for a second time—developed a reputation for being the best hostess in the Broadway area, in fact the "the most bountiful gentlewoman of her degree in all England."[11] She attracted interesting guests to her home—lawyers, university graduates, writers and Londoners, who could provide stimulating intellectual conversation. She would certainly have invited her daughter and son-in-law, Ralph Hubaud, and possibly with them their increasingly famous actor-poet friend, William Shakespeare. Perhaps this guest thanked his hostess in kind. An early copy of his poems was later found among the possessions of her son Walter.[12]

In the latter part of the sixteenth and early seventeenth centuries, other guests at the Great Farm may have included Mistress Daston's Combe cousins who associated with her Savage children and grandchildren, members of the Quiney and Sturley families and the popular Robert Dover who ran the May festival on Kingcombe Hill. An invitation from this renowned lady would have been coveted.

Anne Daston would most assuredly have invited her vicar to her parties. In the year 1610 a new Broadway vicar had just been appointed, Henry Sturley or Strelly* of Stratford and Campden. This young man is

---

It is doubtful if either Greene or Shakespeare was present at the famous scene when old John Combe watched with amusement the efforts of protesters to prevent his hedges going up. He is supposed to have ordered his diggers to throw these people to the ground while "he sat laughing on his horseback and sayd they wer good football playrs..." But regardless of whether he witnessed this protest, Shakespeare emerges from the whole Welcombe controversy simply as a good businessman who cared more about his investment than the vexatious principle of enclosure and its effect on poor people. When he died in 1614, John Combe left five pounds to Shakespeare in his will, possibly as a token of his gratitude to this eminent and influential Stratford citizen for not opposing his enclosure of the Welcombe lands.
*The names Sturley and Strelly were used interchangeably by this family.

the most compelling link of all between Broadway and William Shakespeare.[13] There had been a life-long friendship between Shakespeare's parents and Henry's father, Abraham Sturley/Strelly. Abraham began his career in Worcester, where his eldest son, Henry, was born, and had become a town official in Stratford by 1594.[14] He advised John and Mary Shakespeare on many practical matters. A graduate of Cambridge University, a well-read man and a Latin scholar whose extensive library included Cicero, Pliny, and Plutarch, the elder Strelly encouraged his friends, as well as his son, to read these authors and probably loaned some of his books to the young Shakespeare.

Sturley/Strelly's son, Henry, some twelve years younger than Shakespeare, was an exceptionally able student who had matriculated at Exeter College, Oxford, in 1594/95, becoming Assistant Schoolmaster at Stratford's Grammar School three years later.[15] Although there is no conclusive proof that he taught Shakespeare's younger children, he might well have informally passed on some of his knowledge to Hamnet and Judith while he was still at University.** Their father would have approved of his twin children conversing with an outstanding Oxford scholar. Shakespeare himself would have visited Abraham and Henry Strelly when he came home. University graduates were a rare and welcome source of books and stimulating conversation.

When Henry Strelly was appointed Vicar of Broadway in 1610 and took over St. Eadburgha's Church and parish, he became both minister and neighbour to old Anne Daston. He also started a small private school. In both his capacities, minister and schoolmaster, he would have known the large Sambache family, who were then running the White Hart Inn. He baptised Anne, William Sambache's seventh daughter, in 1610, and, three years later, conducted the burial service of John, William's oldest son, who died young in 1613. Strelly officiated at several other Sambache weddings in the decades that followed, and must have taught some of the many Sambache children. Walter, William and Nicholas were all born between 1597 and 1610 and would have been of school age when Strelly was schoolmaster.[16]

As vicar, friend and schoolmaster, Strelly undoubtedly visited the White Hart Inn. It was during these visits that he met and courted the woman who was to become his wife, Ursula Sambache Chettle. Innkeeper Sambache's fourth daughter was a young widow, who may

---

**Hamnet Shakespeare died August 11, 1596 at the age of 11, a year before Strelly became Stratford's Assistant Schoolmaster.

have helped to serve tankards when the inn was busy. In 1606, at seventeen, she had married Anthony Chettle of London and gone to live there.[17] When Chettle died three years later, Ursula returned home to her father's inn.

On 19th September, 1612, by which time Shakespeare had written his last plays and returned to his native Stratford, Henry Strelly married Ursula.[18] Shakespeare might very well have come to Broadway with the Strelly family for his old friend's wedding and the feast of cakes and ale which followed at the bride's father's inn. In 1614 the first of the five children of Henry and Ursula Strelly was baptised in Broadway and again Shakespeare might have been present for the occasion and the celebrations afterwards, especially since by then he had another good reason to travel in that direction.

In the same year that Henry Strelly married Ursula Sambache, Abraham Strelly sold "a close by Evesham way" to Shakespeare's son-in-law, John Hall, who had married Shakespeare's oldest daughter, Susanna, in 1607. The Halls, with their four year old daughter Elizabeth, were living with the Shakespeare parents at New Place, Stratford, but in 1612 may have lived for a time in a home of their own near Evesham.[19] John Hall*, another Oxford graduate who shared Shakespeare's literary interests, would have welcomed his father-in-law's visits. It is not difficult to imagine Abraham Sturley and William Shakespeare travelling together to see their children and grandchildren in Evesham and Broadway.

There was another less obvious but nonetheless clear incentive for William Shakespeare to have visited Broadway in the last decades of his life. In 1614, the third, and worst, of a series of fires devastated Stratford, causing £8,000 worth of damage. Then, as in 1594 and 1595, the surrounding countryside was called upon to provide assistance.[20] Henry Strelly and Adrian Quiney, even went to London to seek the help of the Queen's Attorney General, Sir Edward Coke. The two men are noted both in 1600 and 1601 "searching records for our town's causes." Their 1601 mission to the Court failed, unfortunately coinciding with the Essex rebellion, although Coke did agree that "it is very reasonable and conscionable for hir majestie to graunt in relief of this towne twise

---

*John Hall probably shared not only literary but medical knowledge with Shakespeare. He is recorded in Stratford after Shakespeare's death as a "doctor of physick" and once cured Michael Drayton, a mutual friend, of a "tertian fever."

afflicted and almost wasted by fire."[21] Quiney was, however, successful in securing a contribution to the relief fund from Shakespeare,[22] as he had been after the first fire, and no doubt was again in 1614, when Shakespeare was actually living in Stratford.

Clergymen throughout the countryside led efforts to raise money for Stratford in what became a cause celebre. The vicar and schoolmaster of Broadway, former schoolmaster of Stratford who had taught the children of many of those distressed by the fires, would have been in the vanguard of this crusade and would doubtless have gone beyond the customary appeal from the pulpit.* Strelly would not have missed the chance do as much as he could, especially when his chief parishioner, Anne Daston, was noted both for her wealth and her generosity. [23]

If Vicar Strelly had wanted to organise a fund raising effort on a wider scale than the church, a logical place to choose would have been Broadway's Great Farm, where the wealthy and influential were accustomed to meeting as the guests of the venerable Anne Daston. Strelly would have made a special point of persuading his wealthy Stratford friend, William Shakespeare, to come to this event and add his name and fame to the prestigious cause.**

When their eighty-six year old hostess, Mistress Anne Daston, retired for the night, Vicar Strelly might have taken her most notable guest and other convivial friends the short distance across the fields by footpath to the White Hart Inn for further talk and refreshment. Shakespeare liked to enjoy himself in hostelries, and Henry Strelly, man of the cloth though he was, would not have been averse to entertaining a local celebrity at his father-in-law's establishment. The group may have been accompanied by other family members and friends—perhaps Adrian Quiney and his son, Thomas. Possibly there were winks and nods about Thomas Quiney and Shakespeare's daughter, Judith, for in two years time the pair would be married.[24]

---

*When natural disasters such as floods and fires damaged towns and villages, as was frequent in a time of mostly timber construction, a royal mandate was customarily issued for a collection to help the victims. This was addressed to the parish incumbent and churchwardens and read from the pulpit. At the end of the service the clerk took the collection at the church door, the funds were handed over to an authorised travelling collector and duly recorded.

**Worcestershire, or Wigorn, is recorded as having made significant contributions to these fund-raising efforts in 1594/95. Though the names of individual contributors are not recorded it is inconceivable that Anne Sheldon Savage Daston would not have been among them. (ER 11/42-3)

Enjoying an evening tankard with friends at the White Hart or staying at the Great Farm, Shakespeare would have been close to the hilly trackways into Gloucestershire. Certainly his plays show knowledge of the Cotswolds in general and of Gloucestershire specifically. A passage in *King Richard II* evokes the "wilds of Gloucestershire":

> Believe me, noble lord
> I am a stranger here in Gloucestershire
> These high, wild hills and rough uneven ways
> Draw out our miles and make them wearisome....
>
> But I bethink me what a weary way
> From Ravenspurg to Cotswold will be found...

Anyone who has climbed from Broadway to Snowshill* on road or track would agree with the poet's repetition of the word "wearisome."

Bumbling old Justice Shallow in *King Henry IV* Part 2 owns a house in Gloucestershire. This house may have been modelled on the home of Sir Charles Percy of Dumbleton, who knew the play well enough to write to a friend while Shakespeare was still alive, on 7th December, 1606: "If I stay here long in this fashion, at my return I think you will find me so dull that I shall be taken for Justice Silence or Justice Shallow...."[25]

Both Shakespeare and his son-in-law, John Hall, may have stayed with Percy in Dumbleton or in a similar Gloucestershire house. Hall, in the year 1631, reminisced in a letter to a friend about a place he had cherished in his younger days: "a knight's house in Gloucestershire to which place I yearly used to come in the summer time** to recreate myself and spend some two or three months in the country..." Shakespeare may have similarly "recreated" himself in such a Cotswold retreat.[26]

---

* The year after Shakespeare's death in 1617, his friend, Henry Condell, purchased some land in Brockhampton. There is, therefore, at least an outside chance that Shakespeare climbed this very hill to where Brockhampton Farm now stands, to look over the land and advise his colleague. (Barnard, 50)

** The poet often transports the spring and summer flowers that he knew in the Cotswolds to "Athens," "Bohemia," or the "Bermoothes" with convincing enchantment:

"Daffodils that come before the swallow dares and take the winds of March with beauty"

"Pale primroses that die unmarried ere they can behold bright
Phoebus in his strength,
Bold oxlips and crown imperial..."

"Where the bee sucks, there suck I
In a cowslips's bell I lie
Merrily, merrily shall I live now
Under the blossoms that hang on the bough..."

One spring holiday in Gloucestershire that Shakespeare is likely to have attended some time in the last four years of his life or earlier is the Dover's Hill Games, held near Campden in Whitsun week. He certainly would have known of their founder, Robert Dover, an attorney, who is thought to have met Shakespeare while studying law at Gray's Inn in London, where Michael Drayton, Thomas Heywood and Ben Jonson were their mutual friends. Both Drayton and Jonson were at Dover's Hill several times and Shakespeare may well have joined his literary friends for some of these jollifications.[27]

Dover, who lived variously at Saintbury, Wickhamford and Barton-On-The-Heath in Warwickshire, had, at the request of James I, transformed this local Campden festival into a major spring social event which drew spectators from as far as sixty miles away.[28] Dover's aim was to emulate the Olympic contests, so he even arranged for a man dressed as Homer to play the harp to add a classical and literary dimension to the lively proceedings. The gentry "in their most elaborate clothes, their horses groomed and plumed feathers flying, could hunt and course, race, gossip, eat and drink to their hearts content while their admiring women folk looked on..."[29]

A contemporary poet, William Denney describes how:

> Each huntsman there, with skill and hope brings forth
> His best bred dogs to show their ablest worth.

Denney makes clear that commoners also enjoyed the occasion:

> Abroad the jolly Sheepheards Bagg Pipes play
> Of whom some leap, some wrastle for the day,
> Some throw the sledge, and others spurne the Barre,
> All act a part that makes them fit for Warre.[30]

As a member of this enthusiastic crowd, Shakespeare would have seen many demonstrations of strength by the local counterparts of "Will Squele, a Cotswold man," and would have watched numerous "fallow greyhounds...outrun on Cotsall." The crowd would have been vast and varied and have included not only "Will Squeles" showing off their physical prowess but Combes, Dastons, Hubauds, Savages and others from the nearby counties as well as from farther away—a rich tapestry for a great poet's imagination.

When darkness fell on Kingcombe Plain, as Dover's Hill was then called, the thirsty participants may have descended on Broadway as well as Campden for food and drink. All nearby towns would have been filled and overflowing so it would have been convenient to be accompanied by a friend who was an innkeeper's son-in-law.

Shakespeare's possible visits to Broadway and the White Hart, whether from Dover's Hill, from Mickelton or from Stratford, plausible as they seem, are speculation rather than firm proof. For those who like to discover new clues about Shakespeare, however slim, we have summarised the facts that exist. Readers can draw their own conclusions.

The one provocative new fact that has come to light, and one worth repeating, is that in the last six years of Shakespeare's life, when he spent more time in Stratford than previously, one of his family's oldest friends, and a former schoolmaster, was the Vicar of Broadway and had married Ursula Sambache Chettle, daughter of Innkeeper William Sambache of the White Hart Inn.

VI

1620-1683
"My House Or Inn... Called The White Hart"

A sharp wind blew down from the hills that brisk November morning in the year 1620, but John Treavis took no notice as he hurried across the village green. He had been looking forward to this day for most of the twenty years that he and his wife Ursula had lived in Broadway. If all went well, the inn and its two and one half burgages of valuable land would soon be his.

Treavis knew the little building well. Three generations of the Sambache family had run the inn and two generations of Whites before that. It had been called the White Hart in the old days, but a few years ago—nobody seemed to know exactly when or why—the sign had been changed to the Swan. He and his wife Ursula would put that right. The oldest inn in the village deserved the oldest name.

Old Will Sambache and his son Walter frequently did business with Treavis. As a member of London's Vintners' Company,[1] he could obtain fine wines to supplement the beer, ale, cider and perry brewed and pressed locally. The Sambaches never bought much, for the inn was a small one, but they were steady customers and good friends. Now Will was seventy-three and ready to retire. Young Walter had other plans.

It had been a long wait for Treavis, but now the time was right. The profits from his London trade, which had kept him away from Ursula and the children for too many months of each year, had been good and he had finally managed, after a long struggle, to collect his share of the large sum that his father had spent to provision the Earl of Essex's expedition to Ireland in 1599.[2] After much persuading on Treavis' part, Lord Mountjoye, the Lord Leftenant of Ireland, had finally agreed to pay the debt and at last his father's estate was settled.

Treavis mused cheerfully that there would be money enough left over after the purchase to enlarge the building, build a proper entrance, add plaster ceilings and oak wainscoting. He would make this a house that Ursula would be proud to live in and reward her for the patient years of waiting.

William and Walter were sitting at a small table beside the stone fireplace. Mulled wine was offered and the transaction was soon completed. For "one hundred pounds, fourscore and four shillings lawful money," Treavis became the owner of "two burgages and one half burgage* being now one dwelling house or inn situate in Broadway, commonly called or known by the sign of the Swan and one little pasture with all houses, barns, stables, orchards, gardens...."[3]

Treavis made a great many changes in the next two decades. One of his first moves was to install an ornate doorway crowned with his wife's name and his own, carved over the date of purchase, 1620, to celebrate their ownership. As the sixteenth century had belonged to the Whites and Sambaches, the seventeenth would belong to the Treavises. The inn was to remain in the family for more than half a century.

The doorway was only a start. Treavis made other substantial changes and enlargements to the inn. He added to the front and side of the old building and built several new rooms on the floor above; these were plastered, with ornate ceiling decorations and fitted with mullioned windows. The enlargements were so extensive that a nineteenth-century antiquarian, Peter Prattinton, made a note beside Ursula Wells Treavis' baptismal record in the Badsey Parish Register that she "married John Treavis who built the White Hart Inn in 1620."[4] He may have meant "re-built," but the changes made by Treavis to the first, much smaller hostelry were impressive enough to look like a new building.

It is not known precisely when the Treavis (Travers, Traves) family first appeared in Broadway. The earliest official record of the family in the Broadway Parish Register is the christening of William Treavis in 1609, followed by his brother Robert in 1611, and four sisters, Elizabeth, Mary, Anne, and Philip [sic], between 1612 and 1616.[5] This suggests that

---

* The term "burgage" evolved from the Medieval open-field system of farming. A burgage plot was characteristically long and narrow and consisted of an acre or at least half an acre. Over the centuries these ploughland strips, which made up the early agrarian settlement, became effectively freehold so that people were free to buy or sell them. It was rare for anyone to acquire as much as three burgages. John Treavis, with his two and a half, apparently bought a sizeable amount of land on or near the present site of the Lygon Arms. Goblets Wine Bar, a sixteenth century building, may well have been part of the first farmhouse and inn.

John and Ursula Treavis had established a home near the White Hart more than a decade before they became innkeepers, although there is no baptismal record for their three older sons, Thomas, Matthew, and John.* Ursula Wells, who was forty-two at the time of the purchase of the inn, was born in Badsey in 1578 and married John Treavis "c. 1600." Her father was Thomas Wells, farmer, of Badsey.** [6]

Although Thomas Habington mentions a Travers family "aunciently of this county" [Worcestershire], the seventeenth-century family connected with the Broadway inn is more likely to have originated in London, according to the Russell archivist and some other records recently unearthed.[7] A John Traves (Travis, Travers, Treavis), who was probably the father of the innkeeper, was a successful member of the Vintners Company of London, and also a victualler there in the late sixteenth century. In this capacity he helped to outfit the Earl of Essex's disastrous expedition to Ireland "in the tyme of our late dreade sovераign Queen Elizabeth,"[8] in 1599. When this John Traves died in 1604, of the £630 worth of provisions he had supplied to the expedition, "Lord Mountjoye, Lord Leftenenant of Ireland" still owed him more than £230. (Mountjoye succeeded Essex in Ireland after the Earl's rebellion and execution in 1601).

Old Traves' will left clear and specific instructions for the recovery of this large debt: "My will and minde is that my sonne, John, shall take upon him the furnishynge of ...greate labour, charge and tyme in the executynge...for the obtainynge and gettinge of the said surplusage..."[9] Since much of Traves' wealth was tied up in this debt, he specified that after the money had been recovered and the expenses for so doing paid, then and only then, his estate was to be divided into three parts—to his "well-beloved wife Anne"; to John, his eldest son; and to Thomas his second son and his two daughters, Anne and Margaret, in equal shares.***

---

*John and Ursula Treavis also had a daughter, Jane, who died in infancy and whose burial is recorded in the Parish Register in 1609.
**We do not know the exact date of Ursula's marriage to John. Vicar Strelly, or some other church official, noted some years later: "Shee is this xth [tenth] day of June 1634, the wife of John Treavis."
***John Traves died 15 January, 1604 and his will was proved 27 August, 1605. His marriage record to Anne Southam, and the baptism of their daughter Anne, have also survived. Therefore, although we can find no baptismal records for John, Thomas and Margaret, we are relying on the Russell archivist for Traves' membership in the Vintners company and his relationship to John Treavis of Broadway, especially since Anne, Thomas, and John are family names which recur in John Treavis large family in the following decades.

Young John was thus burdened with a time-consuming duty upon which his inheritance depended. This task may well have occupied his energies for a great part of the period between his father's death in 1604 and his purchase of the inn in 1620,* which, in turn, would explain why there are few records of his presence in Broadway during the early seventeenth century. Ursula and the children probably remained there while he travelled between London and Ireland.

The Treavis (Travis, Traves) involvement with the brisk commerce of London was a strong one that seems to have been maintained over several generations. Two of John Treavis' five sons later became respected members of the Grocers and Salters Companies. The Grocers and Salters, like the Vintners, were members of the "Twelve Great Livery Companies" of London, originally chartered by King Edward III.** These companies, some of which still exist, were the top layer of London trade and prestige for centuries and are an indication of the Treavis family wealth and general standing. [10]

The close connection of the Treavis family with London may also have been caused by the overseas expansion in the years prior to the Civil War. The East India Company was in full swing, and the American colonies opened up new opportunities for a shrewd man to invest and make money in overseas ventures. In an age when there were no banks and few chances for investments as we know them today, fortunes were often made by anyone in London with the means to put a ship to sea at an opportune time and await its return with a lucrative cargo. Members of the Salters and Grocers companies, and other similar organisations, would have been aware of these possibilities and among the most likely

---

*John Treavis's struggle to recover his father's Irish debt may have gained momentum in 1609 because in that year and the years directly following, King James I made an effort to get the assistance of London merchants, and the Livery Companies in particular to colonize the Irish county of Derry. This had been "depopulated and laid waste" at the end of Elizabeth's reign during the rebellion in which the Earl of Essex played such an ill-fated role. All twelve companies participated in this cause and contributed £60,000 in equal shares. Subsequently the "late desolated cittie of the Derrie" became London-Derry with new masters, the Corporation and Companies of London. (Herbert, I, 222) If the Vintners, Salters and Grocers each invested £5,000 the Lord Lieutenant of Ireland would not have wanted one of their members to continue to complain about a debt of £200.

**All three companies received their original charters in the Middle Ages. The Vintners were first known as the "Wine Tunners" when they were recognized by Edward III. The Grocers, equally ancient, were called first the "Pepperers." The Salters, who received their livery from Richard II in 1384, were incorporated by Queen Elizabeth in 1588. All three of these companies were re-confirmed by later monarchs.

to take advantage of them as did two of the Treavis sons. (The wealth of the American colonies may have already been flowing back to support the inn then, just as it does today).

Old John Traves, with his obstinate struggle to recover his old debt, and his son, John Treavis, who finished the job for him, would have both been proud that two of their successors inherited a measure of their business acumen. William, born in 1609, went into trade in London in 1638 and not only became a member of the well-known Grocers Company, but also the proprietor of "the Three Pigeons" in Watling Street. He died "extremely wealthy" in 1664, leaving his estate to his wife, Rebecca, and three children. His younger brother, Matthew, lived to a ripe old age, and when he died in 1681 was also "very wealthy."[11] His fortune, made as a Salter, was willed to a number of sons and daughters. There is no record of what happened to the other two sons, John and Robert. However, in the year 1634, a Philip Travers is listed as Warden of the Vintners Company at the time of the last confirmation of their charter by King Charles I.[12] As late as 1683 one of John Treavis's grandsons, Gilbert, a son of Matthew, is still listed as a "citizen and Salter of London."[13] So the family tradition of working and prospering in London trade, started by old John Traves in the reign of Queen Elizabeth, continued throughout the whole of the seventeenth century.

Meanwhile, during the two decades between 1620 and 1641, John and Ursula Treavis were living at the inn and bringing up the rest of the family. Thomas, the oldest son, seems to have remained in Broadway with his parents and the initials "T.T." that adorn the mullion window in Room #3 may be his. Other physical reminders of the family's presence include an old apple scoop marked "An Travis," found by the Russell family in the 1920's and the 1620 Jacobean fireback still to be seen in the Inglenook.

A portion of the Treavis' wealth went to keep the churchyard wall in repair. John is listed on the "old velum" Parish Record in 1633 as responsible for this obligation, as Thomas White had been in 1532 and as Francis Phipps would be by 1710. Marriage records also survive for three of the Treavis daughters, Elizabeth to Richard Hope in 1637, Mary to John Taylour in 1641, and Ann to John Baldwin in 1647.[14]

Sixteen days before he died in May, 1641, John Treavis knew he must set his affairs in order for the last time. The old man may have been "weak in body" as he lay there in the Great Chamber reserved for the head of the household or honoured guests, but there was nothing wrong with his mind or memory. He left his widow a life interest in his property, with the stipulation that after her death his oldest son Thomas would receive "all my said house or inn commonly called or known by the name of the White Hart..."[15] He bequeathed ten shillings to each of his grandchildren, forty shillings to the poor of Broadway, and one hundred pounds to each of his younger daughters. He also carefully specified that if Thomas were to die without heirs then Thomas's wife, if any, would inherit but if Thomas should predecease his mother, Ursula would inherit everything. Treavis made provisions for his other four sons, John, William, Robert and Matthew, but they were to inherit only if Ursula, Thomas and any children of Thomas had all died. Matthew and Richard Hope, his son-in-law, were made overseers and Ursula and Thomas executors. One gets the strong impression that the old man respected his oldest and youngest sons more than the rest of his large family.

Just fourteen days after he signed the document he had so carefully drawn up, John Treavis died and was buried in St. Eadburgha's. The slate that commemorates his passing remains there today. It reads: "Here Lyeth the Body of John Treauis, who deceased ye 27th of May an. Dm. 1641 aged 74."

Thomas Treavis never did marry. It appears that he and his mother ran the White Hart from 1641 until his death in 1649, when he too was buried in St. Eadburgha's, as was his mother five years later. Matthew took over the administration of the estate at his brother's request, and all deeds involving the White Hart after 1654 mention only Matthew and his children or Matthew by himself.[16] Whether John and Robert died or were fully occupied and so prosperous in their own businesses that they relinquished any claim to the White Hart we do not know.

Unlike his parents and older brother, Matthew Treavis does not appear to have lived at the inn for any length of time, or to have been involved with its operation. In the year 1670, Matthew leased the inn premises to William Adderley and Joseph and Elisha Biscoe. The price of the lease was £154 with the property described as "all that messuage [dwelling house site] or tenement [land or real property leased or rented of another] of the said Matthew Treavis, used as an inn and known by the name of the White Hart, situate and being in Broadway in the north east side of the street leading from the said town to Worcester...."[17]

Matthew Treavis died in London in 1681, still "seized of" the White Hart Inn. In 1683 the three Treavis heirs, Gilbert, Mary and Katharine, conveyed the property to Thomas Parry, Dyer of Broadway, for £161, which sum was used to pay off Adderley and the Biscoes. Thomas Parry then conveyed the inn to Walter Parry, Dyer, of Harrington, Warwickshire.[18] Both these men continued to be absentee landlords.*

What sort of life were John and Ursula Treavis and their family living at the White Hart Inn in the early part of the century? The family's standard of living would have been fairly comfortable. The enlarged rooms had panelling and plastering, and carpets and mats had replaced rushes on the floors. The old trestle tables had given way to sturdier ones of solid wood, and the bedsteads had feather and flocks [fibre] mattresses.

By this time there was undoubtedly more than one chimney in one central room. The Angel Inn, near the White Hart, was assessed for thirteen hearths in the 1674 Hearth Tax. Although the White Hart was a smaller establishment, it certainly had several hearths and chimneys by this date, and the Treavises may have burned coal as well as wood. Coal had to be transported on pack horses from the rivers, and was more costly, but since the 1680 inventory shows a large supply of coal this may have been used as an alternative source of fuel in earlier years.

The Treavis family and their guests probably did not live on quite so grand as scale as the Verney family in Buckinghamshire, but like the Verneys, their establishment "provisioned itself with little help."[19] Most large houses in this period were self-sufficient, and an inn would certainly have been so. Family members brewed beer and ale, baked bread, churned butter, and made cheese in the "little buttery." They ground corn stored in the Granary and fattened their beeves until time for slaughtering. Swine provided bacon and hams for curing, and the cocks and hens were a ready supply of poultry and eggs all year round.

---

*Important corroborating information about the name of the inn came to light in these deeds for the year 1683. One of these conveyances identifies, very specifically, the transaction that took place sixty-three years earlier between John Treavis and William Sambache in 1620. The sale by Matthew's heirs to the Parrys says:

"The parties named in the first part...do grant, bargain and sell unto Walter Parry all that messuage or tenement in Broadway called or known by the name of the White Hart and also barns, stables, remainders, rents, profits and all deeds and writings concerning the premises, the which said premises were purchased by John Treavis the grandfather of the said Gilbert, Mary, Katharine, unto him and his heirs of one William Sambache of Broadway, gentleman, and Walter the son of the said William by one deed dated 29 November, in the 17 year of the reign of the late King James [1620] and by the name of two burgages and one half burgage and were then used as one dwelling house or inn and called or known by the name of sign of the Swan..." This is conclusive proof of the link between Sambache's Swan Inn in 1620 and the Treavis' White Hart in 1641. The deed from 18th December, 1683 is also the first one which identifies Philip and Susanna Hodges. The Inn was "in occupation of" Philip Hodges in 1670 and of "Susanna Hodges, widow" in 1683.

Treavis, his sons, and their hirelings would have performed the tasks of blacksmith, woodcutter, ploughman, stable boy and farmer, while Ursula and her women not only cooked and cleaned but also spun and wove both flax and wool, cured meat, made perry and cider from pears and apples and prepared herbs for medicinal use. They did a great deal of fine embroidery as well as coarse needlework, kept count in the root cellar to make sure supplies lasted in cold months and ran the distillery when occasion required.[20]

Diet was certainly more varied than in the White and Sambache households, and may have included "salatts," or salad with meat and fowl as well as carrots, leeks, red beetroot and cabbage from the kitchen garden. Clove, gillyflower, and marigold seeds were preserved in vinegar to make winter salads tasty, and celery, cucumber, and radishes were grown as well as lettuce.[21] People were becoming more knowledgeable about health, and efforts were made to prevent the frequent skin diseases caused by lack of vegetables as well as to alleviate the tedium of salt meat in winter.

An annual summer ritual in the White Hart kitchens, involving Ursula and all her women, was the making of jams and jellies. Fruit was also preserved in a number of other ways: syrup for illnesses, sweets, pickles, vinegar and lotions. We can imagine Ursula "almost melted with the double heat of the weather and her hotter employment, because the fruit is suddenly ripe and she is so busy preserving...."[22] Another more frequent ritual was the washing of linen, since good linen was prized by rich and poor alike and was bequeathed with as much care as the best bed and mattresses.

While the women were doing all this daily work to keep the inn running, Innkeeper Treavis was sometimes called away to unexpected and unwelcome duties. The state of the highways is a recurring theme in the Quarter Sessions Records of the time, and road repair was a local responsibility of each parish. Like Sambache in the previous century, Treavis may well have objected to this interruptive forced labour.

In the year 1633 the following presentment appears in the Quarter Sessions Records:

> The highway leading from a place called the Ridgeway* to Evesham at Broadway and the highway in the said town of Broadway to the hill there is in decay and ought to be repaired by the citizens of Broadway....[23]

*There is still a stretch of highway called "The Ridgeway" outside Broadway.

In 1634, the inhabitants of nearby Abberton were enjoined to repair the highway from Broadway to Evesham and in the same year, Wickhamford inhabitants were requested to repair the highway between Evesham and Broadway.[24] There must have been frequent breakdowns in the village of Wickhamford, whose residents could see no reason why they should leave their farming to repair the road to the White Hart Inn.

Despite poor road conditions, the number of guests at the White Hart was growing. Most undoubtedly came on horseback, but those who did not wish to ride could travel in a rough coach with leather curtains to give the passengers some protection from the weather. It was uncomfortable, but a welcome alternative to riding on horses for long distances, especially for ladies.

The White Hart was evidently an honest house, since no records of indictments for violating the licensing laws appear in the Quarter Sessions Records. Even with licenses in perfect order, the proprietors of the White Hart had to deal with brawls and disagreements among disgruntled customers. There are a number of enlightening examples in the Quarter Sessions Records of general unruly behaviour in or near Broadway.

In 1602 one Thomas Wells, who was very possibly Ursula Wells Treavis' father, was summoned to appear before Walter Savage, William Hodges and [Anthony] Brooke of Broadway, for "his keeping of the peace towards Nicholas Lea...."[25] In 1609 there is a citation naming another member of a family later associated with the White Hart: against Edward Stephens of Moreton in the county of Gloucester "for begetting the bastard child with which Alice Phipps now goeth...."[26] (Francis Phipps was running the inn by 1710).

In the year 1637 a member of the Brooke family, who had ruled against Thomas Wells, was himself indicted:

> Indictment against Anthony Brooke, otherwise Weaver, or Wover of Broadway, butcher, for keeping pigs' blood in his butcher shop in Broadway Street to the common nuisance of the inhabitants....A true Bill....[27]

In that year a new outbreak of plague swept through the city of Worcester, causing people to be unusually nervous about any "common nuisance" which might spread disease.

The effects of the approaching war between King and Parliament, Cavaliers and Roundheads, would have been felt to an extent in

Broadway. When King Charles I began his series of desperate attempts to raise money without going to the House of Commons, one of his royal schemes was to force certain landed gentry to accept an order of knighthood, for which they paid an "honorarium;" if they refused to pay they were fined. This practice went on from the year of the King's coronation in 1625 until 1632. Among those fined were several Broadway citizens including "William Sambadge of Broadwaie, Esquire," who had to pay fourteen pounds.[28]

This man was almost certainly the innkeeper from whom Treavis had bought the inn in 1620. Old Sambache did not take kindly to any kind of enforced action, whether it was road repair, for which he was indicted in his middle age, or paying to become a knight, which he refused to do. He might well have supported the Parliamentary side had he lived until the outbreak of war in 1642. He was not averse to controversy

Controversy and uneasiness, if not open conflict, were the order of the day in the late 1630's and early 1640's as England moved closer to the brink of war. Few families, great or humble, remained unaffected. In some cases, members of the same family, like Sir Edmund Verney and his son Ralph, fought on opposite sides. In others, there was merely a lack of trust among friends and neighbours, a deep questioning of loyalties, and a despair that the order of life for generations had been suddenly called into question.

We do not know the politics of the Treavis family. The squires of the village, Savage on the one hand and Sheldon on the other, were certainly Royalists. But John Treavis and more notably his son, Matthew, with business and wealth in London, may well have been sympathetic to Parliament. As in the case of the Verneys, however, political affairs did not divide the family. Sir Edmund, in honest words which were to become historic, said of King Charles as war approached: "I have eaten his bread and served him near thirty years and will not do so base a thing as to forsake him and choose rather to lose my life (which I am sure I shall do) to preserve and defend those things which are against my conscience to preserve and defend. For...I have no reverence for the Bishops for whom this Quarrel subsists."[29]

Verney's son Ralph backed Parliament but he and his father nonetheless remained on good terms. The elder Verney continued his efforts to avert war as far north as the Scottish border, where he was sent to mediate. But Sir Edmund's exertions and those of others like him trying to prevent bloodshed, were to fail. War broke out in the autumn of 1642 and

Sir Edmund, as he had sadly foreseen, perished in the first great battle, still clutching the royal standard as he fell at Edgehill. He remained, to the end, loyal to King Charles and to the traditions that he represented.

Mary Verney, Sir Ralph's wife, who did her heroic best to manage family affairs alone during most of her husband's long exile, had much in common with Ursula Treavis, who was left to run the White Hart Inn single-handed after the death of her husband in 1641 and that of her oldest son eight years later.

Ursula managed alone through the hard years of war, overseeing such servants as were not away fighting, keeping farm, brewhouse and hostelry running as best she could. Ursula and Thomas Treavis, their family, neighbours and customers, divided as they may have been during the fighting and its aftermath, would have been, at bottom, loyal to older customs, to the rhythms of the land and the seasons, to an older England and its preservation for better times.

VII

1642-1645
"The King With All His Army...."

Naked and grey the Cotswolds stand
Beneath the autumn sun,
And the stubble-fields on either hand
Where Stour and Avon run.
There is no change in the patient land
That has bred us every one.

She should have passed in cloud and fire
And saved us from this sin
Of war-red war-'twixt child and sire,
Household and kith and kin,
In the heart of a sleepy Midland shire
With the harvest scarcely in.

But there is no change as we meet at last
On the brow-head or the plain,
And the raw astonished ranks stand fast
To slay or to be slain
By the men they knew in the kindly past
That shall never come again—

By the men they met at dance or chase,
In the tavern or the hall,
At the justice-bench and the market place,
At the cudgel play or brawl,
Of their own blood and speech and race,
Comrades or neighbours all!

Before Edgehill Fight, October, 1642
—Rudyard Kipling

A man can ride from Edgehill to the village of Broadway in less than a day, and it did not take long for news of the first great battle of the Civil War to reach Ursula Travis and her son Thomas at the White Hart. Soon it was all over Broadway—the Royalists were marching on London. The war would soon be over.

But this was not to be the case. London was defended in great force by the Parliamentarian trained bands, and the King fell back on Oxford, which became his permanent headquarters for the rest of the war. His Majesty's army would become a common sight in Broadway.

Standing as it did on the main highway between Oxford, Worcester and Wales, Broadway became a focal point for the contending forces over the next three years. King Charles passed through Broadway at least six times during these years, as we know from several contemporary sources. The first time was in September, 1643, when King Charles and his Commander of Cavalry, Prince Rupert of the Rhine, hot-tempered veteran of the Thirty Years War and superb tactician, were trying to prevent Parliament's General Essex from reaching London.

Essex had surprised the Royalist strongholds at Tewkesbury and Cirencester, captured forty supply wagons to feed his famished troops, and then set off for London, assuming he was not pursued. King Charles followed from his encampment at Pershore, and Rupert from White Ladies Aston. For once the King moved with surprising speed, but was forced to stop and rest for "some hours in Broadway."[1] By then Rupert was a few miles ahead and had his horsemen drawn up on Broadway Down, waiting for orders from the King to pursue Essex. He grew impatient with the delay, knowing that every minute put his enemy closer to London.

The King was nowhere to be found, so Rupert took matters into his own hands and went looking for him. After an exhaustive search in the dark he finally saw him "through the lighted window of a farmhouse, sitting by a fire playing piquet with Lord Percy while Forth, the Commander-In-Chief looked on."[2]

There was a fierce argument and Rupert, having his orders at last, rode off to assemble his men and follow Essex.* Charles marched on later that evening and joined Rupert in Newbury three days later. The first battle of Newbury was fought on September 20th.

It is not clear exactly where the King was resting and playing cards. The home of either of the Royalists Sheldon and Savage (where the King stayed later in the war), and the White Hart Inn, could all have been described as a "farmhouse," especially the inn, which had previously been one. There is thus a strong possibility that the window through

---

*Some historians have objected that it was unlike this fast-moving leader of cavalry to have wasted time looking for the King or seeking orders if he intended to keep up with Essex. But this story was found in Prince Rupert's own papers, so there is no reason to disbelieve the incident if the Prince himself thought it worth recording.

which Prince Rupert looked was in the thoroughfare of Broadway, and that the King had stopped at the hostelry. One likes to think that the fire was in Ursula Treavis' version of today's Inglenook, visible through a mullioned window.

The King's next movements in Broadway and the surrounding countryside are well documented by two contemporary writers. The first is a detailed account of the war by Edward Hyde, Earl of Clarendon in his *History of the Great Rebellion*, the most famous account of the time. Less well known but more detailed is a *Diary of the Marches of the Royal Army, April 10, 1644-February 11, 1645* by Richard Symonds, a Royalist soldier who marched with the King's forces.

Symonds was a well-educated gentleman, interested in the topography of the land as well as genealogy and heraldry. He kept an exact account of the movements of the troops and the places he visited, such as churches, mansions, and more humble dwellings. He was in the King's immediate retinue, he was a keen and accurate observer and his record of the King's movements tallies with Clarendon's.

Broadway saw more than its share of the soldiers of both sides, as the King and Sir William Waller's Parliamentary forces played a game of cat and mouse during the month of June, 1644.

Charles left Oxford on June 3rd and headed west under the cover of darkness, pressing on to Burford with little rest or refreshment, fearing he was being pursued by Parliamentary cavalry. According to Clarendon:

> On Monday the third of June the King with the Prince and those Lords and others who were appointed to attend him...marched out attended by his own troop...the King rested not until he found himself at Burford and then concluded that he was in no danger to be overtaken by any army that was to follow with baggage and a train of artillery; so that he was content to rest his men there and supped himself...yet was not without apprehension that he might be followed by a body of the enemy's horse...Therefore about nine of the clock he continued his march from Burford over the Cotswold and by midnight reached Bourton Upon the Water where he gave himself and his wearied troops more rest and refreshment...[3]

On the morning of Wednesday, June 5th, Symonds notes in his diary:

> The King and all his army marched over Cotswold downes and Brodway hills and came to Evesham, his owne garrison, where Young Colonel Knotsworth was governour; which was the first night's rest of our journey....[4]

On this occasion the King and his men may have stopped briefly at the White Hart or some other watering place (and the inn would have been on his direct line of march from Bourton, his last recorded stop), but pushed on to Evesham because they feared they were being pursued by the crack Parliamentarian commander, General Waller.

The King's fears proved to be well founded. Symonds continues his narrative on June 6th:

> Thursday morning wee heard by one of their captaynes who was taken scowting that morning neare Brodway that Waller was in Brodway with all his army...the King marched with all his army to Worcester that night, being twelve myles the worst way. A woody and durty country...Pershore bridge was pulld down by our forces, because Waller should not follow and forty of our men lost. The bridge fell from them into the river....[5]

Clarendon's account of the bridge action differs slightly as to the number of men killed, saying: "The breaking of the bridge at Parshore [sic] was, unwarily, so near done before all the troops were passed that, by the sudden falling of an arch, Major Bridges of the Prince's regiment, a man of good courage and conduct, with two or three other officers of horse and about twenty common men, fell unfortunately into the Avon and were drowned."

Meanwhile the Earl of Essex joined Waller in an attempt to box up the Royalist army in Worcester. Waller captured Sudeley Castle in Winchcombe and then advanced to Evesham, intent on attacking Worcester, where the King was resting with his men. Worcester was strongly Royalist and provided the King with "shoes and stockings and money for his soldiers," but when Charles learned of Waller's approach he left hurriedly with his troops for Bewdley to keep the Severn between himself and the opposing army. After Waller passed beyond Worcester, the King returned there the next day, "Satterday morning." (This was June 15th.)

With Waller to his north, the King decided to move southward again on Sunday, June 16th, 1644. According to Symonds:

> After sermon in the forenoone ended in the cathedral at Worcester, His Majestie about xii of the clock left Worcester and lay that night at Brodway, com. [comitatu or county] Gloucester, going through

Evesholme. His Majestie lay that night at Mr. Savage, his howse there at Brodway. [6]

This entry is followed by a long description of St. Eadburgha's church.

Since Symonds notes specifically that the King stayed at the house of the Savages in the West End near the church, we can assume that he did not lodge at the White Hart on that occasion. However, some of his regimental commanders and senior officers might have done so, and there is no reason why the King, accompanied by young Savage and possibly Sheldon as well, should not have joined them for a strategy session in what is now the Oak Room.

This strategy was simple—haste. The army was on the move again at daybreak. Both Symonds and Clarendon agree on the morning of June 17th. Symonds says:

> From Brodway the King and all his army marched over the Cotwold downes, where Dover's games were, to Stowe in the Would, six myle. Then that night to Burford in co Oxen, being seven myles further, where his Majestie lay that Monday night at the George Inn in Burford....[7]

Clarendon elaborates:

> Very early the next morning they mounted the hills near Camden; and there they had time to breathe, and to look with pleasure on the places they had passed through; having now left Waller and the ill ways he must pass, (for even in that season of the year the ways in that vale were very deep) far enough behind.[8]

Time to breathe indeed. Charles and his army had narrowly escaped a trap. Waller had been able to go into Evesham because that town had repaired the bridge there, an act that later cost them a £200 fine and a thousand pairs of boots for His Majesty's army.

Even the King realised he had escaped by the skin of his teeth. Lord Digby sent the following dispatch to Prince Rupert from Broadway at His Majesty's order:

> They were raised to comfortable hopes from a state almost of desperation. The truth of it is, had Essex or Waller jointly either pursued us or attacked Oxford, we had been lost. In the one course, Oxford had been yielded up to them, having not a fortnight's provisions, and no hope of

relief. In the other, Worcester had been lost and the King forced to retreat to your highness.[9]

In Burford the King was joined by four thousand men from Oxford who "with their pikes and colours for before there were none, marched with the King." The King, no longer a fugitive, now had a formidable army at his command. This was "unspeakable joy" to the commanders, "acknowledging God's good providence in the preservation of the King, and, in a manner, snatching him as a brand out of the fire..."[10]

The King's next entrance into Broadway was colourful and impressive. Fresh from a triumph over the Roundhead forces at the Battle of Cropredy Bridge on June 29th, Charles marched three days later to Deddington and Great Tew and "thence that night to Moreton Henmarsh where his Majestie lay July 3rd..." Then on the morning of July 4th, "the King with his whole army marched over the Cotswold hills with colours flying, trumpets sounding to Brodway..."[11]

Rupert's cavalry came first, their breast and backplates streaked with mud from long riding, their carbines swinging from wide shoulder straps, and their high leather boots turned down at the knee. Then followed the foot soldiers marching three abreast, each company divided into four divisions, two of pikes and two of muskets formed in files ten-deep.

The pikeman carried eighteen-foot pikes and wore buff leather coats; these were said to be capable of turning a sword or pike thrust and even withstanding a musket ball at a distance of one hundred yards or more. The musketeer's only armour was his steel pot.

The march continued through Broadway and "on to Evensholme that night where he lay."[12] Once again the White Hart would have been a convenient stopping point midway between Moreton-in-Marsh and Evesham to water the horses and refresh the men.

The King's stops in Moreton and Evesham are well documented. There is a plaque in the White Hart Inn in Moreton which commemorates King Charles's visit there on the night of July 3rd.* In the middle of

---

*Richard Savage, the antiquarian from Stratford-upon-Avon, recorded a friend's visit to Moreton in the year 1863:

"Last night (December 12) I slept in a room at the White Hart Hotel in Moreton-in-Marsh, Gloucestershire and I read upon a card, yellow with age, and torn around the edges the following lines and memorandum:
  When friends were few and dangers near,
  King Charles found rest and safety here.

Bridge Street in Evesham is a half-timbered house on which there is also a plaque: "This house is part of the mansion of the Langston family. Here King Charles stayed in July 1644." A local historian corroborates this: "Charles I appears to have stayed at the house of Anthony Langston in Bridge Street, Evesham, early in July 1644..."[13]

Meanwhile the army was quartered at Fladbury. Later in the month, the King left Evesham and once more marched "through Brodway, then over the Cotswold near Shudeley Castle, the seat of the Lord Chandos, from whence the rebels gave us two great shott....This day a soldier was hanged for plundering. That night, at one of the clock, the King got to his quarters, a poor howse in Coverly...."[14]

The fact that Charles did not reach his destination until 1 a.m. leaves time for an extended stop somewhere en route for an early-morning or mid-day meal, and perhaps a council of war. A possible spot for such a stop is Broadway.

King Charles wintered in Oxford and did not reappear in the Cotswolds until the following spring. Symonds chronicles his progress starting on May 7th, 1645:

> His Majestie left Oxford attended with Prince Rupert, Prince Maurice, Earl of Lindsey, Duke of Richmond and Earl of Northampton. His troope and the Queen's lay that night at Woodstock...
>
> Thursday, May 8. This morning at one of the clock an alarme waked us and at daybreake the King marched with his 4 pieces of cannon, 8 boates in cariages etc. vizt. all manner of ammunitiion, his troopes of life guard and foot regiments...Neare Stowe on the Would wee joined Prince Rupert's army of horse and foot, eighteen myles. The King quartered at Stowe on Would. This morning Generall Goring tooke forty of Cromwell's horse prisoners and two colonels near Burford...
>
> Friday, May 9. His Majestie marched to Evesham where he joyned with Lord Asteley's foot consisting of 3,300; in the premier place was Prince Rupert's regiment of foot, consisting of 500, and ten of these

---

KING CHARLES 1st
Slept at this Inn on his way to Evesham, Tuesday, July 3, 1644.
"The ink is faded by time and the handwriting is in that hard style so fashionable in years gone by. Upon enquiry in the hotel I found that the bedroom bore the name of King Charles 1st's room and was still the best bedroom in the hotel...."

colours...300 foot taken out of our garrison at Camden; the howse, which was so faire, burnt...."*[15]

A second account corroborates Symonds:

> When they left Oxford on the 7th of May, the army with the King and Rupert consisted of about 8,000 horse and foot. On the 8th the King was at Stowe on the Wold, on the 9th at Evesham. Here he was joined by Lord Astley's foot, 3,000 strong. The King's own troops were quartered at Childswickham between Broadway and Evesham. With the King came Sir Henry Baird and the Campden garrison, the house having been burnt. Rupert stayed at Bretforton between Campden and Evesham with Mr. Canning. On Saturday 10th the King went to Inkberrow,** Rupert to Alcester.[16]

Did the King stop at the White Hart this early May of 1645? Neither the contemporary writers, Clarendon and Symonds, nor later historians agree on every detail. One modern writer maintains: "the Sheldons were Royalists and it is said that when King Charles was on his way to Evesham on May 12, 1645 he stayed with a Sheldon at Broadway Court and that it was on that night that the flames of Campden House, set alight to save it falling into the hands of the Parliamentarians, lit up Broadway Hill as Prince Rupert marched with his rear guard after the King...."***[17]

---

*Clarendon provides more detail:
When Goring was separated from the King's army, his Majesty marched to Evesham, and on his way drew out his garrison from Campden House which brought no other benefit to the public than the enriching the licentious governor thereof who exercised an illimited tyrrany over the whole country and took his leave of it in wantonly burning the noble structure which he had too long inhabited and which not many years before had cost above thirty thousand pounds the building. (Clarendon, IV, 38.) In this judgement Clarendon may be both prejudiced and incorrect. Another contemporary writer, Sir Edmund Walker, states that the house was burned at Prince Rupert's command.
**One Worcestershire antiquary refers to a tradition at the Vicarage in Inkbarrow. "About 50 years ago (1850) there was still a book of maps of England and Wales with every shire and the small towns in every one of them on six maps, portable for every man's pocket, useful for all commanders, for quartering of soldiers and all sorts of persons that would be informed where the armies be. Never so commodiously drawn before 1644. This was the King's copy and he has said to have left it behind him on that visit to Inkbarrow." It is now preserved in the Worcester County Record Office.
***Algernon Gissing tells us that a newspaper published in Evesham on Monday, May 12th, 1645, recounted the King's visit to Broadway the previous Saturday, the 10th. This may account for the mention of May 12th instead of either May 9th or 10th.

Another latter-day historian goes further. Without naming an exact day, he claims, in describing the modern Lygon Arms, "Over the kitchen is an oak-panelled room where Charles I is said to have met Sheldon of Broadway Court in May, 1645."[18]

Both these writers believe the King met with Sheldon, either at Broadway Court or at the White Hart Inn. It is just as plausible that the King would have met Sheldon and possibly Savage and other "adherents" at the White Hart rather than in the West End, especially if one assumes that the King's route from Campden House and the evacuation of this garrison was more direct over Fish Hill, in which case the inn would have been on the more direct route to Evesham. In neither case is an overnight stop possible because Symonds and Clarendon are both clear that the King marched on to Evesham from Stow-on-the-Wold on that day, arriving by nightfall.

The march through Broadway was a crisis in the affairs of King Charles and his cause. Cromwell and the New Model Army were a strong factor to be reckoned with. Although it may be argued that he needed—and was probably actively seeking—more support from loyal followers like Sheldon, it must also be pointed out that he was in a hurry and that Evesham was to fall two weeks later. Wherever the King stopped, Rupert seems to have spent this night in nearby Bretforton and the rest of the troops in Childswickham, so there is every chance that some of the King's commanders stayed at the White Hart.

On May 11th, the King marched to Droitwich, where he stayed until the 14th and wrote two letters, one to Lord Jermyn, complaining that he had no news of the Queen: "Only take a little more care in writing to me concerning my wife's health," and another to the Queen herself, in which a great deal was written between the lines: "[I]...could not brag for stores of money...so farewell sweetheart, and God send me good news of thee."[19] Charles and Rupert left Worcestershire for good soon after this. While they were campaigning in Staffordshire and Leicestershire, Evesham fell to the Parliamentarians, stormed by Colonel Massey and taken after a fierce fight.[20] Clarendon says ominously:

> The governor and all the little garrison were made prisoners. The loss of this place was an ill omen to the succeeding summer, and, upon the matter, cut off all the intercourse between Worcester and Oxford...there was no more to be done but to prosecute the northern design....[21]

This "northern design" led soon afterwards to the battle of Naseby and the King's final defeat. Charles I had visited Worcestershire for the last time.

Did King Charles I stop at the White Hart to confer with his officers, to meet with local Royalists, or simply to dine? Was the White Hart the "farmhouse" where Charles dallied to play cards with his officers while Prince Rupert fumed on September 16th, 1643? Did he confer with his commanders at the inn on June 16th, 1644, when he hurried from Evesham to Burford? Did the King and his cavalry pause to rest in the middle of a hot day in early July 1644 after crossing the hill from Moreton, or did he stop to dine at the White Hart in the middle of the same month when he made his way more slowly from Evesham to Coverly? Did he make a final plea for political and financial support from Sheldon on May 9th, 1645 as the flames from Campden House cast a red glow on the skyline above Broadway Hill?

All these dates are strong possibilities. The tradition that King Charles I met his supporters in the Oak Room some time between 1643 and 1645 is firmly rooted, and examination of all the known facts only strengthens this important part of the Lygon Arms' story.

"The King With All His Army" 77

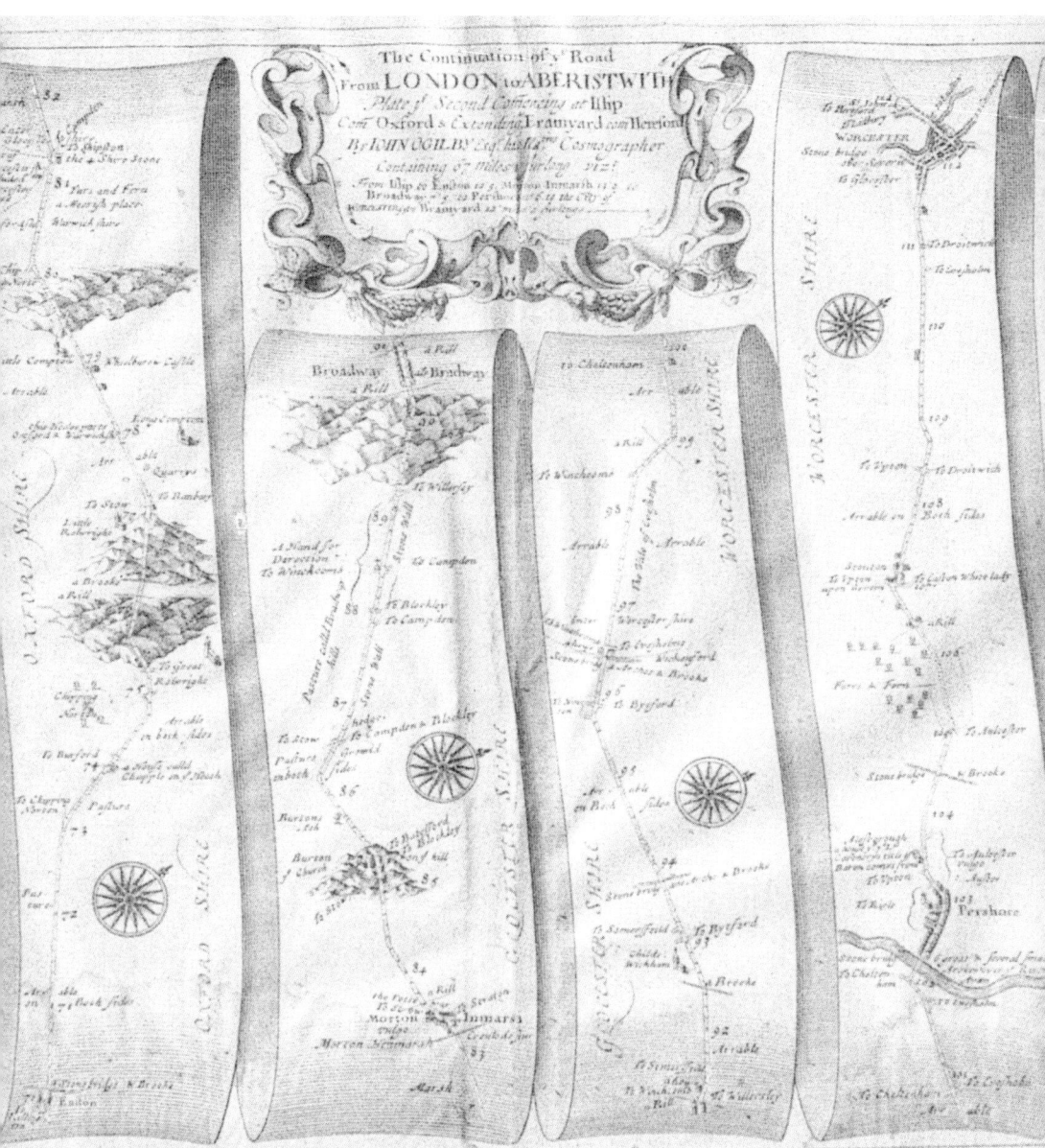

The road from London to Aberystwyth. John Ogilvy 1675. Photo by William Bylund.

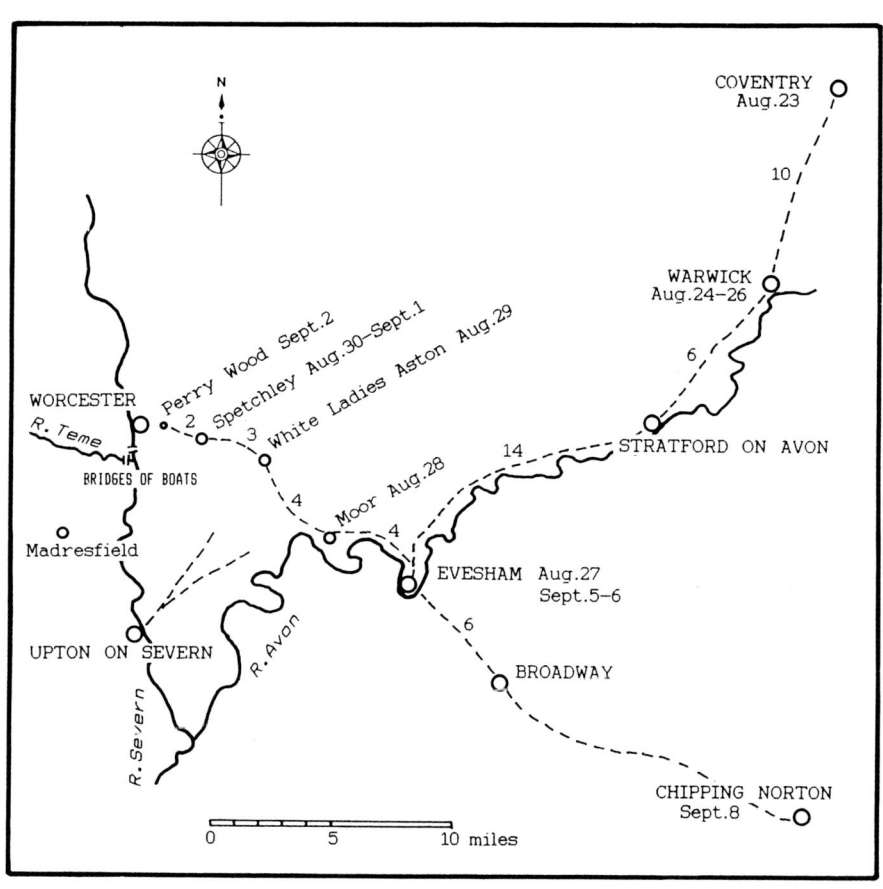

Cromwell's Itinerary before and after the Battle of Worcester, Aug 23rd – Sept. 8th, 1651.

VIII

"A Crowning Mercy"— Aftermath

"When your wives and children shall ask you where you have been and what news, say you have been at Worcester, where England's sorrows began and where they are now happily ended..."

—*The Reverend Hugh Peters to Cromwell's army after their victory at the battle of Worcester, September 3, 1651*

The battle of Worcester, the final and decisive battle of the great Civil War, was fought on the afternoon and early evening of September 3, 1651. Did Oliver Cromwell, Commander-in-Chief of the Parliamentary cause, stay at the White Hart Inn in Broadway the night before this battle in the room which was later named for him? The tradition is a strong one, but is it based more on legend than on fact?[1]

If Cromwell lodged or stopped at the White Hart Inn in the autumn of 1651, it is far more likely that he did so after the battle of Worcester in early September than in the last ten days of August. This conclusion has been reached after a careful study of a large number of sources, including Cromwell's own letters in the crucial days.

To comprehend what Oliver Cromwell might or might not have done in Cotswold countryside in that critical autumn, one must look at the circumstances leading up to the battle. Cromwell had just finished a difficult campaign in Scotland. He had been very ill for nearly two months in the previous spring—May and June—and was out of action completely for much of the summer.* By August of the following year he was weary of the war and anxious to end it all costs.[2]

---

*After the battle of Dunbar on 3rd September, 1650, his great victory over the Scots, Cromwell had written to his wife: "I grow an old man—I feel the infirmities of age marvellously stealing upon me..."

He came hurrying down from the north when he learned that Charles had crossed the border at Carlisle on August 8th, and did not stop "for as long as 24 hours" until he reached Worcester on the 28th. His line of march, much of it in unusual late-summer heat, was through Berwick, Newcastle on-Tyne, Durham and Ripon, then Doncaster, Rotherham, and Mansfield to Nottingham. His objectives were threefold: to place his army between the Scots and London; to cut off the King from Wales and the Welsh Marches, and to fall on the Scottish army with a much superior force and destroy it, once and for all. Above all, he was determined to prevent Charles from reaching London.[3]

On August 23rd, Charles arrived in Worcester where he was proclaimed King "of England, Ireland and Scotland," with much pomp and ceremony. On the same day an exhausted Cromwell rode into Coventry. From then on, his itinerary was abrupt and exact, his movements closely accounted for and documented by letters and military dispatches.*

August 24. Cromwell arrived in Warwick. He met three of his officers—Generals Fleetwood, Lambert and Harrison—to discuss the coming plan of attack.[4]

August 25 and 26. Cromwell and his officers waited in Warwick for the foot soldiers to catch up. Expecting that he would have to lay siege to Worcester, he wrote to the Council of State urgently on August 26th that he wanted a "supply of five thousand shovels, spades and pick axes, thirty tons of match and four hundred barrels of powder sent to Gloucester..."[5]

August 27. Cromwell and his army reached Stratford. From there he wrote to his friend, Lord Wharton "one bold word," explaining he had "no leisure."[6] Also in Stratford he signed a receipt acknowledging payment to Colonel Gilbert Ireland's regiment of horse for three hundred pounds.

That same evening Cromwell pushed on to Evesham to meet General Fleetwood. The combined armies totalled 28,000, outnumbering

---

* Legends about where Cromwell stayed in the countryside have proliferated over the years since 1651. Willis Bund, Worcestershire historian, has this explanation: "While for the sake of subsequent rewards and the honour of having sheltered the King, innumerable persons claimed that Charles slept in their houses before the battle of Worcester, none cared to say they had sheltered the arch traitor. Thus the names of the houses that had the honour of sheltering Cromwell are not recorded." And, to fill the vacuum, other resting places for the General have been suggested, and tales about them have grown to legendary proportions.

Charles's forces about two to one. They were joined there by General Lambert. Cromwell spent that night somewhere in or near Evesham.*[7]

August 28. Cromwell planned to secure the Severn bridges, whose strategic importance was crucial to the coming battle. He spent that night at the Old Manor House at Moor, a village between Evesham and Worcester.

On the 28th, he ordered General Lambert to take a division to Upton, occupy the bridge there, and so control the River Severn. This was accomplished with great difficulty at dawn on the 29th.**[8]

August 29. Cromwell rode to Upton to thank Lambert and his men in person, because he considered the action so important. "As he passed from one regiment to another he was received with abundance of joy and extraordinary shouting." The Royalists (Scots) were cut off from Wales and Cromwell's encirclement of Worcester, which was to prove their downfall, had begun. Cromwell spent this night at the house of a strong Parliamentarian, Mr.George Symonds at White Ladies Aston.[9]

August 30. Cromwell sent General Lambert to collect as many boats as possible from as far away as Gloucester in an unorthodox but, as it turned out, most effective military manoeuvre. He planned to build two bridges of boats across the Teme and Severn Rivers, where they met, to connect his own troops with General Fleetwood's large force and to make communication between them possible during the coming attack. He moved his headquarters to Spikeley or Spetchley, three miles from Worcester, where he probably stayed at the home of Mr. Justice Berkeley.***[10]

---

*Since his exact whereabouts that night are not known, it is possible, if unlikely, that Cromwell could have back-tracked eight or ten miles to the White Hart Inn. Since he had several pressing problems to address early the following morning (the most pressing being the Severn bridges), this theory is improbable.
**When Lambert arrived at Upton the evening of the 28th, he found that the Royalists had anticipated him and broken the bridge, mistakenly leaving one plank across the river. Lambert resolved, despite the swirling currents, to take the bridge anyway. At first light on the 29th, he sent eighteen men to cross this plank. Dizzy from the rapid flow of water below, they accomplished this by "straddling the plank and scrambling and scrabbling to the opposite bank." Occupying a church, they were in danger of being overwhelmed by a superior number of Scots but by nightfall, both the bridge and the church were held by Parlimentary forces. (Bund 231-2).
*** Although there is some doubt about Judge Berkeley's politics and about whether Cromwell spent this night and the following two at his house or elsewhere in Spetchley, he certainly spent these nights on his direct line of march to Worcester. While this very doubt makes it tempting to place Cromwell back at the White Hart, the map makes it logically unlikely. No commander of Cromwell's proven success in the field, would choose to place himself more than twenty-five miles behind his own lines just before a crucial battle,especially during an important bridge-building operation.

August 31. Cromwell wrote to the Council of State: "the enemy is in Worcester and within a few days must fight or fly. On Friday night they made a sally out of Worcester with a considerable body of horse and foot but were repulsed back with considerable loss to themselves. Near Worcester 31 August, 1651."[11]

September 1 and 2. Cromwell remained in Spetchley as the bridge-building continued. The task was nearly completed by September 2nd. Cromwell's forces now controlled both rivers and the approaches to the city itself. Cromwell ordered the attack for the next day, which he considered his lucky day, since it was the anniversary of his victory at Dunbar the year before.[12]

September 2. Cromwell spent this night close to the battlefield, probably in a cottage on the edge of Perry Wood. He may, conceivably, have spent this night at Madresfield Court, which had previously been garrisoned for Parliament under Colonel William Lygon[13] and was then unoccupied. Madresfield was on the west side of the river and some miles further from the battlefield than Perry Wood, and Cromwell would more logically have stayed on the east side of the river where his own troops were stationed. But the possibility that he spent the night at the centuries-old Lygon family seat in Powick, rather than at the inn in Broadway which later became the Lygon Arms, cannot be discounted.*

September 3. It took most of the day to get the bridges of boats in place, and the actual fighting did not begin until the early afternoon. Cromwell crossed the bridge of boats from east to west and back again at least

---

*This interesting possibility is based on more than the proximity of Madresfield Court to the actual battlefield. It is a tradition in the Lygon family. In 1935, Hugh Lygon, the younger brother of the late Earl Beauchamp, told a party of Oxford explorers in the Arctic. that he recalled a tradition that Oliver Cromwell stayed at Madresfield Court some time during the last part of the great Civil War. If Cromwell did, in fact, spend the night of 2nd September, or even part of it, at Madresfield Court, a bed or other furniture may later have been moved to the family inn in Broadway, and so the legend grew up. At the very least, in a day when there was no wireless communication system and commanders in the field were often forced to act on the spur of the moment, Cromwell might have received or sent dispatches from this large convenient house, temporarily commandeered for the purpose some time between 30th August and 3rd September, 1661.

The source for this tradition is Sir Alexander Glen, who was an Oxford friend and colleague of Hugh Lygon and the leader of the Arctic expedition. Another member of the expedition was Evelyn Waugh, who assumed Madresfield Court as a major source for his intended book, *Brideshead Revisited*. Conversations in the long Arctic evenings frequently touched on Madresfield Court and its history and traditions. Sir Alexander Glen is the author of *Under the Pole Star* and *Foothold Against A Whirlwind*. His memories of conversations with Hugh Lygon in the Arctic were discussed in September, 1991.

once, and, theoretically, had time to cross from the west to the east before the full attack.

The battle of Worcester has been many times recounted. Cromwell's own account to the Speaker of the House of Commons, William Lenthall, written late at night on 3rd September, has never been bettered:

> Being so weary and scarce able to write...upon this day, being the 3rd of September (remarkable for a mercy vouchsafed to your forces on this day twelvemonth in Scotland)... we built a bridge of boats over Severn between it and Tame [Teame], within pistol shot of our other bridge...we beat the enemy from hedge to hedge until we beat him into Worcester... the enemy made a very considerable fight with us, for three hours space, but in the end we beat him totally...when we took the fort we turned his own guns upon him. The enemy hath had great loss and certainly is scattered and run several ways...indeed this hath been a very glorious mercy and as stiff a contest for four or five hours as I have ever seen...your forces have behaved with very great courage...the Lord God Almighty frame our hearts to real thankfulness for this which is alone His Doing. I hope I shall within a day or two give you a more perfect account....[14]

Both sides had displayed "very great courage," and only Cromwell's superior numbers eventually turned the tide. The Scots and the Royalists themselves, knowing they were doomed and that only victory or death would prevent death on the scaffold or slavery, fought fiercely for many hours, and their losses were enormous. The young King himself led a vigorous sally through Sidbury Gate and tried desperately to rally what was left of his army. They were pushed back into Worcester, many were cut down, and the King was finally forced to escape through the North Gate.

"A frightful scene of carnage and confusion ensued in the streets. In the days that followed, prisoners and the wounded in their thousands were herded into the Cathedral," Major General Harrison recalled a few days after the battle. "What with the dead Bodies of Men and the dead Horses of the Enemy filling the streets, there was such a nastiness that a man could scarcely abide the Town..."[15]

Carnage in the streets of the city and in Worcester Cathedral was only one part of the aftermath of battle. Confusion spread as looters swarmed through the murk, and bone-tired, desperate men tried to struggle homewards. The cries of the mortally wounded mingled with the roar of fires as soldiers and camp followers from both sides attempted to escape. The countryside was in turmoil, battered and bloodied.

But the fighting, at long last, was over, and no one was more aware that this was a decisive moment in history than Cromwell himself. His second letter to Speaker Lenthall in Westminster, written from Worcester the next day, 4th September, eloquently reflects this sense of destiny:

> Sir: I am not yet able to give you an exact account of the great things the Lord hath wrought for this Commonwealth and for his people and yet I am unwilling to be silent but according to my duty shall give it to you as it comes to hand. This battle was fought with various success for some hours and in the end became an absolute victory...proved a total defeat and ruin of the enemy... what the slain are I can give you no account but they are very many and must needs be so because the dispute was long and very near at hand and often at push of pike...there are about 6 or 7,000 prisoners taken and many officers and noblemen of great quality...indeed it was a stiff business....The dimensions of this mercy are above my thoughts. It is, for aught I know, a crowning mercy...I am bold humbly to beg that all thoughts may tend to the promoting of His honour who hath wrought so great a salvation....[16]

In this mood of great thankfulness and some humility, Cromwell dealt with the aftermath. He dismissed to their homes the militia regiments who had so distinguished themselves, and gave orders for taking down the defences and restoring order to Worcester and the surrounding countryside.

By September 5th, he was again in Evesham, disposing of prisoners and the pay of his troops. The next day he sent two letters, one to a Colonel Thomas Cooper who had come from Scotland with him, and the other a warrant for the army's pay: "Warrant for payment authorizing Sir John Wollaston to pay £2,307-3-6 to John Gladman for the Army. O. Cromwell, Evesham, the vi[th] day of September 1651."[17] —By today's standards a small reward for the bravery of several thousand dedicated men.

By September 7th or 8th, Cromwell's frame of mind was quite different from what it had been when he had hastened from the Scottish border to Worcester in early August. He made a leisurely journey back to London, realising, no doubt, that a great part of his life's work was now behind him, and savouring the countryside through which he passed.

The Vale of Evesham in mellow September sunlight would have been in marked contrast to the events the Lord General had passed through in the preceding weeks. At his roots, Cromwell was a countryman and he would have rejoiced in country fields and smells and sounds as he travelled through the Cotswolds towards Oxfordshire and Buckinghamshire.

Outside Aylesbury he was met by an official deputation from Parliament, sent out as an advance party to greet him. With them, by fortunate coincidence, was a Mr. Winwood, the member for Windsor, who had brought with him his falcons. "Joyfully, as in the old fenland days, the Lord General 'went out of his way a-hawking...' "[18]

The mood of the Lord General and of the country as a whole was "joyful." If he went out of his way a-hawking in Buckinghamshire, might he not have done something similar a few days earlier in Worcestershire and for equally good reasons? Broadway, though largely a Royalist town, would have been less hostile to the Lord General than in previous years. News of Cromwell's victory would already have reached the White Hart Inn as returning soldiers, some of them wounded, trickled into the village from nightfall on September 3rd and during the four days that followed. Some rode horseback, others walked or straggled past the inn clinging to carts and wagons as best they could. Ursula Treavis and her family would have heard all about the last great battle and would have been prepared for whatever else might come down the road in their direction.

Several points support the possibility of Cromwell's presence in Broadway and at the White Hart Inn on this return journey. First, we know he was in Evesham on September 8th and in Chipping Norton later the same day from letters dated and sent on that date. His route from Evesham to Chipping Norton would have led directly through Broadway. If he started early that day he might very reasonably have stopped for the sake of his men and the large number of prisoners and horses travelling with him, including those captured from the Scots in Worcester. Ursula Treavis, who had managed alone as innkeeper through nearly ten troubled years, and had coped with Royalist and Roundhead soldiers sporadically quartered at her hostelry through the entire conflict, would not have been averse to seeing General Cromwell in person.

Second, there is at least a possibility that the Lord General had already heard of the White Hart Inn. Major General Fleetwood, who met with Cromwell on August 24th in Warwick at the Council of War to plan the strategy for Worcester, returned to his troops in Oxfordshire the following day. This means he must have travelled from Oxfordshire to Evesham for the August 27th rallying of forces at Evesham and his route from Oxford and Banbury would have led straight through Broadway, just as King Charles I's path had led seven years earlier. Fleetwood might very well have stopped at the White Hart on this journey and later on, after the battle, suggested it to his Commander in Chief.

Thirdly, it appears from later inventories that the White Hart was already noted for the quality of its horses, and few things attracted Cromwell's attention more than a good horse. If he went out of his way to go hawking in Buckinghamshire a short distance further on, he may well have paused longer than first intended to see some good horseflesh in the Cotswolds, even to ride up on Broadway downs and look back on fields at peace for the first time since he left his own fen country.

It was not East Anglia, but it was green and peaceful and at the heart of the land he had just liberated. It may well have restored his soul in this moment of thankfulness and salvation. Cromwell had just walked through the valley of the shadow of death. He would have been sorely in need of green pastures, still waters, and a sense of goodness and mercy.

There are additional facts to frame this picture of the Lord General looking back towards the Vale of Evesham and the city of his "crowning mercy" from a hilltop just beyond the White Hart. One of these is particularly suggestive. Cromwell left behind in Evesham an order and a letter to Colonel John James appointing him "governour of the City of Worcester and all the Forces....this commission to continue until further order...."[19] This important document*, which is now in the Library of Trinity College, Cambridge, had apparently been dictated before Cromwell left Evesham and left behind with only his signature. It was written in another hand, dated September 8th, and may have been sent after Cromwell himself had left Evesham. Cromwell may, in fact, have left Evesham the afternoon of September 7th, rather than the morning of the 8th which would have permitted him to spend the night of the 7th at the White Hart.

We know only that on the night of September 8th, he was in Chipping Norton, from where a letter, in his own hand, was sent to Speaker Lenthall:

> Sir: I have sent this bearer, Captain Orpyn, with the colours taken in the late fight, at least as many of them as came to my hands, for I think very many of them have miscarried. I believe the number of those sent will be about an hundred...your most humble servant, O. Cromwell.[20]

---

*A note which accompanies this commission in the Trinity College Library says: "This instrument was found among the papers of the above named Colonel John James by his Executor, Sir John Edwards and was afterwards found among his papers by his son and Executor, Richard Edwards, Esquire, formerly a member of Trinity College in Cambridge and by him deposited in the hands of Doctor Colbath for the use of the said College. Signed: Richd. Edwards."

Regardless of whether or not he spent the night of September 7th in Broadway, the distance from Evesham to Chipping Norton is only twenty-one miles, and Cromwell was quite capable of covering twenty miles at a "slow pace" in a day, or thirty or forty when he was hard pushed. So to ride to Chipping Norton for the night, but be able to dine during the middle of the day in the Best Chamber of the White Hart (later the Cromwell Room) and have time to spend riding around Broadway and its environs en route, would not require an early start from Evesham. In sum, both known facts and speculation based on them suggest that Cromwell could very plausibly have spent several hours at the White Hart on September 8th.

Cromwell rode from Chipping Norton to Aylesbury on September 9th and was met there by the group which included Mr. Winwood and his hawks. That night, by invitation of the Mayor of Aylesbury, they all had supper and "much talk," and Cromwell, according to Whitelocke, who relates the whole incident in detail, gave each member of the welcoming committee a "very handsome, gallant young nag" and two Scottish prisoners.[21]

Cromwell reached Uxbridge by September 11th and entered the city of London on September 12th by way of Acton and Kensington. Along his line of progress, streets were lined with enthusiastic crowds, "splitting the welkin with their human shoutings."[22] Salvos of cannon and musketry saluted him as he proceeded joyfully to Whitehall.

As tankards were raised in London on this historic day, back in Broadway, seventy-three year old Ursula Treavis, weary from the rigours of politics and war, may have sipped a quiet glass of claret by the fire in the White Hart and reflected thankfully that at long last peace had been restored to the land and to her hostelry. She had only three more years to live.

Phillip Hodges' Inventory, 1680.

IX

1665-1700
"At The Signe Of The White Hart"

"The signe of the Harte and signpost, two pounds...."

On the morning of the 23rd of June, 1680, Henry Chamberlain, "Clarke," settled himself in the parlour of the White Hart, took quill in hand, and scrawled the following along the top of one of the two long sheets of foolscap that lay on the writing table before him.

> A true and perfect Inventory of all the goodes and chattels of Phillip Hodges of Broadway in the County and diocese of Worcester, Innholder, lately deceased. Taken and appraised by us, Henry Chamberlain, Clarke, John Aynesworth, Gent. and Thomas Austin, Gent. June the 23rd, Anno Domini 1680.[1]

It was the responsibility of Aynesworth and Austin to establish fair value for all the property that Hodges and his widow, Susanna, had accumulated in their more than ten years as innkeepers at the White Hart. It was up to Chamberlain to see that their information was properly recorded. By the time the last item was appraised late that afternoon, he had used one entire sheet of foolscap and half of the other to record the contents of the inn's ten rooms, barns and outbuildings. Despite the fact that he was merely a resident innkeeper and had no interest in the property, Hodges' estate was appraised at £347.

When old Ursula Treavis died in 1654, her youngest son, Matthew, inherited the White Hart Inn. Matthew, who had become a prosperous member of the Salters Company in London, came to Broadway only infrequently, and did not want the day-to-day responsibility of running a country inn. Therefore, soon after his mother's death, or perhaps during her old age, he had signed a long-term lease with Phillip and Susanna Hodges.

The deed that transfers the property from Matthew Treavis' heirs to the Parrys in 1683 shows that Hodges was "in occupation" of the inn as early as 1670, when Matthew leased the premises to William Adderley and Joseph and Elisha Biscoe. Phillip may have been landlord considerably before 1670, and his widow, Susanna, is listed as innkeeper from 1683 until 1700.[2]

Why a substantial innkeeper and his wife, whose possessions at the time of his death in 1680 were valued as worth twice what the Treavis heirs received from the Parrys for the inn itself in 1683, left behind so few written records of their thirty years of stewardship, is a vexing mystery. Luckily, the careful work of Messrs. Chamberlain, Aynesworth, Austin and others gives us a vivid glimpse into the White Hart's rooms late in the seventeenth century. The inventory speaks for itself and the diagram on page 208 recreates the layout of the rooms as they were in 1680.

It is evident, both from the Hodges' will and from the inventory, not only that the landlord and his wife were prospering, but that they were running a farm and a large stable as well as a hostelry. The most valuable item on the whole list is "cropp of corn and all other grains, ninety-one pounds," and the least valuable, "old hay, one pound." The next most valuable item, at thirty pounds, is "horses and colts."

Other livestock include beasts, at twelve pounds, ten shillings; swine in the inn's back yard at six pounds, ten; and sheep and lambs at ten pounds. Farming tools, "implements of husbandry," are worth eight pounds, plate in the house six pounds, "all other trumpery un-named, two pounds, nine shillings," and, most arresting of all, the sign of the Hart and signpost with a value assigned to it of two pounds.[3]

This inventory suggests that the White Hart was a busy place which retained both male and female servants, men to work the land and care for the livestock and women to assist Susanna in the kitchen, little buttery and brewhouse. The mention of luxury items such as ten feather beds, a large supply of linen, a quantity of pewter, a clock at the head of the stairs, and a supply of coal, indicates that Hodges and his wife enjoyed a brisk and profitable trade.

Although the fact is not specifically mentioned in the inventory, the Hodges undoubtedly took advantage of the fertile soil of the Vale of Evesham to improve the orchards and vegetable and flower gardens with new varieties of trees and plants. Fresh vegetables from the kitchen gardens and fruit would have been expected of an innholder of Hodges' standing.

A contemporary order for rootstock included "Venetian peaches, Morocco plums, Roman apricots, French Berry pears, and Portugal quinces."[4] By the end of the next century, a diary shows "apricot tart" on the White Hart table, so that this fruit, at least, must have been in the orchard as well as the more familiar apples, pears and plums.

We can assume that travellers were varied and numerous, ranging from poor scholars who slept three to a room in flocks beds to those who could afford the Great Chamber, the Hart Chamber or the Hill Chamber with feather beds. The guests probably included both fox hunters and fashionable health seekers. Fox hunting became a popular sport after the Civil War because campaigning through the forests had decimated the stag population. The inn may have already begun to gain the renown among hunters that was certainly well established by the middle of the next century.

Some of the guests at the White Hart might have been on the road for a new reason. It had become fashionable late in the century to "take the waters" at least once a year at places like Tunbridge Wells and Bath. Before the English Civil War, people had travelled to the Continent, but noble families began to look for places closer to home "by reason of the roughness of the sea."[5] (Since 1990, it has been unnecessary for a visitor to the inn to travel any further than a few yards, as there is on Lygon premises a country club facility, providing, "waters" both restorative and convenient).

Those who journeyed to Bath from the east and north in the seventeenth century would often have passed through Broadway, just as wayfarers today pass from Campden to Bath on the Cotswold Way. These medicinal trips to Bath became fashionable soon after the Restoration in 1660, and continued throughout the rest of the century. Even a modest household and its entourage would have meant six or eight people staying overnight both coming and going, providing plenty of work for the White Hart's grooms, cooks, and housemaids.

The well-off, moreover, were travelling in style. A bill for a large party for several days at a comparable inn in another part of England gives an idea of what noblemen were eating in 1689:

	£-s-d
For a ham, chickens and eight cauliflowers	1-10-0
For a surloin of beef	13-0
For a frigize (fricassee) of rabbits and chickens	5-0
For salading	1-6
For a dish of mince pies	8-6
For a dish of fruit	3-6
For oil and vinegar	2-6

15 October, 1689 [6]

This bill is for a large party of rank, but is nevertheless revealing.* Even if Phillip and Susanna Hodges were serving smaller parties than the one described above, business would still have been lucrative in seasons of heavy travel and the menu at least comparable.

The fashion in drinks was changing. Beer had been the staple for men and women alike through the sixteenth and early seventeenth centuries, but fruit wines such as cowslip, elderberry, and currant became popular in the late seventeenth, as did "coffee, a berry out of Turkey, ground for a drink." Soon after 1660 Samuel Pepys was drinking "the new China drink, tea," starting a fashion that has accompanied Englishmen all over the globe.

Susanna Hodges and her servants would have had to do a massive "spring cleaning" at least once and possibly twice a year. For this she hired extra servants. This would not have been an extravagance; in London, at that time there could be hired "a woman to scour two days, three shillings, or "a woman six days to scour and wash the rooms and clean the irons, six shillings," or "a woman to help air the bedding when the family came to town, two shillings."[7] These are London prices for the year 1675. Country prices for the year 1663 were roughly equivalent, about a shilling a day for a man's labour, slightly less for a woman's.[8]

Contemporary orders reveal that while some cleaning materials were primitive by today's standards, others have not changed much over the centuries: "for four pounds of soap one shilling," "for oil, ashes and sand to scour, one shilling and eightpence," "for four mops four shillings," "for washing sheets and napkins before the great wash when the two masters were in town two shillings."[9] One can imagine Susanna's purposeful hustle and bustle in the good weather.

During the Hodges era, which may have started during Cromwell's Protectorate, King Charles II was restored to his throne. He rewarded some of those who had helped him in his exile or had served his father

* Some additional details in this lengthy bill are also enlightening:

	£ s d
Bill for wine and glasses broken	4-17-9
Ostler's bill	3-3-10
Coachman and groom's bill, all night	1-12-6
Shoeing a horse by the way at Mr. Brown's	1-0
Cheese for the servants	1-0
Bread and beer	6-19-8
To the poor at the inn when Your Lordship took coach	7-6

before him, with the Order of the Knights of the Royal Oak. Among their number for Worcestershire were Thomas Savage of Elmley Castle and Sheldon of Broadway.

Another royal innovation that became visible in Broadway was King Charles II's new coinage. All coins issued between 1642 and the Restoration were recalled to London in the 1660's and new coins were issued. Among those newly minted were copper tokens struck by Hodges himself. These halfpenny tokens, dated 1669, depicted a hart. Michael Russell* of Broadway struck similar tokens depicting a dog, the initials M.A.R. and "1670".[10] One of these was found in the 1920's during the restoration of the Lygon Arms. Michael Russell's son or grandson appears as an overseer of highways in the next century.

King James made what seems to have amounted to a royal progress to Worcester in 1687.** As far as we know he did not pass through Broadway on this visit. An overseer's account for 1691, however, includes an entry for the Angel Inn: "Paid for expenses at the Angel when horses were pressed about the time of King James's progress." [11] (The Angel was at that time owned and run by John and Thomasine Phipps, the parents of Francis Phipps who ran the White Hart by 1700). Horses may also have been pressed into service from the White Hart's stables, which would, presumably still have had a large number of mounts a few years after the death of Phillip Hodges, who stabled thirty. (Since King James had abdicated in 1688 at the time of the Glorious Revolution, the accounts seem to have been three years in arrears.)

Phillip Hodges' widow, Susanna, was running the inn during the reign of King James II; and she continued to run it when William and Mary replaced him in 1688. She was still in charge when the sale to Francis Phipps took place in 1700.[12] By then she was an old lady, leaving most of the work to underlings and spending her time with her children and grandchildren. Certainly her husband had left her well off.

Although he was merely a long-term tenant of the inn, Hodges himself was by no means a poor man. His clothes and the money in his purse at

---

*Mr. and Mrs. Gordon Russell, whose first child, Michael, was born in Spencer Cottage next to the Lygon Arms, was named after this Michael Russell because his parents found one of the coins at their cottage just before his birth. The two families were not related.

**In his visit to Worcester, King James II was not greeted with the same pomp and circumstance as Queen Elizabeth, and the accounts of wool subsidies in the years following his visit do not show that Worcester was favoured. However, one interesting act was passed which was designed to help the wool trade: everyone was required to bury their dead in a woolen shroud or face a five pound penalty.

the time of his death, came to a value of twenty pounds. He apparently owned property of his own, since his will left to his "well beloved wife Susanna and his deare sonne Luke all his freehold and leasehold lands and houses whatsoever and all my Goods and Chattels." To his "dear Daughter, Ann Hodges," he left one hundred pounds.[13]

We do not know what happened to Susanna, Luke and Ann, although the Hodges family remained prominent for generations to come, both in Broadway and in Snowshill, and their stewardship "at the signe of the White Hart" is noteworthy and enlightening.

Phillip Hodges' Inventory

A true and perfect inventory of all the goodes and chattels of Phillip Hodges of Broadway in the County and diocese of Worcester, Innholder, lately deceased, taken and appraised by us, Henry Chamberlain, Clarke, John Aynesworth, Gent. and Thomas Austin, Gent. June the 23rd, anno domini 1680.

	£	s	d
Imprimis all his wearing apparell and money in his purse	20	0	0
Item all the brass and pewter and other goods belonging to the kitchen	9	0	0
Item three barrels and all other things in the Little Buttery	1	0	0
Item in the Hart Chamber two beds and that belonging to them with other furniture	10	0	0
Item in the room over the Hart Chamber two beds and other furniture	9	0	0
Item in the Pantries the goods there	0	10	0
Item the goods in the Parlour	2	0	0
Item in the Chamber over the Hill Chamber two beds and the furniture with trunks and other things	6	0	0
Item in the Servants two Chambers the goods of	1	0	0
Item in the Hill Chamber two beds and all the furniture	7	0	0
Item in the Great Chamber two feather beds and other the furniture	9	0	0
Item in the Scholar's Chamber three beds, flocks and all other things	4	10	0
Item in the Sun Chamber one bed and all other things	1	10	0
Item in the Cockloft old trumpery	0	6	0
Item the Little Chamber two old beds and all other goods	4	0	0
Item in the Green Chamber one feather bed and flocks beds with all other goods there	4	10	0

Item in the Chamber over the Green Chamber one feather bed and all the furniture	5 —0 —0
Item at the Stayres head a clock	0—15—0
Item two chests of linen containing thirty pairs of sheets flaxen and homespun with napkins, pillow cases and other linen	16 —0 —0
Item barrels and beer in the Cellar with all other things	10 —0 —0
Item in the brewhouse one furnace, a maltsmill and tubs with all things other	4 —0 —0
Item Malt, Wheat and all other grains in the house	20 —0 —0
Item Wheat and pulse to thresh	12 —0 —0
Item saddles and all racks in the Stables	1 —0 —0
Item Wood and Coal	8 —0 —0
Item 1/2 cwt. oats and harness	6 —0 —0
Item all the bacon and provisions in my house	6 —0 —0
Item the swine in my backsides	6—10—0
Item the sheep and lambs	10 —0 —0
Item seven beasts	12 —1 —0
Item horses and colts	30 —0 —0
Item all the implements of husbandry	8— 0 —0
Item the cropp of corne of all grains	91 —0 —0
Item all the old hay	1—10—0
Item the plate in the house	6 —0 —0
Item the signe of the harte and signpost	2 —0 —0
Item all other trumpery unnamed	2 —0 —0

                Sum total in this page etc. 174—10—0
                    In the other page etc. 173 —1 —0
                         the sum total is 347—11—0

                               Henry Chamberlain
                               John Aynesworth
                                 Thomas Austin

18th Century Posting Yard. Drawn by Gordon Russell.

X

1700-1780
"A Common Inn, Situate In Broadway..."

Egad, to be sure, Squire Lumpkin was the finest gentleman I ever set my eyes on. For winding the straight horn or beating a thicket for a hare or a wench, he never had his fellow...he kept the best horses, dogs and girls in the whole country...but come, my boys, drink about and be merry...[1]

—Sir Roger has the custom of saluting everybody that passes him with a "good morning" or a "goodnight." This the old man does out of the overflowings of his humanity...it renders him so popular among all his country neighbours that it is thought to have gone a good way in making him once or twice a Knight of the shire...as we rode along, the farmers' sons thought themselves happy if they could open a gate for the good old knight...[2]

Country customs, like country seasons, do not change much over centuries. The fictional Squires Lumpkin and de Coverley were typical of England in the early eighteenth century. Whether chasing wenches or saluting their neighbours or both, squires were part of their tenants' accepted fabric of life. Although this was an era in which England played a major role in stirring events abroad, in most rural parts of England, such as Broadway, life remained, on the whole, placid and predictable, everyone in his appointed place and doing his proper job. At the White Hart, where Squires Averill, Taylor and Winnington mingled with Hodge, Corbett, Purser and Clemens as they drank their evening potations, there would have been familiarity without disrespect and knowledge of the wider world without direct involvement in it.

Customers at the White Hart and the other inns and taverns that lined the long, straight way that led to Fish Hill might have heard of the Duke of Marlborough's triumph at the battle of Blenheim, the Jacobite rebellions, the revolt of the American colonies and of Lord Cornwallis's defeat by the American General Washington, and of the storming of the Bastille by the revolutionaries in Paris, but they would have been more concerned about how the financing of these wars would affect each man's purse. Broadsheets were posted in public places for all to see: "an Aid to His Maj. for defraying the expense of his Navy Guards and Garrisons for one year (1701),"[3] or "an Act for granting to her Maj. a land tax for carrying on the war against France and Spain (1702),"[4] or King George III's hefty Land Tax to help settle debts caused by the war with the American colonies (1787).

During most of this century, the White Hart's customers were more familiar with its parlours than was the management. The inn changed hands many times between 1700 and 1790, beset by a veritable plague of mortgages, loans, inheritances, and conveyances.

The confusion began with Francis Phipps, who bought the White Hart on April 5, 1700.[5] He purchased it for £159 from Thomas and Walter Parry, who had bought it from the heirs of Matthew Treavis in 1683. At the time of this purchase, Phipps was a fairly wealthy man. His parents, John and Thomasine Phipps, who died in 1674 and 1676 respectively, had left him the Angel Inn, which had been in their family for some time. According to a 1673 inventory, the Angel was worth £491-03-10,[6] an impressively high figure.

Francis Phipps, therefore, took over the White Hart in 1700 as the already prosperous landlord of the Angel. He is listed on the "old velum" in the year 1710 as the owner of both properties and thus responsible for two separate sections of churchyard wall. Some time after 1710, Phipps must have sold the Angel, because there is no mention of it in his will.

Francis Phipps had little chance to enjoy either his inheritance or his new investment. He died in 1713, leaving the bulk of his large estate to his nephew Francis Mitchell. Phipps' sister, Anne, had married James Mitchell on April 28, 1672[7] and their son was probably named after his uncle. Phipps, who had no children of his own, was evidently fond of the young man, bequeathing in his will: "To my nephew, Francis Mitchell, who hath for many years lived with me in Broadway, my house...where John Griffiths, Clerk, now dwells, and also all that house or home stall called the White Hart being a common inn situate in Broadway now inhabited by one John Cormell...and all my yard lands and all my odd lands and commons in grass and pasture...all tenements and hereditaments [any property which can be inherited] whatsoever...."*[8]

Phipps's total estate, including both his house and the White Hart Inn, was valued after his death at nearly seven hundred pounds. With this sort of inheritance behind him, it is hard to understand why, in 1732, Francis Mitchell started a series of mortgages that was to take the White Hart out of the Phipps and Mitchell families for good.

In November, 1732, Mitchell mortgaged the White Hart to one Sarah Taylor for £100. This lady may have been related to the well-to-do barrister William Taylor who lived at Middle Hill.** Less than two years later, in October 1734, Mitchell next conveyed the White Hart and "all its houses and outbuildings" to Ann Cormell, subject to the mortgage by then jointly held by Sarah Taylor Corbett and her husband, William Corbett.[9]

Ann Cormell was the wife of the John Cormell*** mentioned in Phipps's will as the landlord of the White Hart in 1713. This man, who was the illegitimate son of John Cormell and Hannah Neale, was born in Ebrington, Gloucestershire in 1687, and married Ann Smallmann of Willersey in 1706.[10] She became not only his wife but his business partner in the White Hart, and later its owner. The inn was owned by the Cormell children, three daughters, and subsequently by their children and grandchildren for most of the rest of the century.

The three Cormell daughters were Elizabeth, Mary and Sarah, who

---

*Phipps appears to have been a prudent businessman and kind human being. He left "forty pounds to the poor of Broadway who receive no weekly allowance from the Parish," ten pounds to each of three nieces, and generous gifts to two old servants, his sister and another nephew.

** John Morris's *History of Middle Hill Estate* gives us a glimpse of this period and what was going on in the lives of the inn's neighbours. The Taylor family, of which Sarah, who married William Corbett, was a member, was an important one in the area. In 1729, William Taylor had bought the Middle Hill estate from Walter Savage's sister.

When Taylor died in 1741, he left, among other bequests, one hundred pounds to his Clerk, John Purser, the same Purser who loaned fifty pounds to Ann Cormell, his future mother in-law.

***An elderly spinster named Ann Cormell was brutally murdered on 4th February, 1701 in what became a sensational murder case. This killing was followed by the murder of another old lady, a widow, in Upton, Snodbury, ten months later. In both instances the victims were robbed and the houses were burned by the murderers. This resulted in the arrest of four men at the Worcester Assizes in 1708, three of whom were found guilty and hanged. We have not been able to discover any relationship between old Ann Cormell in Bretforton and the White Hart landlord, John Cormell, despite the fact that they lived near one another in the first quarter of the eighteenth century.

grew up at the inn. Elizabeth married a William Touch and moved away, but Mary, Sarah and their mother remained in Broadway and apparently found themselves in financial straits after John Cormell died in 1733. In 1739 Ann Cormell borrowed "fifty-one pounds sterling" from John Purser. She put the entire property in trust for the two daughters who had stayed in Broadway, retaining a life interest for herself. She later borrowed an additional £220, 12s and 6d from a rich neighbour, Isaac Averill.* Mary Cormell married John Purser, her mother's "banker," and Sarah married a John Higgins. In 1740 Ann herself died intestate.

What happened in the next fifty years has come to light only by the discovery of a large number of intricate deeds, which are summarised in Appendix D. These show complex financial transactions but reveal very little about the human beings who owned the property. They describe a long and disjointed series of borrowings by Cormell heirs and their possibly grasping spouses, who used the inn as collateral whenever they needed ready money between 1740 and 1790.

In 1790 one Christopher Holmes bought the White Hart for £500. In less than half a century, the inn had risen in value from the £159 that Francis Phipps paid Parry in 1700 to the £500 Holmes paid to clear the title in 1790.[11] In 1793 Holmes died and his widow, Martha, inherited the inn. About 1807 William Law Phelps, solicitor of Evesham, began searching the title. Given the complex network of previous owners, it is no wonder that Phelps took two years to satisfy himself that he was free from encumbrances before he bought the inn from Mrs. Holmes in 1809.

Although little is known about the specific landlords of the inn during much of this century, a variety of other records, such as Constables' Accounts, newspaper advertisements, excise tax permits, and Parish Awards provide brief insights into what was going on behind the legal language at the White Hart Inn. It was a busy and flourishing hostelry.

In 1704 the Constables' Accounts, allowed by Walter Savage and Richard Wood, show that John Brunton, constable, had expenses at the inn for two prisoners, John Wilson and John Davis, of sixpence, and nine shillings and sixpence respectively. Their crimes are not recorded. In 1707, young Francis Mitchell was a church warden, trying to help the needy people of the parish, and involved in signing papers on their behalf.

---

*The 1771 enclosure map reveals that Isaac Averill owned the land directly behind the White Hart and that he and other members of his wealthy family controlled a large amount of property all over Broadway.

On April 1, 1736, the *Berrow's Worcester Journal* for that day informs us that someone offered a reward of two guineas for the return of "a shirt wrapped in two linon [sic] handkerchiefs and a small parcel wrapped in Paper in which were three mourning rings, one glass ring and other things." These items are to be brought to "the White Hart Inn at Moreton, the White Hart Inn at Broadway or the Three Tuns in Evesham" to claim the reward.[12]

In the year 1752, and probably in many other years, highwaymen were on the prowl. The constable's expenses for that year record "men warding at the White Hart on highwaymen—10 shillings."[13]

The landlord in 1757 was probably Anthony Stratton. An excise permit, found under the floorboards of a second floor bedroom of the inn in 1904, says: "Permit Mr. Staite of Broadway... to receive...five gallons...part of the stock of Mr. Anthony Stratton of which an account has been taken and duties charged as witness my hand and seal this fifth day of April 1757...W. Brunt."[14] (We are not told what the five gallons consisted of).

There is one solitary record for 1767. In the schedule for the Willersey Parish Award the following item occurs: "To Giles Atwood, White Hart Inn, Broadway, on the several Commission days, £84 15s. 2d. Bill for entertaining the Commissioners and Proprietors." The same account shows "£5 5s. to the servants of the White Hart..."[15]

The White Hart Inn was a meeting place for business matters of all kinds. On October 20, 1781, a Court Leet was held at "the house of Christopher Holmes, commonly known by the sign of the White Hart before William Phillipps, gentleman, Deputy Steward."[16] (This man was the father of Sir Thomas Phillipps, the bibliophile, who becomes part of the story in the nineteenth century as a friend of the Lygon brothers). This Court Leet record suggests that, ten years before he became owner of the inn, Christopher Holmes was already living there as landlord. In the year 1787, King George III's land tax shows an assessment for Christopher Holmes for one pound, sixteen shillings and twopence.[17]

Regardless of who was owner and who was landlord, the White Hart Inn was a major stopping point for travellers throughout this century. When Queen Anne died in 1714, some Englishmen may have been discomfited by the advent of the German Georges, but they still travelled. Copper coins "from all the Georges" were found at the Lygon Arms in the early 1900's.[18] George III's son, the Prince of Wales, stayed at Farncombe House with his friend, Squire Porter, and both gentlemen visited the White Hart in the years before the Prince became King George IV. Porter was "very liberal, kept a good house, carriages and livery servants."[19]

Talk over the tankards through the decades may have touched on the Battle of Culloden, Wolfe's siege of Quebec, and Lord Nelson's victory at the Battle of the Nile, but more intense gossip would have centred on the latest village scandal—who had been arrested for poaching or smuggling, what local boy had run off with someone else's betrothed, whether Parson Griffiths or Parson Palmer had just had a row with a member of his flock. Among the gentry, perhaps the latest news from London:

> Ned Goodyear has killed Beau Fielding as reported and made his escape. The quarrel began at the Play house in Drury Lane. The same night a captain here did the like friendly office for young Fullwood so there will be two Warwickshire beaux the fewer . The captain is in Newgate ....[20]

In London society drinking, gambling and duels were commonplace. Duels were not, for the most part, the fashion in the country. Shooting, fox hunting, fishing, and riding the estates occupied the gentry, while races on the village green, football, and wrestling matches served as diversions for the yeomen.

By the middle of the century, cricket had become popular all over the country. Summer Sunday afternoons were often spent, as they still are, in village cricket matches in which all took part. "Squire, farmer, blacksmith and labourer, each with their women and children, came to see the fun, and were at ease together all the summer afternoon...If the French nobles had been capable of playing cricket with their peasants,. their châteaux would never have been burnt."[21]

On such pleasant days of rest and recreation, Broadway residents, along with travellers, may have repaired to the White Hart to dine. We know from a later diary that the White Hart's fare was good by 1787, but can only make comparative guesses for the earlier part of the century. The menu offered to guests probably was not on quite so grand a scale as that described by Parson James Woodforde when he attended a banquet at his Oxford college in the year 1763:*

---

*Parson Woodforde was a graduate of Oxford University, living in Essex, who kept a minutely detailed diary of his travels to and from his alma mater, his costs, his food, village affairs and life in general in the mid-18th century. He is a valuable source of detailed information.

[Stewed tench [fish], veal soup,] a ham and fowls and two pies...custard puddings, baked mutton pies, roots, scallop shells brown'd over...roasted duck and green peas...trifle, blamange, small raspberry tartlets...peaches, nectarines and three kinds of plums....[22]

Woodforde had an annual stipend of £400. A less affluent traveller, a visitor to England from the Continent, complained that "an English dinner for such lodgers as I am generally consists of a piece of half broiled or half roasted meat and a few cabbage leaves boiled in plain water with a sauce made of flour and butter...."[23]

The everyday fare at the White Hart was probably somewhere in between these two extremes. It may have more closely resembled the menu planned by a would-be innkeeper:

At the top, for the first course, a pig and prune sauce...next, a pie, a boiled rabbit and sausages, a florentine, a shaking pudding and a dish of taffety cream...at the bottom end a calf's tongue and brains....[24]

Well-to-do travellers who arrived at the White Hart after a long day on the roads might well have agreed with one of their number who said of a similar inn: "Upon my word, a very well-looking house, antique but creditable...after the disappointments of the day, once more the comforts of a clean room and a good fire... travellers must pay in all places—the only difference is that in good inns you pay dearly for luxuries, in bad inns you are fleeced and starved...."[25]

In winter and bad weather, horsemen travelled only with difficulty and few carriages were on the roads. But between the middle and the end of the century Parliament at last began to pay attention to the long-neglected problem and the responsibility for the upkeep of the roads was finally transferred from unreliable local authorities, to a national system which relied on the purses of those with the most incentive to keep the roads in repair: the travellers themselves.[26] This was a radical change.* Once those in power had grasped the magnitude of the problem and granted powers to independent turnpike companies to erect gates and toll bars, road conditions improved and travel greatly increased.

Travellers to the White Hart would have journeyed in greater comfort, because as the roads improved, so did the quality of the conveyances.

---

*Four hundred road acts were passed in the first fifty years of the century and sixteen hundred more in the next forty.

The light "charet" of the Hodges' day and the "glass coach" pulled by six horses at a walking pace in Queen Anne's reign were both vehicles of the past.[27] By 1750, stage coaches pulled by two or four horses were more common; these had no springs, uncomfortable seats, and were often pursued by highwaymen. But they carried red-coated guards as well as passengers and at least moved rapidly from place to place. For the affluent, the post chaise became the most comfortable mode of travel. This new ease of travel made it possible for men and women to move about more, not just for business reasons but because travel itself became pleasurable, even fashionable. Roads were thronged.*

Even before the 1771 turnpike was built over Fish Hill, there were at least two routes into Broadway: "The main road from London used to pass by the Church of St. Eadburgha by way of Pie Corner, Connygree Lane and the Seven Wells but there was...always an alternative road through Broadway village over the hill...."[28]

This "alternative road," which would have led directly past the White Hart, and which almost certainly goes back to Thomas Habington's travels and even earlier, is specifically mentioned in a Quarter Sessions record from the year 1752, the fourteenth day of July, at the height of the travel season:

> Ordered that every Waggon or other Carriage drawing up the Hill from the Signe of the White Hart in this town of Broadway to the topp of the Hill soe far as it is in the County of Worcester, may be drawn with Ten Horses if the owner thereof shall think proper....

And what owner would not "think proper?" Those who have walked, ridden or even motored up today's Fish Hill, with its steep incline and many twists and turns, can imagine the horses struggling up these same inclines with a heavy load more than two hundred years ago, especially in the heat of July. Fish Hill is indeed a ten-horse hill if ever there was one. After 1771 vehicles taking this route were subject to the turnpike toll, as were those tak-

---

*Some contemporary writers lamented the good roads and fast carriages as a spur to dreams of London and an exodus of country people to the city: "Young men and women in country villages fix their eyes on London as the last stage of their hope. They enter into service in the country for little else but to raise money enough to go to London which was no such easy matter when a stage coach was four or five days in creeping an hundred miles. The fare and expenses ran high. But now! A country fellow one hundred miles from London jumps on a coach box in the morning and for eight or ten shillings gets to town by night..." (Trevelyan, III,86)

ing the other roads into Broadway—the old road up Connygree Lane, starting at what is now Broadway Court and another turnpike route on what is now Leamington Road. A tollbook of 1799, discovered some years ago, documents the existence of this third toll route.

This toll book was signed by Michael Russell, overseer, who was undoubtedly a descendant of the Michael Russell who struck coins in the year 1670. He received the money "of one John Barker, the Gate Keeper, the sum in full." The first column recorded coaches drawn by six horses, which were charged ninepence. There were fewer of these on the roads than the others, only twelve at this toll gate in the forty one weeks of this record. Four-horse coaches paid sixpence and one or two-horse coaches threepence. There were 693 of the former and 1,371 of the latter recorded in the period between January and December of 1779. Not surprisingly, the busiest months were May to August.

There is a fourth category in this toll book, "Waggons with nine-inch wheels for hire." These monsters had begun to replace pack horses for the transport of goods and some passengers at a cheap rate. They paid ninepence to go through the toll gates. According to the toll book log, these were "huge and cumbrous machines with immensely broad wheels, so as to take a good grip of the road, and make light of the ruts. Slow and laborious was their work, but these machines and the few canals then in existence did the inland goods carriage of the whole of England."[29]

These wagons and their teams took precedence over all other traffic, and when the chime of the bells hung from their horses' great collars heralded their approach, other carriages gave way. Travellers on horseback and on foot took pains to get an early start to avoid being stuck behind them, much as modern drivers try to avoid being stuck behind a slow-moving lorry headed up Fish Hill.

One can sit in front of the Lygon Arms today and picture the crowds going in and out of Broadway by the various approaches, hear the rumbling of wagons, the jingling of harness bells and brasses, and the shouts of the coachmen, drovers, and shepherds. Post chaises, carts and stage coaches crowd the roads, and the Royal Mail rushes through at great speed, paying no tolls.

Flocks of sheep, herds of cattle, hogs, and asses trudge through the wet, sloshy mud of December or sweat patiently in the midsummer heat. Solitary horsemen and people on foot make their way to and fro, to markets and to fairs, on business or for pleasure, and for many, their paths lead—at least for a time—to the White Hart Inn.

XI

1785-1813
"A Most Comfortable, Cleanly House...The White Hart"

> When first imagination fills the Mind
> And Hope delusive leaves slow doubt behind,
> The eager Tourist hastens to begin
> His fancied Journey to a pleasant Inn;
> Where many a Traveller in days of old
> Has trod good Roads and good Adventures told:
> The Prospects fine and the Horizon gay
> Speaks lucky weather and a prosp'rous day....[1]
> —John Byng

So wrote one traveller on the improved roads in the spring of 1787 as he started off on a journey. It was an age when people loved to travel, and many descriptions of various parts of England have come down to us, from Daniel Defoe, who was recording impressions for Robert Harley in Queen Anne's reign, from old Parson Woodforde describing his trips to Oxford from his Essex village, and from William Cobbett inveighing against the encroachments of the industrial revolution in his *Rural Rides*. Unfortunately, none of these well-known wanderers seems to have passed through Broadway. But luckily for posterity, a less famous, but good-natured and fluent traveller not only passed through Broadway several times, but stayed at the White Hart at least once and recorded his visit for all time.

As John Byng, later Viscount Torrington, rode through the Cotswolds in the high summer of 1787, his comments about the inn bring to full and joyful expression the chorus of sentiments many another traveller must have felt on the same road and at the same inn in previous years and centuries. History had been waiting for John Byng.

The man who jogged about England's green and pleasant land for recreation in the summer months was at first a lieutenant in the Foot

Guards, and lived in Duke Street in London. He was later a civil servant, Commissioner of Stamps, by 1782, and moved in sophisticated circles. But his chief delights were reading Shakespeare and riding about the country in the good weather. He was unpretentious, well-read, wrote poetry for fun, and had a keen sense of humour. He did not seek publicity, thinking that travel journals were too much of a fad in his day, and said of his own diaries:

> If my journals should remain legible, or be perused at the end of 200 years there will, even then, be little curious in them relative to travel, or the people; Because our Island is now so Explored; Our Roads, in general, are so fine; and our speed has reached the Summit.[2]

His innocence amazes us, but he lived at a moment when, for the first time, it was possible to reach Edinburgh in three days instead of three weeks; when one could reach Bath overnight by the "Balloon Coach travelling so fast, making it a point to be before the Mail Coach;" and when the arrival of the Mail Coach itself was a "great gala...[that] assembles as ignorant a crowd of starers, and admirers as there did of Mexicans about Cortez..."[3]

Although the journals were written when England was at war with the American Colonies, as well as with France, Spain and the Dutch, was besieged in Gibraltar and was fighting in India, Byng pays little attention to events in the larger world except for chance references.* He is a typical countryman enjoying his country.

Byng mentions Broadway and the White Hart on four separate occasions, each time favourably. His journal also contains a number of disparaging references to other White Hart inns in various parts of the British Isles which suffer by comparison.

His first mention of Broadway is in 1784:

> Friday, July 23, 1784: I was now again let loose in the world, but not quite alone as Mr. B. follow'd my steps. Round Evesham the country has been lately enclosed, and continues so to the village of Broadway, which, tho' in a dirty soil, is tolerably built of good stone, contains many decent houses, and is larger than many market towns.
>
> Broadway Hill is very long and steep, abundant of stone quarries, and leads to a fine hunting country, over which I seem'd to bound

---

*Byng mentions King George III "domestic, despotic and insecure," and refers briefly to the war across the Atlantic, when he has been "prosing over the American war" with a Colonel York, who "was captured with Lord Cornwallis" (April 31, 1782).

along. On the left I saw the town of Campden, and to the right the seat of Mr. Coventry, famously placed for hare hunting. Bourton on the Hill is a small village in which are two hunting houses, where I fancy I could pass three winter months much to my satisfaction. Two miles farther is the town of Moreton-In-Marsh...[4]

Three summers later he returned to Broadway.

Sunday, August 12, 1787.
Having now got into the high Worcester road, six miles
brought me to Bengworth—from the Bridge of Evesham (leading into Bengworth) I viewed that famous tower (still existing) of Evesham Abbey, call'd the Abbott Tower; a most elegant Gothic beauty. On the opposite side of the wall leading from the Tower, is this curiously carved arch, which probably was a grand gate way of approach to Evesham Abbey.

"I did not stop at the Unicorn Inn at Bengworth (altho' I knew its goodness,) because it was too early for my dinner stop; so kept on to Broadway, in hopes of finding there another inn as good; and did put up at a most comfortable cleanly house, the White Hart, where a delicious loyn of veal was ready to be served, and I was ready for eating it; which I did in ample quantity, and had then a superabundant temptation by an apricot tart; nor cou'd I determine upon going away, til my manager T.B.* called upon me, `Why Sir, you will stay here all day!' `And why not, T.B. it is a good house?' 'Aye, so it is Sir, and the hay is so good and everything so neat and the dogs so fat!'

At last off I went, but e're I had rode 40 yards, I said `T.B., I must return—I am tired—am too full—and can't ride,'—so I came back, and hoped I had done well.

After tea I climb'd by a very pleasant foot-path to the hill-top where Sir John Cotterell has built the most extraordinary gaze-about house in the world, at the summit of an exceeding steep; without a tree about him, and fronting the west;—there it stands, looking to Wales—but farther than sight can reach.

I seated myself at the brow—straining my eyes at the view;—whilst the distant church bell from the valley, sounded soft'ned and melodious:—and then return'd near the turnpike road, after a pleasant saunter of two hours, and lolling upon every stile.

At my return to my spacious and clean parlour, I was at a loss for employ, till I borrowed some books of my landlady;** which, with

---

*"T.B." is a friend-companion of Byng's who seems to accompany him on most of his travels.
**The landlord and landlady Byng refers to are probably either Christopher and Martha Holmes, (who were "in occupation" of the inn by 1790 and may have been there by 1787) or Daniel Clemens and his wife, who were there previously.

writing, supping and some attempts at thinking, kept me awake until eleven o'clock.

There cannot be a cleanlier, civiller inn than this is; which bears all the marks of old gentility, and of having been a manor house; walls very thick, floors oaken and wide, with a profusion of timber, and the remains of much tapestry, for carpeting, whereon was well told instructive church historys.—My bed room was very large with black oaken boards, a wrought sieling [ceiling], a wide cornice, with a lofty mantle-piece: in short, I appear'd to be in the grand bedchamber of an old family seat*.—In the kitchen hung a picture which appear'd to me the work of a great master, (perhaps of Rubens,) but the landlord, having had a hint of its value, did not seem inclined to part with it, unless some foolish sum had been offer'd him.

Most inns will do during the summer's heat, but there are not ten endurable in the winter, when you come out of London from register stoves, and turkey carpets; tho the inns now mend in their rooms and stabling, as we here begin to enter a fine fox, and hare-hunting country to which many gentlemen resort in winter; nor are their charges unreasonable, as you may perceive by the following bill:

	White Hart, Broadway
Tea	0 9
A chicken &c.	2 0
Tart (apricot)	0 2
Liquors	2 3
Breakfast	0 9
	5 11 [5]

In the years that followed, the White Hart remained fixed in Byng's mind, and seems to have become the standard by which he measured the comforts of other establishments. In 1790, travelling in another county, he observed:

Monday, June 14, 1790: A week is already gone, but no one can say unemploy'd, or that I have been idle. My bed room of last night was one of the oldest I have ever slept in, all pannell'd with black oak; the finest and oldest I ever slept in was at Broadway in Worcestershire; and in one of the best inns....[6]

---

* This "grand bedchamber" is almost certainly the Cromwell Room of today. In the Hodges inventory of 1680 it was known as the "great chamber"; in the Giles Lawrence inventory of 1814 it was called "the Best Bedchamber."

Later on he finds another inn to his taste because it manages to equal the standard of the White Hart, even in a "black" [industrial] town.

> Disley:
> And Now I was soon delighted at finding myself at the snug little comfortable inn of Disley, where the highroad is re-enter'd: a neater and more cheerfully situated inn I never saw; (for who should, but from force, stop in a black town:) I do not in my praise even except the inn at Broadway; the room I chose looking upon a small garden, and up to the pretty church, is like one of a good rectory...[7]

In the ensuing years, Lord Byng stayed at several other White Hart inns which certainly didn't measure up to expectations:

> September 7, 1782.
> Arrival at Andover, at the White Hart, where I ...dined very uncomfortably—never dined worse or was in a crosser humour about it...little miserable stale trout, some raw, rank mutton chops and some cold, hard potatoes...[8]

> August 24, 1788. Sussex, near Ashdown:
> ...there cannot be an inn of worse description than is this White Hart and the Star looks as badly—if ever I should come this way again the Bear must be my trial.[9]

> June 20, 1790. Buxton in the Midlands:
> By T.B.'s advice I put up at the White Hart, one of the lodging house inns...and was there as much slighted as could be—which I bore with philosophy, knowing that I meant to go on—I could scarcely get a room and I could scarcely eat the dinner put before me....[10]

> May 26, 1792. Kent:
> ...in the pretty village of St. Stephens, just above St. Albans, where I put up at the White Hart at 1/2 past 3. Such an inn is scarcely to be found (tho perhaps the best here) of filth, inattention and charge... I did not afford them much scope by only taking some cold beef (such stuff) on my return from the walk around this once famous abbey....[11]

> May 24, 1794. Ampthill, Bedfordshire:
> We put up at the White Hart, a mean, miserable Inn....[12]

John Byng was very much a man of his time, and reflected that time in its many aspects with both honesty and zest. He was not self-conscious, as some diarists tend to be, but wrote from the heart without affectation and without fear or favour.

Byng said that he did not want his writings to be "tricked out with false taste and French trimmings, but to be what most of my country women are—elegant, neat and engaging; full of decency, simplicity and fancy."[13]

And so they are. Writing at night by a rushlight in the inns, he mirrors for us the haymakers in the "golden glow of a Gainsborough landscape," "the first smoke from copper [mines] at Neath," or "the milkmaids near Oxford [who] looked and dressed like London Strand misses."[14]

As well as reading Shakespeare, Milton, and Cervantes, Byng read the authors of his own day—Swift, Fielding, Pope, Goldsmith and Johnson. He moved in the same circle as the distinguished lexicographer, and wrote to a friend when Dr. Johnson died: "This account [from a Mr. Cawston who sat up all night with Johnson before he died]... has given us the satisfaction of thinking that the great man died as he lived, full of resignation, strengthened in faith, and joyful in hope...."[15]

Byng wrote his experiences, such as this reference to Dr. Johnson's death, as he felt them, with refreshing spontaneity, and he covered a great deal of the contemporary scene as well as many miles of the landscape.*

Perhaps in his later years, too old to ride long distances, sitting in his London house with his wife Bridget and son Frederick, regretting the long, drawn-out wars with France, Viscount Torrington may have re-ridden in his imagination the pleasant roads through the Cotswolds and once more been welcomed at the White Hart Inn in Broadway at the close of day.

> Why in the Close of Day, perhaps too late,
> At this old Inn he stops to take a Bait;
> Hopes,—after too long bounding on his Crupper,
> He has some Chance to get a bit of Supper;

---

*Torrington's editor observes:
"His object was to ramble on, seeking new delights as he chanced to meet them, with no fixed purpose other than to enjoy and to record. His narrative wanders on from one thing to another—the decay of the landed gentry, their dilapidated country-houses... the new fashionable world huddled together in the growing falseness of London life... the busy turmoil of the new manufacturing towns and of an industrial population which before long would be trained to make more than the world could possibly need. There is good and there is evil.

"The new turnpike roads, ugly and straight, encourage people to rush around the country, importing a sameness into every district and eating their meals, brought from London, by the roadside instead of patronizing the local inns. That is bad and inhuman."

Has heard somewhere, or else has somewhere read,
That lucky Poets have procur'd a Bed—

Our Manager his Waiter; and it suits
We should suppose The Prompter Mister Boots;
Who will, we doubt not with officious care,
Procure him slippers and an Easy chair:—
Let him;—His jolting ended, if ye can,
Retire with your Applause, The Warming Pan.
                                    —John Byng[16]

Viscount Torrington died in 1813, two years before the Battle of Waterloo.

Giles Lawrence Inventory, 1814

Total Amount of Household Furniture, Linen, China, Glass, Stock of Wines, Liquers, Ale, Horses, Carriages, and other Effects at the White Hart Inn, at Broadway, in the Co. of Worcester, is the Sum of One Thousand, three hundred and five Pounds, ten shilling & sixpence—valued on the 21st, 22nd, 23rd, and 24th days of March by us—W. Handy & Wm. Moore

Front Attic
Attic Chamber No. 2
Double Bedded Attic
White Room
Landing
Back Bedroom next the Yard
Chintz Room
Best Bedroom
First White Room
Best Double Bedded Room
Dressing Room
Stairs and Landings
Parlour No. 1
Parlour No. 2
Soldiers Room
Room over Kitchen
Room over No. 3
Maids Room
Back Stairs

Mens Room
Parlour No. 3
Bar
Larder
Kitchen
Back Kitchen
Back Larder
Dairy
Small Beer Cellar
Granary over Wine Cellar
Yard
Second Granary
Post Boys Stable
Ale Cellar
Wine Cellar
Garden
Front of the House (bell to Post Boys room)
9 Horses

XII

1815-1867
"Spring Hill Manors" and "The Lygon's Arms"

Some time between 1839 and 1841 a workman, hammer in hand, leaned a ladder against the sturdy signpost in front of the old inn. Carefully he took down the sign of the White Hart which had presided over Broadway's main street for more than two hundred years, and replaced it with another, the ancient arms of the Lygon family.

Two proud red lions passant with forked tails dominated the centre of the shield. They were supported by two other royal beasts—a chained black bear and a chained white swan. On the reverse, a Saracen's head couped blazed forth in red, white and gold colours, paying tribute to the family's role in the twelfth century Crusades. These supporters were inherited from the Beauchamps, the hereditary Earls of Warwick, and from Urse d'Abitot, an eleventh century Norman overlord.

Exactly when this new sign began to swing is not recorded. We know only that it was before 1841 when a census list for that year refers to the inn as "the Lygon's Arms."[1]

The first half of the nineteenth century brought great change to England and all of Europe. The relative peace and complacency of the late 1700's in England were shattered by the French Wars between 1793 and 1815. Although Broadway was far from the coast, the echoes of this conflict were felt here as they were all over England. There is a record from 1804 of volunteers who were ready to serve at a moment's notice should England be invaded, a very real possibility as the long war dragged on.[2]

The new century meant change for the White Hart as well. Innkeeper Christopher Holmes died in 1793, leaving his middle-aged widow, Martha, with the onerous task of running the hostelry on her own. She soon began to think of selling the inn. When an Evesham solicitor,

William Law Phelps, bought the property in 1809, it was legally described in the document as:

> A freehold estate called the White Hart Inn situate in Broadway in the county of Worcester...one messuage [dwelling house], four stables, two Coach houses, one Brewhouse, two Curtilages [buildings and yards], two Gardens, two Orchards, two acres of land and Common pasture for all manner of Cattle with the Appurtenances....[3]

Phelps felt that the inn was a good investment. It still grew most of its own food and was reasonably self-sufficient. Despite the war, the local gentry continued to enjoy their sports and pastimes. *Bailey's Monthly Magazine*, some years after the fact, chronicled their patronage of the White Hart in 1808: "Colonel Berkeley, afterwards Lord Seagrave and Earl Fitzhardinge...hunted the Broadway country regularly once a week on Saturdays. The members used to dine and sleep at the White Hart on the Friday where they always had lampreys for dinner and excellent claret..."[4]

The White Hart was clearly a leading hostelry, despite the fact that, in 1800, the town had thirty-two other establishments for the traveller to choose from. Its rooms were well-appointed, with fine furniture, hangings and carpets. Its best bedroom (now the Cromwell Room) contained, among other items, a handsome mahogany four-post bedstead with fluted front pillars and striped hangings, a large mahogany Cumberland dining table with six matching wing-back chairs and a solid mahogany wardrobe. A pair of Kidderminster bedside carpets and a five-yard-square Persian rug covered the floor, and striped curtains with fringes hung at the windows. In a corner, an angled mahogany basin stand held a yellow ewer and basin and two chamber pots.[5]

Other Broadway inns of the time, according to John Morris, included the Spinning Wheel and the Old Swan, both dating from the mid-eighteenth century, the Kettle, the Farmer's Glory, the Milking Pail, the Woolpack and the Angel. Most of these disappeared when coaching declined after the railway reached Evesham in the 1850's.

In the coaching days, Broadway was on the main road between Worcester and London as it had been for centuries, and the White Hart was a favourite stop for watering and changing horses. The *Imperial Guide*, in 1802, and the *Traveller's Companion* in 1812 both show distances from London to Broadway Hill and Broadway as 93 and 94 miles respectively, and list the White Hart as the stopping point.

Phelps, whose legal practice was in Evesham, evidently did not himself act as host. During his ownership, several landlords are listed, John Starling in 1813 and Giles Lawrence in 1814, among others. Lawrence, who already owned the Northwick Arms in Bengeworth, may have considered purchasing the White Hart as he had its contents valued in March, 1814.*[6]

Giles Lawrence and his customers undoubtedly welcomed the historic news that sounded like a bugle call through the countryside in the summer of 1815. On June 18th, Wellington's allied forces of Great Britain, Prussia, and the Netherlands crushed Napoleon at Waterloo, inflicting nearly 40,000 casualties while sustaining 23,000 of their own. Laurel-covered coaches came clattering to Broadway as to villages all over the country, bringing news of this great triumph for England.[7] The nation breathed a collective sigh of relief. Peace at last after more than twenty long years.

There was special cause to celebrate in Worcestershire. Captain Henry Lygon, commanding a unit of the 2nd Life Guards, and his brother Colonel Edward Pyndar Lygon, commanding the 13th Light Dragoons, both distinguished themselves in the battle. They were the younger brothers of William, Earl Beauchamp, who presided at the family seat at Madresfield Court near Malvern. Some years after the war, both Edward and Henry, who suffered a severe wound at Busaco during the Peninsular War in 1809, were promoted to the rank of general.

Meanwhile at the Middle Hill Estate in Broadway, near the White Hart Inn, a young man named Thomas Phillipps had just completed his first degree at Oxford. He had a passion for books and book collecting and

---

*This inventory gives us a picture of the contents of the old hostelry's rooms as the coaching era was drawing to a close. Three attics are listed, one of them with double beds. There were eight bedrooms, including: "White Room, Chintz Room, First White Room, Best Bedroom and Best Double-bedded Room," as well as a "Soldiers Room" and several maids' rooms. All were well-furnished with such items as "pull testor bedstead with blue and white hangings," "linen window curtains," "Scotch carpeting," "oak dressing table with drawers and looking glass," "mahogany elbow chair with hair seat and arms," and "oval looking glass in gilt frame."

Downstairs there were three parlours, one with an eight-yard by five-yard Kidderminster floor carpet and "six handsome matching chairs with satin hair seats, brass nailed and a pair of elbow chairs to match." The bar contained a mahogany escritoire and copper kettle and among other items in the larder were "a beer machine and jars of pickled walnuts." Also inventoried were two kitchens, a brewhouse, a granary, ale and wine cellars, a yard, a dairy, a post boys' stable, and nine horses. The latter may have been on hand to help pull the heavy coaches up the steep slopes of Fish Hill.

was keenly interested in local affairs. His voluminous correspondence, most of it preserved, provides a clear view of much that went on in his neighbourhood in the first half of the century.[8]

In 1818, Phillipps succeeded to his father's title. There are two letters in the collection for that year which refer to the White Hart. William Bylund Bedford, who had evidently been staying at Middle Hill, wrote after his departure:

> After ten minutes conversation with your blunt, surly White Hart landlord,* I got on the Mail and was much amused by the guard, an intelligent young man who had been employed by Bonaparte in a medical capacity....[9]

The other letter, from Phillipps's cousin, William C. Phillipps, passes on some local gossip:

> I assure you that the Broadway gentry have been extremely gay during your absence. Last Tuesday was held at the White Hart a very splendid ball, two and fifty people attended, Mr. J.R. Griffith sole manager. But what spoils it all is the Ladies and Gentlemen greatly complained about his inattention towards them. Poor S. Averill** is put in the background by the Misses Griffith's two gents....he swears he will have no more to do with them. The manager complained very much about the great trouble he had but I understand that it was his own fault as he would not accept of Mr. S. Averill's assistance who would have been very happy to have joined him in the fatigue. They say it will be a long time before there is another ball here...[10]

Three years after the war ended Sir Thomas Phillipps had developed a friendship with the two younger Lygons that may have prompted their brother William's eventual purchase of the White Hart five years after Waterloo. Edward Pyndar Lygon shared with Sir Thomas an interest in horses and hunting; Henry shared his enthusiasm for politics,*** county affairs, and books. Visits between Middle Hill and Madresfield Court appear to have been frequent.

---

*This surly fellow could have been Giles Lawrence or more probably one of his servants.
**Both Griffiths and Averill were old Broadway families. It was Vicar Griffiths who first unearthed the "Old Velum" from the chapel coffer in 1710, and copied and preserved it. A former "Squire Averill" loaned money to Ann Cormell when she owned the inn.
***Henry Lygon was already a member of Parliament for Worcestershire.

"Spring Hill Manors" and "The Lygon's Arms"

On January 7th, 1818, Edward wrote to Sir Thomas:

> Dear Sir:
> Should you be disengaged on Tuesday next my brother will be very happy to see you at Madresfield for some days. He regrets it is not in his power to mount you and hopes you bring your own horses.
> Very truly yours,
> Edward P. Lygon

Later in the same month, Henry wrote in the same vein:

> Jan. 18, 1818, Madresfield
> Dear Sir:
> The election being fixed for Monday next, I hope you will give me the pleasure of your company at dinner on Tuesday. Lord Beauchamp will be very happy to see you. Believe me, dear sir, very sincerely yours.
> Henry Lygon.[11]

A few months later, the elder brother, Earl William, himself wrote to Sir Thomas to remind him of a dinner engagement:

> My Dear Sir:
> I hope you will not forget your promise of dining here on Sunday next at half past four o'clock. Of course you will sleep at Madresfield.
> Beauchamp[12]

The Earl himself was a comparatively young man at the time and probably enjoyed, as did his military brothers, the company of a young scholar and antiquary in touch with experts who could put in his way "eight original letters of Napoleon when commanding the army of the French Republic to his wife Josephine."[13]

By the winter of 1822 the brothers were visiting in the Broadway area and may have already been leasing the Spring Hill estates in Snowshill which they subsequently purchased*.

Edward sent a quick note to Phillipps on February 2nd:

---

*The Spring Hill estates, then and now, are on the hill between Broadway and Snowshill, about three miles from the Lygon Arms. They adjoin the Middle Hill Estate owned by Sir Thomas Phillipps in 1822.

My Dear Sir Thomas:
I propose hunting in the neighbourhood of Snowshill on Tuesday at 11 o'clock and I hope to have the pleasure of meeting you in the field.
My dear sir, very faithfully yours, E.P. Lygon.[14]

What eventually led to William Lygon's purchase of the White Hart is a matter of conjecture. It may have been partly the friendship of all the brothers with Sir Thomas Phillipps, their fondness for the hunting and other recreations at Spring Hill, or just a good investment in a going concern, similar to other property purchases he and his brothers made over the years. Whatever the motives, on June 15th, 1820, Earl William, the oldest brother, purchased the White Hart from William Law Phelps.

The Lygon era began with a great many legal flourishes. The carefully penned deed was bedecked with red sealing wax, green ribbons, and the mention of many previous owners. For the sum of one thousand five hundred and eighty pounds, "The Right Hon. William Earl Beauchamp, Viscount Elmley and Baron Beauchamp of Powick in the county of Worcester...shall have, hold, occupy, possess and enjoy...all that Messuage or Tenement situate and being in Broadway, commonly known by the name or sign of the White Hart with the stables, barnyards, gardens, outhouses, rights, paths, ways...and appurtenances whatsoever...."[15]

This purchase of property was swiftly followed by others. Some time before April, 1824, Henry and Edward Pyndar Lygon bought Spring Hill, and their unmarried sister, Lady Louisa Lygon, purchased Seven Wells Farm. Sir Thomas Phillipps detailed these transactions in a letter to an unidentified friend on April 20th of that year. After thanking the friend for a book and discussing other books for his collection, Phillipps adds:

> I beg to send you a little information with respect to the change of property at Spring Hill. Col. Edward Lygon has bought Spring Hill estate with the house and Lady Louisa Lygon has bought the Seven Wells Farm and I have bought the Tower Farm, all in the parish of Broadway.[16]

Lady Louisa Lygon spent a great deal of time at Spring Hill and appears to have acted as hostess for her bachelor brother Edward. She quickly made friends with Phillipps, and on November 3rd, 1824 wrote him a note of thanks.

> Lady Louisa Lygon presents her compliments to Sir Thomas Phillipps and begs to offer her very best thanks for his kindness and

attention for which she is most grateful. The access of drives at Middle Hill is a great indulgence and will add greatly to the enjoyment of Spring Hill. Lady Susan Lygon [Henry's wife] is at the moment not within or she would also write to express her gratitude to Sir Thomas Phillipps for his very great civility and good nature.*[17]

No doubt not only Phillipps, but Broadway society as a whole welcomed the new owners of the White Hart Inn and the Spring Hill estates. The Lygons were an old and distinguished Worcestershire family, descended from the Normans. Urse d'Abitot, a powerful and controversial Norman nobleman who was Sheriff of Worcestershire for forty years held Madresfield at the time of the Domesday survey in 1086, as noted in the Prologue.

Later the mansion was owned by the de Bracys who started the tradition of public service as county sheriffs, members of the Board of Assizes, and knights of the shire as far back as 1298. About the year 1420, Joan, the heiress of the de Bracys, married a Thomas Lygon, establishing the link between the two families. One of their descendants was knighted at the coronation of Queen Anne Boleyn in 1533, and in 1593 Sir William Lygon and his wife, Elizabeth, put up the stone panel archway adorned with their initials still to be seen in at Madresfield Court.

The family continued to be prominent as the centuries passed. Colonel William Lygon fought for Parliament in the Civil War, but his descendants were loyal to the crown, and the family which bought Spring Hill was made up of devoted Tories.

The brothers' father, William Lygon, M.P., was the first Lord Beauchamp of Powick and Viscount Elmley. He died in 1806, and was succeeded by his oldest son, William, purchaser of the White Hart, who died young in 1823. John, the second son, inherited the title, but when John died unmarried in 1853, Henry became Earl.[18]

---

* Lady Louisa evidently so much enjoyed the drives on the Middle Hill estate that soon after this she wrote a note of apology to her neighbour, Lady Phillips:

> I am shocked at my stupidity yesterday in not recognising your carriage, which must, I am certain, have seemed very extraordinary to you... it did not occur to me until after you had passed that the livery was yours... I was in earnest conversation with Mr. S___ at the time... I did my best to mount the bank to overtake you but you had driven on... I must trust to your good nature to forgive me...
>
> Very truly yours,
> Louisa Lygon.

The two Spring Hill Lygons, Henry and Edward, were both distinguished men. Edward Pyndar Lygon joined Wellington's army as a young man in 1812 and served in the Peninsular campaigns of 1813 and 1814, receiving a medal for his role in the battle of Vittoria. At Waterloo, he commanded the 2nd Life Guards, "eminently distinguished himself," and was made a Companion of the Order of the Bath.[19] He was a colonel when the war ended and a full general by 1846. He never married.

General Edward Lygon was sufficiently interested in commemorating the battle of Waterloo to plant extensive spinneys on his Spring Hill estate in the shape of troop formations at the battle. The Duke of Wellington is supposed once to have visited Spring Hill and the two old soldiers may have walked the land and reminisced together.[20] (The outline of the battle in trees is not clearly visible today).

Henry Lygon is most noted for his public service. He served as M.P. for Worcestershire from 1816 until 1831, and for West Worcestershire from 1832 until 1853. When Spring Hill was purchased, he had just married Lady Susan Caroline Eliot, daughter of the Earl of St. Germans, by whom he had six children. Shortly before his death in 1863 he was made Colonel of the 2nd Life Guards and Gold Stick in Waiting to the Queen.

Henry was obviously a good politician who knew that taking care of the people he represented was the key to his continued success. The editor of a Worcestershire newspaper penned this tribute to the Lygon family in 1863:

> ...their moderation, courtesy and constant attention to the local interests of their constituents has been ever such as to generally elicit the approbation and esteem of their opponents so that since the passing of the Reform Bill a Lygon has always been 'safe' for West Worcestershire....[21]

Although one of their forebears had fought for Parliament during the Civil War, the Lygons since that time had been loyal supporters of the monarchy and aristocracy. Taking his seat in the Commons in 1816, Henry continued that tradition, and after the passage of the First Reform Bill in 1832, supported the new Conservative Party under Sir Robert Peel "with warmth and fidelity," perhaps with increasing warmth as this party became more progressive. In any case he served through years of rapid change and intense political debate, and under several Prime Ministers, the most notable of whom were Wellington,* Melbourne, Peel, and much later, Palmerston.

---

*Wellington had become Prime Minister because of his renown as the victor at Waterloo. From 1822, thanks to Sir Robert Peel, the Tories became the Conservatives and shed much of their reactionary image. They retained power until 1830.

The Lygon family was well respected in Broadway and throughout the North Cotswolds. When Earl William, who had bought the White Hart in 1820, died in 1823 at the age of 40, his obituary occupied a full double column in *Berrows Worcester Journal* and included this detailed description of the funeral:

> This departed nobleman lay in state the whole of yesterday in the Grand Saloon which was entirely hung with superfine black cloth...coffin lined with rich white satin, foiled and ruffled...covered with rich crimson Genoa velvet...and numerous escutcheons....

The procession to Madresfield Church included the Dean of Worcester and other distinguished members of the clergy; the Steward; Earl John, William's brother the chief mourner; Col. The Hon. Henry Lygon M.P.; Col. The Hon. E.P. Lygon and Lord Deerhurst.[22]

General Edward Pyndar Lygon's funeral in 1860 and his brother Henry's in 1863 were just as impressive and well documented. This was a period when England revered the members of her aristocracy who symbolized the prestige of the realm, the more so if they had fought at Waterloo.

William, Earl Beauchamp died in 1823, just three years after he acquired the inn. It is not clear whether his surviving brothers took an active part in its management.* The correspondence with Sir Thomas Phillipps makes it seem unlikely, especially since Henry and Edward Lygon divided their time between Madresfield Court, Spring Hill and various fashionable addresses in London.

When they were in their own county, however, Spring Hill's owners and their guests undoubtedly entertained at the White Hart, especially during the hunting season. Their letters are full of references to the state of the game, renting estates for hunting, feeding costs, and all the details of their favourite sport. There is a lengthy exchange covering nearly two years about the possibility of the Lygon brothers renting Sir Thomas Phillipps' lands for hunting in the winters of 1826 and 1827. This exchange began in August 1826, with some hard-headed advice to the often impractical Sir Thomas from his brother-in-law Thomas Molyneux:

> How about the manors? I do not think you will be able to prevail on any person to give you the price you require for them unless Col. Lygon will do so as they are, for various reasons, a greater object to him than to

---

*The names of all the landlords of the inn during this period have not come to light, but one who was there for some time was Thomas Stanley. He was married to a widow Taylor named Elizabeth. On the baptismal record for their son, Charles, in 1831, Stanley's occupation is listed as "victualler, White Hart."

any other person. You must also recollect that, never having been properly preserved [stocked], you have a very scanty supply of game....I was offered a manor in Norfolk wherein you might kill, I imagine, as many head of game in a day as you have at Middle Hill altogether....[23]

Phillipps followed Molyneaux's advice, and wrote to the Lygon brothers. But in the epistolary fencing match that followed he seems to have pushed his rental price up to £150. After numerous polite suggestions that £100 was his limit, Edward Lygon cursorily resolved the matter by a refusal in February, 1827. Phillipps tried again, writing in an injured vein:

> Middle Hill
> Feb. 22, 1827
> My Dear Sir:
> I intended to offer you this morning the whole of the manors but not yet having offered them to any other person except yourself, nor had put any advertising in the papers reflecting them and I intended to let you have the whole of them at the 100 which you offered. But if I judge rightly by your conversation, such a proposal comes too late. I consider it most advantageous to both of us to let you have them at a low rate than to a stranger at a high one...—T. Phillipps

Lygon's patience in the haggling match, however, was exhausted. He wrote by return of post:

> Spring Hill, Feb. 23, 1827
> My Dear Sir:
> Thank you very sincerely for your kindness in offering me your manors on such very advantageous terms but my ardour in the preservation of game is much abated, which has induced me to form a resolution not to extend my beat beyond its present limits and with this view I am obliged to decline your proposal...—E.P. Lygon [24]

Phillipps's correspondence with the Lygons chronicles the warming and cooling of the relationships between the two families, much of it involving this skirmishing over the price of shooting rights.* Phillipps, whose mind was more on his book collection than his bills, was always in debt and constantly trying to raise money in every way possible.

---

*A copy of the entire correspondence between Sir Thomas Phillipps and Henry and Edward Lygon between the years 1822 and 1855, including the argument over shooting rights, is contained in Appendix E. These letters form a part of the Phillipps Robinson Collection at the Bodleian Library.

Possibly due to Sir Thomas's ever-growing pecuniary troubles, Henry Lygon's letters to his friend began to show restraint as well as warmth as the decades went on. Lygon's own life, divided as it was between duties in Parliament and social responsibilities in London and Worcestershire, was undoubtedly frustrating at times. He had to keep abreast of national cross currents and still deal with his Worcestershire constituents.

In 1842 he tried to help the impecunious Phillipps settle a dispute about his taxes. Later that same year Phillipps was so beleaguered that he "knocked a tax gatherer to the ground." For a time after that the Lygon family kept their distance socially. Some examples from January, 1843:

> Spring Hill 7 January 1843:
> I am sorry I cannot dine with you tomorrow. I am going to London at six o'clock on Wednesday and it is very inconvenient to be from home late the night before starting.
> Yours Faithfully, Henry Lygon.
>
> Spring Hill Monday Morning 8 Jan. 1843
> Nothing in the world would give me more pleasure than dining at Middle Hill but the truth is I have just recovered from a severe cold and I am advised particularly to avoid going out at night and this, I am afraid must be my excuse for not accepting your kind invitation.
> Very faithfully yours. Edward P. Lygon.[25]

An additional source of friction between Phillipps and the Lygons was the fact that some years after the death of his first wife, Henrietta in 1832, the Baronet re-married. His second wife, Elizabeth, was not readily accepted by the county people and Phillipps was testy about this as well as about his unsuccessful appeal to tax officials. In 1845 he once more appealed to Henry Lygon:

> Although you were not able to prevail against the Philistines of the Tax Office yet I hope you have more influence in your own county. A friend of mine is very desirous to be put into the Commission of the Peace for Worcs....he has more value on the Bench at Campden than all the others...I am buried in snow which has remained on the trees for three days without melting, which, I suppose, is not the case with you, surrounded as you are by fires and steam engines....[26]

Henry apparently did exert himself for this magistrate, a Mr. Steele, because in February of the same year Phillipps wrote again to his M.P., a letter combining thanks and pique:

I was not aware until recently that you had executed your promise of applying to Lord Lyttleton for Mr. Steele's appointment...I regret you were unsuccessful and would now ride up and thank you in person for your exertions in his favour were I not prevented by never having yet had a visit of congratulation on my marriage from your brother, by which I infer he has no desire I should visit any of you at Spring Hill. I am now therefore only returning you my best thanks by letter which I now beg to do and remaining my dear general yours truly. Thos. Phillipps.[27]

Despite the intermittent cooling of relationships, the ladies of both estates continued to take the air in daily drives and the gentlemen exchanged letters on matters both political and social. In the following decade, after Henry Lygon had succeeded to the title, Sir Thomas wrote to him, offering to show his book collection to Frederic, the heir apparent, possibly aware that it would be wise to remain on good terms with the future Earl:

My dear Lord Beauchamp:
Not having had the pleasure of shewing the Hon. Frederic Lygon my topographical collections... I fear he has been waiting for an expression... If such is the case, may I beg you to deliver the enclosed to him and to state that I am now disengaged and shall be most happy to see him if he will be content with my humble style of life. I have long sacrificed for the pleasure of collecting books for the use of my literary friends.
Believe me always, my dear Eral Beauchamp, Very Faithfully, T. Phillipps.[28]

The Lygon family style of life in those decades was comfortable, even luxurious. A brochure of the time describes Spring Hill as a large and palatial mansion, complete with park and "pleasure grounds."*[29] We can assume that the Lygons' London residences at Hyde Park, Grosvenor

*A Mansion beautifully situate on an eminence in the centre of a small park of about sixty acres surrounded with Plantations, altogether tastefully laid out and forms one of the most delightful Residences in the county of Worcester...the occupiers have the liberty of sporting over three thousand acres of land...an entrance hall, Dining and Drawing rooms, Library, Morning room, seven Best Bed rooms and two Dressing Rooms, Music room, Nursery, five Chambers for servants, Servants hall, Butler's Pantry, Housekeepers Room, Kitchen, Bakehouse with oven and troughs and excellent Wine and Beer cellars.
The outbuildings consist of...Stabling for Seventeen Horses, with Saddle Room and Lofts, Barn, Bullock Sheds, Cart-House, Pig-sties...Bailiff and Gardener's Cottages, a good walled Garden, in which are Peach and Green-houses, Pinery, with succession Pits, Melon Ground...In the shrubbery and pleasure grounds are an Ice House and a Summer House.

Square, and St. James's Place were equally opulent. The wills of Edward Lygon in 1860 and his brother Henry, in 1863, show that the former had goods valued at £60,000 at the time of his death and his brother, the Earl, a total of £180,000.[30] The family of Henry Lygon employed a large number of servants, including one Charles Drury, who would later figure prominently in the history of the Lygon Arms.

Meanwhile the mail coaches continued to rumble up and down Fish Hill and beyond, carrying post and passengers between London and the White Hart and other inns in Broadway. As early as 1825,[31] *Pigot's Directory* showed that a number of coaches were passing through Worcester, Evesham, Broadway, Chipping Norton, Oxford, and High Wycombe to London every day except Sunday. "The Royal Mail calls at the Northwick Arms, Evesham, every evening at 6:15, the Telegraph calls every evening at 5. The Aurora calls every morning (Sundays excepted) at 6:30, the Sovereign at 7:30. All go through Broadway, Chipping Norton, Oxford and Wycomb...."[32]

The railway, which had started in England in the 1830's, reached Evesham in 1852. In the long run it would have an adverse effect on the Lygon Arms' business, but in the beginning its impact was minimal. Coaches were still very active in 1845 when Sir Thomas Phillipps offered an expected guest some advice about the best way to reach Middle Hill: "Your best mode of conveyance will be to Cheltenham by coach and from Cheltenham a coach to Broadway called the Stevens Coach. This leaves on Tuesday, Thursday and Saturday only about four or four and a half and arrives in Broadway in about three hours. A fly from Broadway will bring you to Middle Hill to dinner."[33]

Some time during these years when Henry and Edward Lygon were exchanging business and social missives with Sir Thomas Phillipps, by 1841 at the latest, the Lygon coat of arms became a familiar sight, both to the local gentry and to visitors from other parts of Great Britain. It was to become even more well-known in the second half of Queen Victoria's reign.

XIII

1839-1898
"One Of The Finest Hunting Districts In The Kingdom.."

On a darkening evening of a market day some time in the 1840's, Charles Drury had every reason to be pleased with himself. He was mounted on a fine hunter, and the leather money pouch tied to his belt had a reassuring weight, thanks to the successful sale of some Lygon Arms livestock at the Moreton-in-Marsh market.

As he rode along the lonely "Five-mile-drive" from Moreton toward Broadway, the sound of horses' hoofbeats in the distance caught his ear. As they grew increasingly louder, Drury realised that they must be highwaymen who had taken note of his successful transactions at the market and were bent on relieving him of his purse.

Approaching the top of Fish Hill, where the road to Broadway passed through a small quarry near where the Fish Inn now stands, Drury decided that the pursuing horsemen were too close for comfort. Untying the money pouch, he threw it as far as he could into the quarry's depths and spurred his hunter down the hill to the safety of the village, where the highwaymen could only ride quietly by. The following morning, Drury rode back up the hill and retrieved his money.[1]

The late Charles Stuart Drury delighted in telling this tale of his grandfather, the ambitious son of a poor Cotswold farmer who worked his way to the position of butler and steward to the Lygon family, and who purchased the Lygon Arms in 1867.

Baptised in Weston Subedge on 31st May, 1801, the son of Henry and Elizabeth (Rimmell) Drury,[2] Charles apparently entered the service of the Lygon family at Spring Hill and later at Henry Lygon's London house in St. James's Place. While still a young man, he rapidly became one of Henry Lygon's most trusted retainers.

On 7th March, 1839, when Charles married Jane Richardson of Eaton Square at St. George's Hanover Square, his occupation is listed as "gentleman" and his father's as "farmer."³ Soon after this, his master, either by lease or appointment, made him innkeeper of the Lygon Arms for he is so listed in the baptismal record of his first son, Charles Richardson Drury, on 6th September, 1840 in Broadway.⁴

The 1841 Broadway census lists Drury, his wife Jane and son Charles, six months, three female servants, a mason, two guests and an older lady, Elizabeth Drury, "independent," Charles' mother. This is the first official record in which the former White Hart is listed as "the Lygon's Arms." Drury must have re-named it as soon as he took over its management, in tribute to the family who had promoted him from butler to innkeeper.

In the decades that followed, Drury expanded his interests beyond innkeeping. He is listed in various local directories as a "victualler," as one licensed to rent horses (*Billings*, 1855), as "the proprietor of a posting and commercial house," (*Cassey's*, 1860) in addition to "Innkeeper, Lygon Arms Inns."*⁵

By the late 1840's coach travel began to decline. According to the 1855 Broadway Census List: "In the good old coaching days Broadway was a place of considerable note, having been one of the stages on the road to Oxford and London but since the introduction of the rail into the country it has lost much of its briskness, and has settled down into a very quiet place, many of its chief inns being closed. The population in 1851 was 1620 inhabitants, being 58 less than in 1841."⁶

But Drury's Lygon Arms was soon to have an advantage that competing hostelries did not, the hunt. The White Hart, now the Lygon Arms, had always been one of the gathering places for huntsmen, and old habits persisted. When the Earl of Berkeley's hunt was subdivided in 1867 the Lygon became the meeting point for the North Cotswold Hunt, and Drury did a brisk business putting up and fitting out the field, who came from as far away as London.

Hunting rights to Cotswold manors were evidently much in demand, even though game was not always plentiful. Witness the correspondence between Sir Thomas Phillipps of Middle Hill and a Londoner named B.

---

*The *Billings Directory* provides some insight into what Broadway was like when Drury's family was growing up. "There is a Free School, endowed in 1686 by Mr. Thomas Hodges for the education of twenty poor boys...a national school for boys and girls, supported by contributions and the childrens' payments, average number of scholars: Boys, 15; Girls, 25." In the days before elementary education became compulsory in 1870, Broadway was comparatively lucky in having two schools. Drury's son would have had to pay to go to the national school.

"One Of The Finest Hunting Districts In The Kingdom..."

Littlewood, who proposed a lengthy stay at the Lygon Arms during the 1855 hunting season.

> Norton House, Nr. Stourbridge, 12 May, 1855 to a solicitor near Broadway:
>
> Sir: In a letter I have received from a Mr. A. Walker of Grays Inn, London, he says that you will kindly meet me at the Lygon's Arms, Broadway, and give me the information I wish concerning Sir T. Phillipps manors. I now write to say that I intend being there on Thursday next about half past eleven and shall be happy to meet you. I am sir, your obed. B. Littlewood.

Later in the summer, Littlewood wrote to Phillipps:

> Norton House, Nr. Stourbridge. July 13, 1855
>
> My Dear Sir: I am sorry we could not have the pleasure of paying our respects yesterday at Middle Hill, being much pressed for time and my wife feeling fatigue from the weather. We have made arrangements to take apartments at the Lygon Arms and I shall therefore be happy to take the shooting and if you think well to have any agreement drawn up I will sign it. My dear sir, yours faithfully, B. Littlewood.

Phillipps made note of his arrangements at the bottom of the same piece of paper: "Gen. Lygon and Wm. Gist declined letting their houses. Mr. Walker of 13 Kings Wood will draw up the agreement. Thanked him for his offer of commission."

Evidently Phillipps didn't bother to check on the abundance of game at the manors. Two weeks later, Littlewood sent his gamekeeper to assess the situation, and fired off this testy note to Phillipps:

> Norton Nr. Stourbridge, July 28, 1855.
> Dear Sir: I am quite aware that you know nothing of the state of the game and also that you would not wish me to waste my time living at an inn at great expense and walking 20 miles a day without seeing any game of any sort, as my keeper expresses he has done....B. Littlewood.

This note is followed by another on 16th August with the season only a few months away:

Dear Sir: I must also satisfy the landlord of the Lygon Arms, one way or the other. B. Littlewood.[7]

One hopes that not too many of Drury's prospective long-term winter guests were similarly put off by Sir Thomas Phillipps's lack of game or that of neighbouring estates. Winter huntsmen were a major part of the Lygon Arms' income, and Charles Drury delighted in their company. During his years of stewardship for the Lygons, Drury had been saving his money, and in 1867, when a series of deaths in the family prompted Earl Frederic Lygon, who had succeeded his father, Henry, in 1863, to put several of their freehold properties on the auction block, Drury purchased Lot #14, "The Lygon Arms Inn, an important and valuable freehold property, now and for many years past in the occupation of Mr. Charles Drury."

The notice of Public Auction at the Crown Hotel, Broad Street, Worcester, on 23 October, 1867, further described the property:

> The premises contain Entrance Hall, Commercial Room, Sitting Room, Bar, Bar Parlour, Smoke Room, Kitchen and two cellars, capital Double Coachhouses, Harness Room, Saddle Room, Loose Boxes and Stalls affording accommodation for upwards of forty hunters and other horses.
>
> Two Roods and 21 Perches situate fronting the road from Moreton to Evesham...the Lygon Arms is in the centre of one of the finest Hunting Districts in the Kingdom, is a frequent meet of the Cotswold Hounds and is well known as the favourite headquarters of Gentlemen hunting with the several Packs of Foxhounds in the neighborhood of Broadway.[8]

On completion of the sale, Drury at once began to make his inn even more attractive to the huntsmen. Since his purchase coincided with the founding of the North Cotswold Hunt, more space was needed. One of his first acts was to design and build an "Assembly Room" for their gatherings and balls.* A Mr. Christopher Hensley was apparently the lowest bidder. His estimate, dated February, 1869, totalled £238-10-10 for such jobs as "cost of materials and labour for unroofing and taking off timbers of Store Room, Brewhouse, Stables and Saddle Room, and erecting new room on old walls."[9] Hensley specified that the work would involve a labourer, a digger, a foundation builder, a bricklayer, a carpenter, and a slater. The room was completed in time for the hunt season the following winter.

*This room has been replaced by the present Great Hall.

Drury's new assembly room quickly became popular. In 1871, the *Evesham Journal* recorded: "The Hunt Club Ball (North Cotswold Hunt) will be held on February 15th and will be held at the New Assembly Room at the Lygon Arms, Broadway. Patronesses: Countess of Coventry, Lady Northwick, Lady Clifford, Lady Rushout, Mrs. Knowll, Mrs. Henry Griswood. Patrons: Earl of Coventry, Lord Sudeley, Sir Thomas Phillipps, Bart." (Phillipps died the following year). Ticket prices are listed as "Gent. 21s. and Ladies 15 s."[10]

Drury saw to it that the room served other purposes besides the hunt balls. In 1875, the *Evesham Journal* chronicled: "a very enjoyable evening of entertainment," which took place fortnightly in the winter months, and included a variety of duets, solos, and part-songs accompanied by the pianoforte. "The room was well filled with a respectable audience and the proceeds were in aid of the funds of the Broadway Cricket Club."[11]

Private concerts for good causes were also held at the Lygon. A receipt from 13th April, 1888 signed "C. Drury, Prop. Family, Commercial and Posting House, Broadway," has survived. It was given to the Reverend Mr. Morgan for a concert held in the Assembly Room on April 3rd, for the following items:

	£-s-d
Fires in the Ante Room	1-5-0
Conveying organ from Vicarage and back	0-2-6
	1-7-6 [12]

The last census listing at the Lygon for Charles Drury and his wife is in 1871, with a staff consisting of a barmaid, a cook, and a general servant. After that he apparently retired to nearby Farnham House, and his son, Charles Richardson Drury, took over the inn. Jane Drury died in 1875 and her husband in 1879. She was seventy-nine and he seventy-eight.

Since there is no will or inventory of Lygon Arms property on record, it appears that Charles Drury Sr. ceded the inn to his son in his lifetime.* Charles Richardson Drury may have chosen not to live at the inn, as he is listed on the 1881 census as occupying the Old Vicarage, with his wife Laura and seven sons. In the same year a Caroline Caldwell is listed at

---

*In so doing he followed the example of an earlier innkeeper, Thomas White, who had given the inn to his son-in-law, William Sambache, before 1556.

the Lygon Arms as "housekeeper and manageress" along with a barmaid, domestic servant, and retired farmer.

Charles Richardson Drury had been born at the Lygon Arms in 1840 and educated at Coventry School and Chester College. He married Laura Griffin, a local girl, and had eight sons, one of whom died in infancy. As a young man, he farmed for a short time in the Swansea valley in Wales, but soon returned to help his father with the inn and eventually took it over. In his father's time, the heyday of coaching, the Lygon Arms had been "considered the best hotel between Worcester and Oxford for anything that could be desired by travellers. That old reputation was well kept up during Mr. Drury's [Charles R's] management....genial and hospitable, he was liked by all with whom he came in contact and made a large circle of Broadway friends."[13]

A frequent visitor in the 1880's was Allan Fea, who mentioned the inn twice in *The Antiquary*. In 1881, Fea referred to a "princely pigeon pie" he had eaten at the Lygon Arms, and in 1887 he declared: "The Lygon Arms is little less than a palace, tall, majestic, sombre, with a look of romance about it." He also mentioned grey stone walls, and doubts that "we could see such happy roses anywhere else in the country...."[14]

An equally enthusiastic literary visitor was James John Hissey, who travelled from London to St. David's and back by dog cart in 1891. He passed through Broadway, stayed at the Lygon Arms and thus described Drury:

> The landlord...was an ideal one in true sympathy with his romantic surroundings. Seeing the great interest we took in his delightful, old-time inn, he kindly showed us all over it; and fortunate indeed is the chance that was given to see such a rare old building. A proprietor who so highly prizes his possession...Mine Host...showed me an old oak panelled room with a little staircase all to itself...that opened into it through a corner of the panelling....[later] mine worthy host entertained me in the bar with pleasant gossip and local information over a glass of whisky and a friendly pipe.[15]

Possibly inspired by these visiting authors, Charles Drury himself published a small brochure entitled "Picturesque Broadway" which includes his own description of the Lygon Arms. The brochure tells the public: "This picturesque old house, anciently the White Hart and for many generations the hostelry of the village, is situated about the middle of North Street, has a South aspect, and is, as a place of accommodation, of considerable antiquity."

It points out encouragingly about Broadway:

> The neighborhood is extremely healthy and the air very pure and bracing. After having been in succession, a `Royal Demesne' to the Mercian Kings and their successors, and the productive and health-giving estate of the monks of Pershore Abbey, the village bids fair to become a sanitary resort of some note....those who have enjoyed the breeze on the hill at over a thousand feet above sea level, close to the Village, bear witness to the fact that there is a sustaining property to the air which wards off and dissipates fatigue and refreshes the nervous system in a very remarkable degree...the *Evesham Journal* says: "The palm goes to Broadway, which is one of the most salubrious towns in the kingdom and has in the last quarter sustained its reputation as an exceedingly healthy place by registering the low death rate of 6.4 per thousand." The village is readily supplied with shops of various kinds....[16]

What a commercial for young and old alike!

Another regular visitor to the Lygon about this time was a retired clergyman, the Rev. J.S. Stone, an antiquary who wrote prodigiously. His writings appealed to history lovers as well as those concerned with their health and Innkeeper C.R. Drury doubtless made sure that they were spread about in circles where they could do him the most good. In the year 1893, the Reverend. Stone waxed eloquent, if somewhat fanciful, in an article entitled "Over the Hills to Broadway:"

> Now there is in the village of Broadway an hostelry of some 400 years* standing....where, over a mug of nut-brown ale and with a church warden pipe—if you choose to smoke—one can easily transplant one's self from the prosaic and comfortable present into the stirring Commonwealth times or even into the brilliant days when bluff Harry reigned, nay, for the matter of that with scarcely great effort, into earlier ages still. The very look of the place is to the history lover an inspiration...the house was well known as the White Hart Inn...and here in the main thoroughfare of Broadway stands, as I repeat it has stood for the last four or five hundred years,* the quaint old inn...a good plain dinner of roast mutton, green peas and new potatoes, served up in a style that old John Travers would have delighted in...the manse [Prior's Manse] is as old as the days of the Mercian kings and from the tenth century it belonged to the good fathers of Pershore. In those days of Clerkly ownership, Broadway flourished. Indeed until the coming of

---

*Reverend Stone, writing in 1893, seems to date the inn as existing by 1393 or at least by 1493.

the railway into the land, the place was a "bustling thoroughfare." The horn of the post boy awakened the echoes and the coach filled with passengers from far off 'Lunnon' and drawn by four sturdy and well-rubbed horses, rumbled and rattled twice a week along the road...."[17]

Like his father before him and his sons after him, C.R. Drury was a lover of horses. When he was not conducting the affairs of the Lygon or entertaining his guests, his chief sport was riding to hounds or driving a coach and four to Cheltenham. He was well-known as a fine huntsman with the North Cotswold Hunt, "riding straight, fast and fearlessly." He was also one of the best of whips, and for several years drove a small, four-in-hand coach between Cheltenham and Broadway, earning himself the reputation of being "one of the smartest turn-outs and liveliest drivers in England."[18]

Drury was also a good shot and an expert fly fisherman, which made him popular with the local gentry. He did more than any innkeeper thus far to make Broadway and the Lygon Arms known to the world, and was hailed for his "enterprise and management in bringing to the village a large number of Americans and Colonials...."[19]

Most interestingly, in the last two decades of the nineteenth century, he helped to make Broadway a Mecca for writers, painters and philosophers. A widely-read man himself, with a talent for remembering quotations, Drury enjoyed art and music. He joined enthusiastically in the launching of a distinguished art colony.

It began with three major figures in Victorian art and letters: William Morris, who stayed for a part of each summer in the Broadway Tower, and his friends Edward Burne-Jones and Dante Gabriel Rossetti. It was there, in 1877, that Morris was inspired to write his manifesto for the Society for the Protection of Ancient Buildings.

This luminous trio was soon followed by the American author, Henry James, who called Broadway "the perfection of old English tradition" and probably included the village in his "happy belief that all the world is an English garden and time a fine old English afternoon." Francis Millet came next, renting Farnham House, and also later the Abbot's Grange for studio space. John Singer Sargent, Edward Gosse, and Edwin Austin Abbey joined the group. One of Sargent's best known impressionist paintings, "Carnation, Lily, Lily, Rose," named after his hostess, Lily Millet, was created in Broadway.[20]

During C.R. Drury's last years of proprietorship, one of the Lygon

Arms' most famous guests gave a dinner party there for a cricket team. In 1897 the playwright James Barrie started his "Allahakbarries" team, so-called because "Allahakbar" means "God Help Us" in Arabic. The players included such literary figures as Conan Doyle, creator of Sherlock Holmes, the novelist A.E.W. Mason, and several members of the staff of *Punch*. Barrie's team played a team of painters organized by Mary Anderson Navarro, the famous American actress who had settled in Broadway. What the two sides lacked in athletic prowess they made up for in high spirits.[21] Barrie's Lygon dinner was followed by a dance at Francis Millet's studio, attended by Mr. and Mrs. Drury.

At the time of Queen Victoria's jubilees in 1887 and 1897, the flower beds in front of the Lygon Arms burst forth in red, white and blue blooms, as did the flower borders all over Victoria's England. Her popular rule of more than sixty years was also the era in which the Drury family had prospered. Two years after Queen Victoria came to the throne, Charles Richardson Drury's father, the son of a farmer, had been promoted from butler to running a prosperous inn. Drury and his family would have been proud of their heritage as they celebrated the Queen's long reign.

Charles Richardson Drury lived the last two years of his life in Cheltenham, and died there in August, 1900, at the age of 60, survived by seven sons. Six employees, including Lygon stable manager Charles Jarrett, carried his coffin into St. Eadburgha's church, followed by a large family gathering. Newspaper reports took notice of wreaths from "Ernest," "Arthur and Minnie," "Frank and Nada," "Stuart and Louie," "Lloyd and Annie,"[22] as well as from widow Laura Drury and many family friends.

Unfortunately, Drury's sons were more interested in horses and gambling than they were in continuing their father's and grandfather's tradition of providing hospitality at the Lygon Arms. According to a great grandson, Stuart Lloyd Drury, Ernest was a horse trainer in Cheltenham, and another brother, Hugh, was a skilled polo player who went to America and eventually settled in Texas. In a letter to one of his brothers in 1926, he rejoiced: "I play polo all the year round here. I tell you I ride, still ride...."[23]

Two sons settled locally. Charles Stuart Drury married a member of the Broadway Morris family and ran a farm at Mill Hay, and Roland Lloyd Drury, a surveyor and keen horseman, died in a riding accident in 1926. Roland's son, Donald Lloyd, still alive in 1991, was a Director of a School of Architecture, and his son, Stuart Lloyd, is a landscape architect who has collected much historical material about his large family of uncles and great uncles.

"The whole family had horses in the blood," he said in 1991. "My great uncles, who had been brought up to respect huntsmen, coachmen and expert horsemanship, were simply not interested in the demanding business of innkeeping. Horese became, in fact, their business. I think my great-grandfather knew this, which is why the inn was not given or sold to a member of the family."[24]

In 1898 the Lygon Arms was taken over by Charles Drury Lane and Robert Cordell. Charles Lane appears to have been a relative by marriage, but the innkeeper of record in the years between 1898 and 1903 is Robert Cordell, who is listed as a "wine and spirits merchant at the Lygon Arms family and commercial hotel and posting house."[25]

Just as Queen Victoria's reign, with its tradition of elegance and propriety, was coming to an end, so the tradition of gentility and hospitality begun at the Lygon by William Earl Beauchamp began to give way to the rancid odors of stale beer and tobacco smoke and customers of the hard-drinking, hard-smoking variety.

Travellers of the old sort were few during these years. Fortunately, one of the few was J.J. Hissey, who describes the old hostelry in his book, *Across England in a Dog Cart*:

> An ideal old hostel, a romance in stone, more like what one would expect to find in a painting or described in a novel, than to meet with actually existing by the roadside in these present prosaic times.

This passage and Hissey's other remarks about the inn fired the imagination of at least one discerning reader, who would not only purchase the Lygon Arms, but restore it to its former glory.*

---

*J.J. Hissey's entire description of The Lygon Arms is contained in Appendix F.

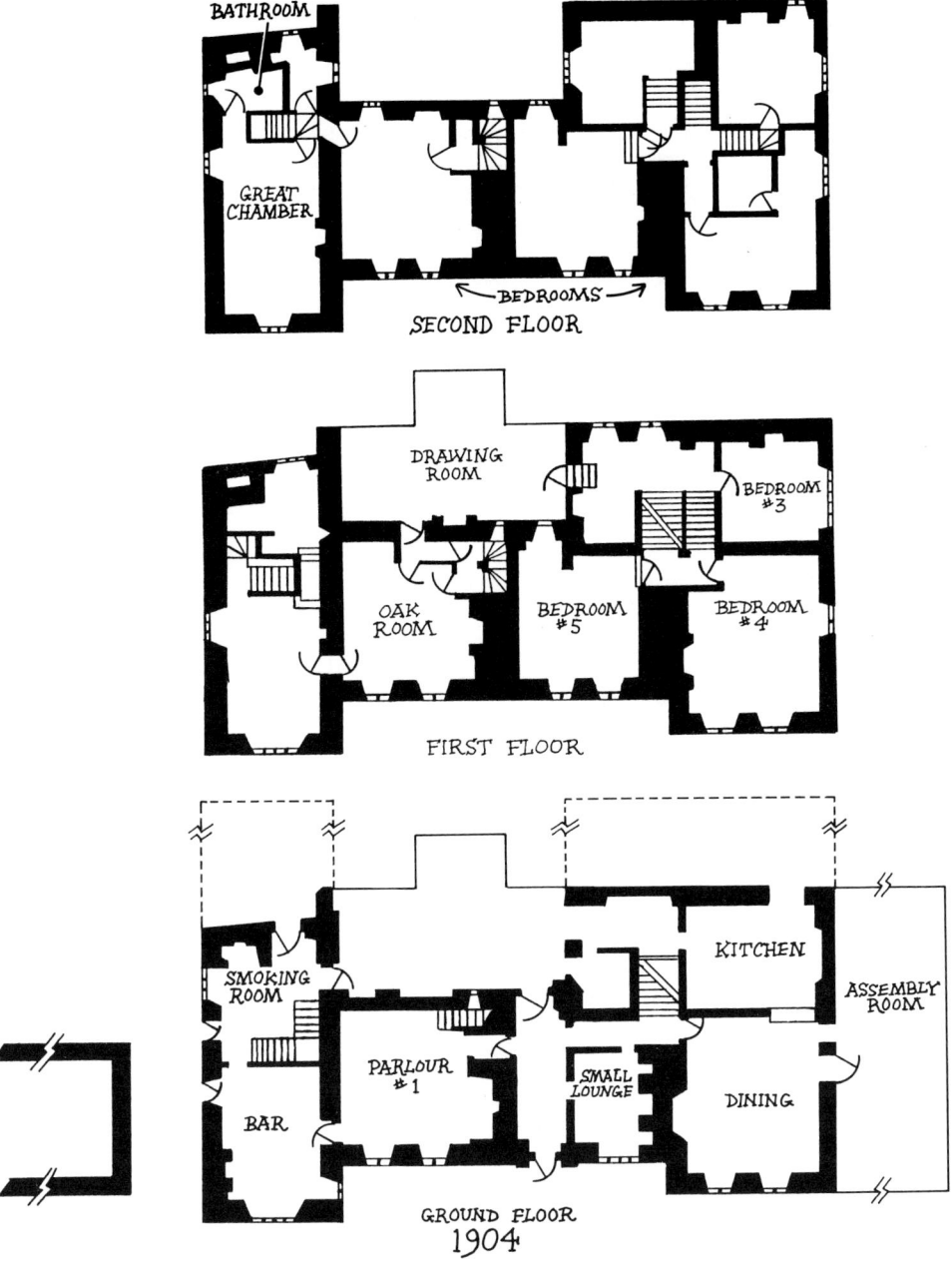

An artist's interpretation based on inventories and structural observations.

XIV

1903-1938
"Ha'pennies Make Pennies and Pennies Make Pounds."

> "Only a rather odd family would appreciate that it was better to live an interesting life of this kind than to make a lot of money."

These two apparently conflicting philosophies were spoken roughly forty years apart by two members of the same family. Sydney Bolton Russell and his oldest son, Gordon, viewed events between 1903 and 1940 with different eyes. Sydney Russell was famous for making both pennies and pounds go as far as possible in the early days of his ownership of the Lygon Arms and, indeed, for most of his life. His remark about ha'pennies is well remembered by those who knew him in Broadway and Snowshill.[1]

Gordon Russell, Sydney Russell's oldest son, viewed the early struggles at the Lygon in his boyhood as anything but a mere money-making project. To Gordon it was all a glorious adventure and great fun, as the whole family pitched in to make a go of it in a joyful, enthusiastic hurly-burly atmosphere that left all the members of his family with remarkable and probably unique memories.

Gordon's witty accounts of this adventure in innkeeping read like a series of theatrical romps, but they chronicle one of the most crucial and formative periods in the inn's long history; a twentieth century turning-point that transformed Earl William Beauchamp's old country inn into a hostelry of international repute.

Sydney Bolton Russell was a former banker's clerk with a keen financial sense. His role in saving the Lygon Arms and fostering its growth between 1903 and 1938, cannot be overestimated. He is the bridge between the Victorian era and modern times.

In the five years following the death of Charles Richardson Drury in 1898, the Lygon fell upon hard times. During the tenure of Robert

Cordell and Charles Lane, it relied on a "brisk bar trade" for the locals. It was full of "tawdry furniture, garish, dirty wallpaper, an atmosphere of stale beer and tobacco." One had to see the "inconvenience and squalor of the kitchen and back premises and the stark ugliness of the Assembly Room"[2] to appreciate the challenge that lay ahead. Despite all this, Sidney Russell purchased the Lygon and moved in during the winter of 1903. A lone bin of madeira was the only stock remaining in the wine cellar.[3]

A Londoner by birth and background, Sydney Bolton Russell was ambitious, and not content to be stuck in a rut. He had left school at the age of fourteen, following his father's death, to earn a few shillings a week in a coal merchant's office. He was a clerk at the London and County Bank for seventeen years, marrying on an annual salary of £150. His sons remembered Queen Victoria riding by in an open carriage to lay a foundation stone, and the sense of personal loss when black-edged newspapers announced her death in 1901.

Russell left the bank at the age of thirty-five to accept a position as agency manager for Samuel Allsopp and Sons, brewers. In this capacity, he travelled up and down the country inspecting public houses, many of which had foundered as a result of the Boer War.

It was during one of these visits that he saw, for the first time, an old house about which he had previously read in J. J. Hissey's *Across England in a Dog Cart*—the Lygon Arms—and immediately saw its potential as something more than an ordinary public house.

He urged Allsopps not to treat it as a regular country beer bar, but to carefully develop it for people to stay in. When the brewery, unimpressed and unconvinced, failed to follow his recommendations, Russell approached R. C. Drew, a businessman with hotel interests whose books he had kept while working for the bank. He asked for financial backing, and suddenly found himself an innkeeper.

"To my mother the whole business must have seemed an extraordinary cock and bull story"[4] Gordon Russell recalled. But the three children were elated by a move to the country. Allsopps accepted an offer, and the Russells moved. Gordon, the oldest son, was twelve, Donald was ten and Dick was six weeks old.

"Twenty times a day we looked up Broadway on the map. We found out that there was a tower on the top of Broadway Hill, that the nearest station was Evesham, that Stratford on Avon, Cheltenham and Worcester weren't very far away, and that the villages nearby had pleasant English names—names which haunt one when far from England: Childswickham, Aston-sub-Edge, Willersey, Hidcote Bartrim, Mickleton, Saintbury, Chipping Campden, Didbrook, Winchcombe..."[5] Gordon and his brothers could not know then how many visitors to the Lygon would look up Broadway in exactly the same way in the years ahead.

Sydney Bolton Russell moved his family to the Lygon on 1st February, 1904, driving the six miles from Evesham station to Broadway in a brougham. Tawdry and run-down though it was, to the Russell brothers the old hostelry was a land of limitless adventure. They met the "Boots" and the "Ostler," explored the "Glory Hole," used for smoking bacon, discovered the "Bogey Hole" which led to mysterious attics, and found "glorious haylofts" above the stables.

They were immediately befriended by Charlie Jarrett, Drury's former stable manager and a coachman of the old school, who detested "newfangled moty cars," and had "the smell of the stable about him." It was Jarrett who drove the boys to places of interest around the countryside, including a crossroads where four counties meet.

Gordon and Donald were sent as weekly boarders to the Chipping Campden Grammar School, but their weekends were far from free. After walking over the hill to Broadway they were set to various tasks, including making out bills, booking orders, typing and duplicating menus, writing advertisements, and marking the stock in a small antique business Sydney Russell had started.

Sydney Bolton Russell's idea of taking an English country house as his model for an inn, with the best materials and sound English cookery instead of the "bastard French hotel tradition" popular in the Victorian era, did not always find a receptive audience amongst his suppliers and staff. "Everything had to be done differently, by blood and sweat, and we found our own solutions as we went along," Gordon recalled. "All the forces of commerce seemed to be marshalled against him and he was made to feel that his requests were odd and unreasonable. Not that he was discouraged by this attitude. It seemed to act as a spur!"[6]

Meanwhile the mundane task of washing away the years of accumulated grime, and repairing and replacing out-of-date equipment, proceeded, and the Lygon's untrained staff soon learned to expect the unexpected from the new landlord. Gordon Russell recalls:

> Just to liven things up a bit he was liable to pull down the ceiling with very little notice and the whole place would be deep in dust. Through the murk he might be seen with wet cloth tied over his nose

> looking for old clay pipes, coins and similar things which had fallen through the chink in the boards...we were quite unable to see why the women made so much fuss about this.
>
> I don't think my mother viewed this adventure in quite the same light he did. He told her in the beginning that she would not have to take any part in the business but he spoke too optimistically...my mother was soon drawn into the kitchen after it was cleaned up, and it nearly engulfed her, but being a strong-minded woman she came to terms with her fate.
>
> Among other things, I recall that she said she must have a half bottle of champagne every night for dinner, after she had supervised the serving of the guests' dinners. For years she had it and well she deserved it. God bless her....[7]

The first ten years of the Sydney Russell administration were a whirlwind of activity for both parents and children. The Lygon was a going concern, but many improvements needed to be made, and money to finance them had to be found somehow. For this reason, Sydney Russell would spend a day or two each week administering properties in London, but his sons quickly learned to expect a barrage of questions about the operation of the Lygon when he returned.

> Up to 1909 my mother used to drive him into Evesham in the dog cart with the bay mare to catch a train before seven in the morning. When he got back at dinner-time, very tired, he would start an inquest on the day. Have they finished unloading the truck of coal? What's Jim Turner* been doing? How much did the pigs make at Campden Market? Any developments on the building?
>
> As soon as a question could NOT be answered, my father went off the deep end. 'Always the same when I go away. No one does anything. No one cares. That's where the system breaks down...' In fact, there was little system. My father believed in personal supervision of every detail rather than a carefully thought out plan of delegation. Years later, the whole family chortled at any mention of 'The System' and my father chortled with enjoyment at his own expense....[8]

Sydney Russell was determined to restore the inn to its early Victorian state, as the coaching inn that it had once been, but he also understood the value of modern architecture. One of his first and most significant

---

* Jim Turner, who lived in Snowshill, was one of the Lygon's most valued workers, Gordon Russell deemed him "a sound, conscientious workman who hated scamped work." He was indispensable for such tasks as putting up the supper marquee or polishing the dance floor.

moves was to rebuild the 1869 Assembly Room of which old Charles Drury had been so proud. This was described in 1910 as "a kind of enlarged railway waiting room."[9]

Sydney Russell commissioned a local architect, C.E. Bateman, to design a room that could be used as a ballroom in the winter and a dining room in the summer season, but the project floundered in the early stages with five different sets of plans made and discarded. Finally, and by sheer chance, Sir Aston Webb, the noted architect, was dining at the Lygon Arms and looked over the plans at Russell's request. Webb immediately suggested a radical change, proposing to relocate the entire room parallel to the street, to achieve more space, as well as to make room for a garden behind. Thus the Great Hall was placed where we see it today.

The next step was to renovate the old kitchens, and to add bedrooms above. An entire new wing was built in 1911, replacing an old nineteenth-century stable block, and making room for increased catering and more overnight guests.

Unfortunately, neither of these improvements entirely overcame the problem of how to make ends meet during the lean winter months. A few hunting people stayed then for long periods, and there were several balls, including the North Cotswold Hunt Ball, but these alone could not sustain the inn.

Luckily the increased use of the motor car for touring provided exactly the new influx of guests the Lygon so needed at this trying time. Sydney Russell was quick to grasp the importance of the car. Despite his old-fashioned views about money, he was interested in mechanical gadgets (he had been one of the first in Broadway to install both a telephone and a crystal wireless set), and was especially keen on cars.

Consequently Russell made friends with Lord Montagu of Beaulieu, a car enthusiast with great influence. Both men shared the dream of the motor car reviving the glories of the English inn, which had waned when the railways drove the coaches from the roads.[10]

Russell visited Montagu in Beaulieu, and Montagu, an authority on all forms of transport and a qualified railway engine driver, who was probably the only member of the House of Lords to drive a locomotive during the General Strike in 1926, spread the word about the Lygon Arms to all his friends. He wrote about it in *The Car*, a magazine of which he was the editor:

> Mr. Russell has wisely grasped the fact that a new species of tourist is now using the roads, one who is not pleased with the somewhat coarse fare of the farmer's ordinary and who equally doesn't like that kind of messy cooking termed by many English hotel keepers 'French.'
> He has also realized that visitors arriving in cars costing from £500 to £1,000 each are likely to appreciate good wine and like to drink something better than the ordinary 'gooseberry' bottled in the village or neighbouring town and labelled according to taste. In fact, he has laid himself out for a superior class of visitor, and however refined the motorist's home may be, he will find in the Lygon Arms just those little touches that show that Mr. Russell knows what refinement means, whether that word be used with reference to food and drink, service of meals or the furnishing and equipment of the sitting and bedrooms.
> At the Lygon Arms there is an undeniable atmosphere of Olde and Merrie England, combined with modern comfort. In the course of time, other inns will doubtless arise, which will imitate Mr. Russell's efforts, but it is unlikely that any will surpass this pioneer of the hostelry of the future.[11]

Coming from an expert on motor cars and a member of the House of Lords, this enthusiastic praise was a great boost to the inn's business and may have prompted the re-printing of Lord Montagu's article five years later, accompanied by the following Editor's Note:

> We feel that Lord Montagu's remarks exactly express the opinion that we ourselves have obtained in the course of many visits to the Lygon Arms. Motorists—with whom we class ourselves—do not now travel from town to town, but from hotel to hotel, and we have often covered many an extra mile so that we may have the undeniable pleasure of a night's stay at the Lygon Arms. For visitors to the Lygon Arms always come back; whether it be the wealthy American from the States or the jaded dweller in the metropolis, there is a subtle and magnetic influence that brings the visitor again and again to the hospitable porch and good cheer of the Lygon Arms...when spring once again gladdens the earth. This is a delightful haven of rest nestling under the friendly shelter of green-clad Broadway Hill.—E.J.B.[12]

Perhaps prompted by such encomia, many other notable visitors came to the Lygon by motor car in this pre-war period. These included the Prince of Wales (the future King Edward VIII), George Bernard Shaw, A.J. Balfour, Rudyard Kipling, and Henry Ford.

But not all notable travellers arrived by motor car. J.J. Hissey, whose book first led Sydney Russell to the Lygon Arms, became a good friend and often travelled to Broadway, driving the horse and trap in which he explored remote towns, villages, and old houses in search of vintage port. Another visitor literally dropped from the sky. One early morning in 1911 Sydney Russell was awakened by the night porter to discover that balloonist M. Aumont Theville, who spoke no English, had come from Paris and landed his balloon on Broadway Hill, having found the Thames valley shrouded in fog. After giving him breakfast, Russell accompanied Theville to his landing site, where the balloonist showed Russell the balloon carefully folded and hidden in the bushes. Theville stayed at the Lygon. Sixteen years later in 1927, the Master of Sempill spent the night at the inn during a tour of Great Britain by plane. "He was the first guest to arrive by plane," said Sydney Russell in an article in *The Countryman* magazine.

The antique business that Sydney Russell had started soon after acquiring the inn, and which his sons helped run, turned out to be good for business, and frequently led off in strange directions. Donald Russell once bought an Arabian carpet for £50 and was sternly rebuked by his father for extravagence. This carpet, now in the Cromwell Room, has greatly increased in value over the years.

Sydney Russell himself, on an expedition in the countryside, found a large refectory table out in a barn with a pig being cured on top of it. He reluctantly gave £132 for it—an unusually large sum for him to spend on any one article of furniture.[13] This table still stands in the Great Hall and has, in recent years, been much sought after by collectors willing to pay many times its purchase price. Sydney Russell's instinct in purchasing was almost invariably sound.

A few of the artists, writers, and craftsmen who frequented Broadway and the Lygon during the tenure of Charles Richardson Drury were still sharing village life when the Russells took over the inn. The painter Francis David Millet shared Gordon Russell's passion for restoring and renovating; the American actress Mary Anderson and her husband, Anthony Navarro, made Court Farm their permanent home, and many of their old friends came back to visit them. Gordon Russell remembers Alfred Parsons, Phil May, Vaughan-Williams, and Edward Elgar enjoying festive evenings with the Navarros at the Lygon before World War I.

In 1920, Mary Anderson Navarro decided to organize a concert for charity. When Sydney Russell questioned the stiff five-pound price of the tickets, the former first lady of the theatre quietly but firmly set him straight. "Mr. Russell," she said, "When I organize a concert, the tickets WILL sell."[14]

And sell they did. Lifford Hall was packed on the night of the concert, which raised a large sum of money. There is a photograph of Mary Anderson in the room to the right of the Lygon Arms front door, inscribed with her personal thanks to Sydney Russell.

One of Sydney Russell's remarkable qualities was his open-mindedness about things new, especially things American. He was, in most ways, a product of the Victorian age, but was prepared to experiment and take advantage of new inventions. Henry Ford visited in 1912 and again in 1928, and became a good friend. At one point, Ford purchased an entire blacksmith's forge and moved it from Snowshill to Dearborn, Michigan. All the roof tiles for his son Edsel's house were brought from a Cotswold quarry.

In later years Russell enjoyed telling a story against himself about his visit to Ford in Dearborn. When he arrived to inspect a wall, Ford was away but had left instructions that his guest was to be driven to the office. He was met by a burly giant who rudely asked him his business.

Russell was most annoyed, and announced that he had come in Mr. Ford's own Lincoln, which he had left at the top of the road, and he would report the discourteous way in which he had been received. The man replied: "That's a bloody likely story,—out you go!"[15] When Russell finally reached the office, there were profuse apologies, and explanations that each entrance had a bouncer to deal with gate-crashers.

Gate-crasher or not, Sydney Russell was a favourite of the American press. *The Christian Science Monitor* pronounced: "A coaching inn in the hills...an ancient hostelry whose whole aim and object is to supply real comfort and beauty combined is an experience not only to be appreciated, but joyously remembered. In this last category is the Lygon Arms at the foot of the Cotswold hills...."[16]

On July 9, 1905 the motor car brought royalty to the doors of the Lygon. While motoring from Batsford to Stanway House, King Edward VII stopped outside. A journalist travelling with the royal entourage describes the trip:

> Leaving Campden, the party proceeded down Aston Hill, through Aston Subedge, along the bottom of Saintbury, through Willersey and on to Broadway. Numerous groups of people had assembled at all these places and at Broadway flags were displayed. The royal car proceeded at a moderate pace through Broadway and stopped for a few moments outside the Lygon Arms Hotel to which Lord Redesdale called His Majesty's attention so that everyone could get a good sight of the King.[17]

A few years later in 1913, the Prince of Wales and the Princess Henry of Battenberg were guests, and in 1922 Queen Mary stopped at the Lygon on her way to have tea with the Countess of Wemyss at Stanway House. In 1927 Princess Marie Louise stayed at the inn, and the following day her lady-in-waiting sent a personal note of thanks to Sydney Russell. He wrote a courteous note in return, hoping that: "the asparagus reached you in good condition and on time," and recommending its grower to the distinguished ladies.[18]

Shortly before World War I, Sydney and Elizabeth Russell moved to the village of Snowshill, two miles above Broadway, where at first they lived in a house owned by friends, the Milvains, at the far end of the village. When she returned from her honeymoon in Alaska, Mrs. Milvain gave Sydney Russell the large moose head which still hangs in the Great Hall.

Just before war began, Russell bought three old cottages which he converted into the present Tower Close. Gordon Russell remembers receiving, copies of the plans for this conversion when he was on service in France. He wrote home urgently, stipulating: "the quoins must be substantial and properly worked." His advice was heeded.

In 1914, Donald and Gordon and many of the inn's staff, left to go into military training and the brothers ended up in some of the most brutal fighting of the war. Gordon's service included Ypres, the Somme, and Passchendaele Ridge. The innkeeper and his wife kept the home fires burning as best they could.

As hostilities accelerated, a small and tactful note appeared in the Lygon lobby:

> Defence of the realm. Food rations. April 1917. The Lygon Arms is an old English inn; the present owner has always employed an English staff and its visitors are mainly English people. It is therefore felt that a sympathetic and patriotic attitude towards the present legislation may be looked for.
> Visitors are asked:
> 1-Only to cut off the actual bread they will consume; any smaller broken pieces sent out on their plates cannot be used again.
> 2-To ask for their meat either fat or lean and thus prevent similar waste.
> 3-To remember the actual sugar allowance only amounts to two small lumps, or their equivalent, per meal.[19]

A local newspaper preserves a story of hospitality under the headline: "Wounded Soldiers at Broadway:"

> Mr. and Mrs. Sydney Russell entertained a group of convalescent soldiers from the Military Hospital in Stratford for an afternoon. This included a tour of the Lygon, high tea in the garden and music. The soldiers all expressed appreciation of the change of surroundings and "Mr. and Mrs. Russell's thoughtful kindness."

The innkeeper and his wife made up for their lack of staff with old-fashioned hard work and long hours. A lady motorist, writing for the *Caterer and Hotel Keepers Gazette*, observed:

> The Lygon Arms, Broadway. The weary war worker from London who is able to snatch a few days from his arduous duties cannot find a more ideal or restful spot in which to recuperate than the quaint little old-world village of Broadway...It was my good fortune to be motoring thither recently, leaving in the ninety-odd miles behind me, the dust and noisy traffic of town...although since the war things have changed very much, the comfort of the guest is still the first consideration. Mr. and Mrs. Russell's two sons have joined the Colours and every available man of the staff has been released for a similar purpose, so the host has to take the place of many, and although his duties must be arduous, he performs them with alacrity, feeling that in this way he is, in a measure, 'doing his bit.'[20]

Meanwhile, in Snowshill, the local people's opinions of Mr. Russell were mixed. He did not hunt, shoot, ride, fish, or engage in any of the activities considered "suitable" for local gentry. He did not tip the odd sixpence to little boys who rushed to open gates for him. He took half-pennies off cheques instead of rounding up. He earned the nickname of "Old Rock" for his habit, when bargaining, of asking: "Is that your rock bottom?" and then trying to negotiate an even lower price.[21]

Mr. Russell however, did his best, according to his own lights. He knew, from his own curtailed experience in boyhood, the value of a good education. So he started a Sunday morning class in reading and essay-writing for the village children, to supplement to what he considered the too limited education at the local school. In 1991, a Jack Hodge of Snowshill still had a bound copy of *Puck of Pook's Hill* which he won as first prize in an essay contest run by Mr. Russell more than sixty years earlier. But Russell was a hard taskmaster, and the class languished when some pupils refused to rewrite essays he considered less than first-rate.[22]

Russell also realized the importance of history, and was the first innkeeper to make a point of finding out as much as he could about the origins of The Lygon Arms, its owners, and the events which had taken place there in past centuries. Just before World War I, he decided that he and his sons should bring out a small history of the inn and "sell it for a shilling."

Russell was as good as his word. The ensuing publication, researched and illustrated by Gordon, well-printed and without advertisements, cost far more to produce than its shilling price and was a novel venture for a hotel or inn of the time. The first edition came out in 1914, and was immediately popular, especially with Americans, who often bought several copies at once and posted them to friends.

As the years went by, friends of Sydney Russell who were working on historical ventures of their own made it a point to write to him with any fresh discoveries about The Lygon Arms they came upon. One of the first of these was Richard Savage, Curator of the Shakespeare Birthplace Association, who forwarded a list of Treavis wills and a complete tracing of the Treavis line of ownership from "John Travis, born before 1575, mar. c. 1600 & died 1641 'very wealthy.' "[23] Savage unfortunately did not provide Sydney Russell, nor future historians, with the source of this information.

A second strong ally was Dr. Rees Price, a retired dentist from Glasgow, who made his home at "Bannits" in Broadway and whose hobby was collecting antique glass, an interest shared by Sydney Russell. It was Rees Price who first re-discovered, in 1924, the old Broadway Parish Register, which showed on "old velum" the line of innkeepers from Thomas White in 1532 through John Treavis in 1633, to Francis Phipps in 1710, all proprietors of the White Hart Inn, and all charged with keeping a portion of the churchyard wall or "perch" in good repair. As new information came to light, revisions were made, and two new editions of the history followed in 1924 and 1929.*

By the 1930's, Sydney Russell had more time to pursue the Lygon's history, because he had turned over most of the responsibility for managing the hostelry to his second son, Donald. He spent his time in such varied projects as counselling prisoners in Gloucester Gaol, taking part in church services as a lay reader, and bee-keeping in his Snowshill garden.

---

* In this history, *The Story of An Old English Hostelry*, the Russells refer to the inn, for the first time, as "The Lygon Arms," with a capital "T," not "the Lygon Arms" as it was previously called. The authors have done likewise in Chapters XV and XVI.

Bees were such an enthusiasm late in his life that he was known to rush out of Lygon board meetings if informed that his "bees had swarmed." He was proud of the little pots of "Tower Close" honey he gave to friends. Money seemed to mean less and less as the years went on, so much so that he was heard to exclaim in exasperation that all he needed was "a pound a week and the *Daily Mail*,"[24] to the complete mystification of his family and friends.

A slight stroke in 1916 failed to slow down these activities very much, but in January, 1938—thirty-five years after taking over the management of The Lygon Arms—he died suddenly in Snowshill at the age of 74. His son Gordon remembered the funeral procession:

> We took him from Snowshill to Campden on the bed of a farm wagon strewn with daffodils... his three sons, grandsons and people he had known... walked behind it the five miles of lonely road... we laid him overnight in the splendid church... built by another Cotswold pioneer, William Grevel, 'the flower of the wool merchants of old England,'... it seemed to me in very truth the end of an age, as indeed it proved to be.[25]

"Ha'pennies Make Pennies and Pennies Make Pounds"   153

The Tower Close, Sydney B. Russell's home in Snowshill. (Photos courtesy of Susan Byrd and Hans Schad.)

Early Workshop. Drawn by Gordon Russell c. 1927.

XV

1938-1957
"A Family Business"

In June 1957, Sir Arthur Morse stood before a dignified gathering of celebrities and friends of the Russell family and The Lygon Arms to open the Russell Room, a large elegant dining room which replaced the temporary summer function room installed in the 1930's. "The whole venture has been very much a family business," said Morse. "How could this room be called anything else but the Russell Room?"

How could it indeed? It had been fifty-three years since Gordon, Donald and Dick Russell had ridden the six miles from Evesham station to Broadway in a brougham to the delicious adventure of exploring—and eventually restoring—a run-down country inn; and twenty-one years had gone by since the three brothers and many friends and members of the inn staff had trudged the "five miles of lonely road" between Snowshill and Chipping Campden behind the farm wagon bearing their father's oak coffin. The memories of all those years must have been in their minds as they listened to Sir Arthur continue:

> This magnificent inn, as we know it today, is largely the creation of the Russells, father and sons. The father was a man of vision, with a knowledge and love of architecture and a passion to create the perfect English inn. His two sons, Gordon and Donald, who are members of the board of The Lygon Arms, shared and extended his interests. Both have made their names in different fields: Gordon in the field of industrial design and Donald in the no less exacting world of hotel keeping. The third son, Professor Richard Russell...is actually responsible for the replanning, furnishing and decorating of the Russell room. Their joint interests have come together in this room.[1]

In a few short minutes on this notable occasion Morse had succinctly summarized more than fifty years of collaboration among the three brothers which had formally begun when Gordon and Donald returned from military duty in 1919.

When he was demobbed after long service in the trenches, Gordon recalled "wondering what on earth I was going to do next." His father solved that problem for him, inviting both boys to join him as partners in the inn business, and altering the name of the firm from S.B. Russell to Russell & Sons.

Fresh from the world of war where their decisions were made for them by superior officers, both Gordon and Donald Russell welcomed any sense of direction in their new world of freedom. Although each had certain responsibilities, there were "no very clear lines of division" at first.

It was arranged that Donald, who had been apprenticed to Baileys in Cheltenham before the war and who had a good working knowledge of antiques, would buy suitable items, and Gordon would be "responsible for building and repair work at the Lygon."

Gordon was twenty-seven and Donald twenty-five. Neither had any training or experience except that gained by working with their parents at the Lygon while they were at Chipping Campden Grammar School. The brothers were merely continuing, on a formal basis, what they had been doing informally before the outbreak of war.

Father and sons did not always agree. Sydney Russell still regarded "The Public" as a group of well-off people who dressed for dinner every night and expected an inn to be run as a country house. He was born in the Victorian age, and could not grasp that his sons, fresh from war service, wanted to widen the appeal of the inn and not merely to rely upon its traditional affluent clientele.

When it came to running the Lygon, however, most differences were forgotten and all three pulled together and buckled down. More bathrooms and lavatories were added. There were more cars on the road and comfortable quarters had to be provided for their drivers. The pre-war plans for lock-up garages were abandoned, and a large new garage was built, with chauffeurs' quarters over it. Since Broadway at that time had no public electricity, a power house was built to supply the Lygon. Water was scarce in years of little rainfall, and finally the local council was persuaded to install a small emergency tank, which quickly became known as "Mr. Russell's little tank." Central heating was added to save servants the drudgery of carrying coal up several flights of stairs.

From the first, Donald Russell appreciated the importance of each guest and employee. He argued that recognition of a customer's wishes was "the very life blood of an inn." He used the same methods to train his staff as the army used to train recruits, and took a close interest in working conditions. If a waitress complained of aching feet, he insisted on paying for a visit to the chiropodist. ²

Gordon turned his attention to restarting the antique business. There were "several sheds full" of old pieces of furniture acquired before the war which, with the help of Jim Turner and his sons Edgar and Clarence, he began to repair and sell. An old farmhouse 100 yards west of the inn was acquired and turned into a furniture showroom. Gordon became "buyer, manager, salesman, packer, book keeper, transport manager and workshop manager," all rolled into one, although at first on a fairly small scale.

On leaving school, Richard Russell joined Gordon's side of the business. Soon after this, Gordon persuaded "The Guvnor" to send him to architectural school, since the brothers felt that this would add another dimension to the business.

More 'help' was hired in the summer of 1920, and one of those who answered an advertisement was a young lady named Constance Elizabeth (Toni) Denning,* who wanted to get out of London and live in the country. In the summer of 1921, both Donald and Gordon were married, Donald to Effie Bowker, the Lygon's efficient housekeeper, and Gordon to Toni. So began two lifetime partnerships.³

Donald and Effie lived in the Lygon; Gordon and Toni in Spencer Cottage next door. Both couples' lives were ordered to an extent by Sydney Russell. He insisted that Donald and Effie could not both leave the Lygon at the same time, in case there was an emergency. A few years later, he refused to allow Toni to hire a nursemaid at ten shillings a day and still kept tight control of the family purse strings. One day, after a particularly fierce disagreement, Donald rebelliously stalked out and bought a hunter so that he could get away and relax on long rides. Uneasy repercussions from this incident rumbled on for months.⁴

Meanwhile, Gordon Russell's cabinets were beginning to gain attention and were exhibited at the British Empire Exhibition at Wembley in 1924. A walnut cabinet on an ebony base was purchased there by an important customer for £200. This sale impressed Sydney Russell and "got us a good deal of publicity."⁵ By the mid 1920's, Russell was exhibiting his furniture not only in England, but also in Paris, Stuttgart, Dunedin and Glasgow.

---

* Constance Elizabeth Denning, who married Gordon Russell, was always called "Toni." Eventually she became Lady Gordon Russell. The authors refer to them both by the names that were used in the Cotswolds throughout their lives.

Gordon Russell started evening classes in cabinetmaking and arranged for various well-known people to lecture to his staff, on the grounds that one "should keep the men in the ranks informed about the work in hand." These classes were accompanied by lantern slide shows. One of the operators of the magic lantern was a young man named A.V. Freeman, who was to spend most of his working life with Gordon Russell. The workshops in turn led to amateur theatricals, with Freeman and Ted Darley and their wives as prime movers. "Gordon Russell often played the blushing heroine," recalled A.V. Freeman.[6]

When Richard Russell returned from architectural school, he took over the drawing office from Gordon, and the two brothers proceeded to "mix theory with practice—architectural students and cabinet makers...art and technical education in close integration. It was small wonder that people found our showrooms an interesting place to visit, although many seemed to think we were crazy."

Some visitors could not understand why the furniture was not stained to make it appear old. A fundamental principle of Gordon Russell's work was to use natural wood, which conflicted with public opposition to modern architecture and modern furniture design. Russell wrote a satirical pamphlet with the headline: "Wonderful isn't it? Only an expert would ever guess it wasn't old."[7]

But there were some discerning people who approved of the new ideas. Among these were Charles Laughton and Elsa Lanchester, regular Lygon visitors; Mrs. Pope Riddle, a wealthy American who designed a whole school in Avon, Connecticut, around a village green with everything handmade to resemble a Medieval village; Queen Mary, who gave a set of "wooden building bricks, hand lettered" to Princess Elizabeth; and Lloyd George, who ordered a chest of drawers made from a blown down holly tree on his estate. There was also Lady Maud Bowes-Lyon, who lived in Broadway, where her niece, Elizabeth, before she became Duchess of York, often spent holidays. Both ladies visited the showrooms.

Gordon Russell separated the furniture business from the inn operation in 1926, forming a small private company called Russell Workshops Ltd. in collaboration with R.H. Bee. Later, as its founder became well known for his writing and lecturing, the name was changed to Gordon Russell Ltd.[8]

The Lygon Arms and the Russell furniture showrooms served complementary purposes; those who came to the one often also spent time at the other. Visitors who bought cabinets and other high quality furniture would be likely to enjoy good food and fine wines as well. American visitors frequently planned their vacations and furniture-buying forays around a stay at the Lygon, stays that often lasted for several weeks.*

The 1929 Wall Street crash was disastrous for both the inn and the furniture business, as many regular American customers stopped travelling. It would be five years before they reappeared, but the Lygon weathered this setback and gradually recovered.

Meanwhile Donald Russell was slowly but surely upgrading the Lygon's facilities. Between the two world wars he rebuilt the kitchens, and transformed the old kitchen area into a temporary, canvas-covered supper dining room for parties, fortnightly dances, and other special events. This increased the income, but the canvas had to be put up on each occasion and suffered from wind and weather.

By the 1930's, Donald had more or less taken over the management of the inn. He had inherited his father's instinct for things English: food, cooking, and country hospitality, but he also sent a promising local boy, Francis Hollington, an apprentice in the Lygon kitchens, to France to be trained as a chef. Upon his return, Hollington was to be in charge of the Lygon menu for many years to follow.

Donald Russell believed in seeing first-hand what he was going to buy, and made several trips to Scotland to "see his beef on the hoof." Donald also inherited his father's strong sense of economy and dislike of high prices. In the mid-1930's he worried about increasing the price of a Lygon lunch by half a crown. The luncheon was then 12s 6d but Russell eventually raised it to 15s.[9]

World War II broke out shortly after Sydney Russell's death, and provoked a crisis of a different sort. It appeared at first that The Lygon Arms would be commandeered by the government for some sort of wartime housing or offices. This threat was averted, but little more than a year later, in November, 1940, the following notice was posted in the lobby:

> In order to meet the constant demand for accommodation by members of H.M. forces on leave, and professional and business people from raided areas who are seeking a brief respite from their necessary work, we are not accepting reservations for a longer period than one week.

---

*A case in point is that of Col. Frank A. Scott, a businessman from Cleveland, Ohio, who visited the Lygon with his wife and family several years in a row during the late 1920s and early '30s. He placed regular orders for furnishing his Mentor estate and A.V. Freeman remembers him in the showrooms ordering furnishings for entire rooms at a time. Freeman was responsible for packing the orders. "Nothing ever arrived broken," he recalled. "And he wrote to thank me for it."

The Lygon Arms has always been an Inn and we feel our customers will appreciate the reason for its remaining so, rather than becoming a residential hotel in war time.

Donald Russell's efforts to cheer the lives of servicemen were unremitting. By the time the war ended, he had corresponded with more than 300 soldiers, sailors and airmen, all of whom had been entertained at the Lygon's expense. Despite staff shortages, rationing, and insufficient fuel, Donald and Effie, by backbreaking work that often included doing the cooking, shepherded the inn and its guests through the war and so saved it for future generations.

Among the visiting servicemen was a young naval officer from Perth, Australia, named Douglas Barrington. He was an accountant and was very interested in the operation of an inn, especially in wartime. He and Donald Russell struck up a warm friendship, and Barrington was invited to return after the war was over. So began a twenty-five year relationship which was to have a decisive impact on the inn's future. In Donald Russell and Douglas Barrington, the traditions of the Victorian era and the innovations of a new age effectively meshed. This gradually transformed Lygon Arms policy and operation.

Meanwhile, Gordon Russell, who had volunteered for war service as a policeman and later served in the Home Guard, delegated responsibility for the furniture business to R.H. Bee. (Little furniture could be made anyway as timber was rationed and was needed for the war effort.) Bee reorganized, and soon the staff was busily turning out wooden parts for Mosquito aeroplanes. Later Gordon Russell would admit that Bee's ingenuity had saved the business from disaster.

Disaster of another kind struck one October night in 1940, when a German bomber en route to Birmingham was attacked by British fighters over Broadway and jettisoned its load of incendiary bombs. One of these made a direct hit on the barn behind the Russell showrooms, which contained an immense amount of furniture and 20,000 yards of textiles brought from London for safe keeping. The light from the fire could be seen as far away as Kingcombe, Gordon Russell's home in Campden. The barn and its contents were a total loss.[10]

Gordon Russell's Home Guard headquarters for the Fourth Worcesters were at the Fleece Inn in Bretforton, which he reached by bicycle most of the time, since petrol was rationed. He recounts the night he returned from London as far as Oxford by train and then "walked the twenty-eight miles to Moreton through a glorious starlit night, arriving at Campden for breakfast."[11] During the war years, he also raised pigs and grew vegetables, and took up his father's beekeeping. He learned to carve in stone, seeking solace from wartime tensions through creative work with his hands.

Richard, the youngest brother, was on active duty with the navy and his wife, Marian Pepler Russell, a designer in her own right, was living first with Gordon and Toni at Kingcombe and then in Didbrook. Elizabeth Russell, Sydney Russell's widow, spent the war years at the Lygon as her sons did not want her to be alone at the Tower Close when invasion was expected.

When the war ended, The Lygon Arms faced new problems and another reassessment. By the start of World War II, Donald Russell had upgraded staff training and had given up employing part-time catering staff. Consequently it was necessary to pay the Lygon's own staff full-time, which was difficult in the lean winter months. New stratagems had to be developed.

Douglas Barrington arrived, as promised, in the autumn of 1945, and was appointed to the Board of Directors. He suggested that the Lygon undertake cocktail parties, wedding breakfasts, and other activities which would bring local people into the inn and help defray some of the high costs of the full-time kitchen staff. Barrington also approved of the fortnightly dances, which brought in more people and led to a demand for catering at private houses. At the same time the Lygon began to accommodate small conferences of up to fifty people.

The increasing number of visitors led to other changes. More bathrooms were added, and Richard Russell, back from the Navy, designed completely new kitchens. He also converted the old kitchen space into a large permanent supper room in the 1911 wing, at right angles to the Great Hall and served by the same kitchen. French windows opening on to the garden were added. Completed in 1957, this became the Russell Room with portraits of Sydney, Elizabeth, and Donald Russell hanging on adjoining walls.

In 1956 Douglas Barrington was appointed Managing Director by the Lygon board and took on many of Donald Russell's responsibilities. Although he still came daily to the Lygon, Donald spent more time with the District Council, the Worcestershire County Council, the British Legion, and other organisations. Particularly interested in the Catering Institute, he helped to set up training centres all over England and took trainees at the Lygon for short periods. In 1964 he was asked to lecture at the Royal Society of Arts on British Catering, and was awarded the Society's silver medal.[12]

Meanwhile, Gordon Russell and Dick Bee were getting back to the business of making furniture. At the end of the war Gordon had been involved in a plan for making 'contract furniture,'* and had participated in the 1951 Festival of Britain. Lord Ismay, who was the Chairman of the Council for this Festival, was a family friend of the Russells, having done much of his courting in earlier years at The Lygon Arms. He took a delight in reminding Gordon that Sydney Russell had once reproved him sternly for keeping the innkeeper from his rest one night when the porter was ill and off duty.[13]

In 1955, Gordon Russell received a knighthood, and in 1963 he received the Royal Society's gold Albert medal "For Services to Industrial Design." He travelled extensively, at home and abroad, but was happiest at Kingcombe. Kingcombe itself was a work of art, a long labour of love for both Gordon and Toni Russell, from the day they acquired the land in 1925 for more than half a century.

There was always one more job that needed doing, and, when he had respite from his national and international commitments, Gordon enjoyed this work as much as anything else he did. He was a craftsman who liked to work with his hands, and was particularly proud of the garden pool he designed and built himself. In spring, summer and early autumn, guests at Kingcombe would be invited to sip wine outdoors and admire this pool, inspect the wall made of empty wine bottles, walk through the flower borders, and look out over the fields to the distant tower of the old church.[14]

Gordon's wife Toni, Lady Russell as she became, was an incomparable hostess who had a way of putting even shy people instantly at ease and drawing out from them their own special interest or ability. Thus Gordon Russell's humour and knowledge of the world and Toni's quiet charm

---

* Sir Gordon recounts the story of meeting a hawk-nosed woman furniture customer whose first question was: "Will it stand up to it?"

"Will it stand up to what?" Russell replied.

"Well my daughter's just got some—she was blitzed you see—and when 'er 'usband 'eard about it—'e's been in India for four years—'e wrote 'ome and said 'e'd seen some pictures of it in the papers and some of it looked a bit spidery."

"Spidery? I wonder what piece of furniture he was thinking of?"

"Well, I dunno, but the only piece 'e mentioned was the bed. And that's what I want to know so as to write to 'im. When 'e comes 'ome, will it stand up to it?" (DT, 203)

complemented Donald Russell's down-to-earth qualities as innkeeper and Richard's skills as architect and designer. Together they combined to make a visit to the Cotswolds and The Lygon Arms an unforgettable experience through four decades.

One man's dream in 1903 had evolved into a unique and widely-known "family business" popular with all ages and kinds of people, an inn that continues to thrive and grow, blending the best of the old with the new. Sydney Russell would have been proud. His dream had been fulfilled by his sons, and The Lygon Arms was and is known all over the world.

Lieut. Barrington, RANVR

H.M.S. *Eggesford*, World War II.

XVI

1945-1988
"The Fortunate Proprietor of Britain's Most Famous Inn"

"**H**e's the fortunate proprietor of Britain's most famous inn...an urbane and courtly man who, at the same time, retains the salty wit of his homeland." So stated the *Los Angeles Times* in October, 1974, at the height of Douglas J. Barrington's innkeeping career at The Lygon Arms. His story is almost as compelling as the story of the inn itself.

This "fortunate proprietor" is Australian. He first came to The Lygon in 1941 as a young naval lieutenant on leave from the Royal Australian Navy. Donald Russell had a policy fostered by the Victoria League, of providing hospitality to overseas servicemen and, as it happened, Barrington was one of them, number 47 out of a total that grew to 310 by the war's end. The two became great friends and wrote regularly throughout the war while Barrington was on duty aboard the destroyer *Eggesford* in the Mediterranean.

He returned whenever he could in 1941 and 1943, and with each visit became more fascinated with the Lygon and its operation. During these visits, he and his naval officer friends held their rendezvous in what is now "Gin Corner," so called because the naval officer's traditional drink is gin. The little ante-room with its stone fireplace, opposite today's gift shop, still reminds some older guests of World War II.

In July, 1945, an important conversation took place. While Barrington was on leave from a gunnery course in England, he and Donald Russell discussed the future of The Lygon Arms. By this time Russell had decided to form a private company with his brother Gordon and his niece as directors. "In a late night session," Barrington recalled, "the idea was floated that I might become manager at the end of the war. But then it looked as if the war with Japan would last a long time."

Soon after this Japan surrendered and Barrington found himself back at The Lygon Arms as Manager, carrying on his duties in naval uniform until demob suits could be ordered. "That was the beginning of my career in the hotel industry," he recalled. "At the age of twenty-four, I started near the top."[1]

The Lygon could accomodate only forty-four guests when Donald Russell appointed Barrington to the Board of Directors in 1946. By the end of Barrington's tenure, thanks largely to his unremitting energy and foresight, the inn's capacity was one hundred and twenty-five. "Don Russell deserves enormous credit," Barrington maintained . "He took on a person ignorant of hotel keeping with just an accountant's training and naval background. Yet from the first day, he never queried or cancelled any instructions given by me. He let me learn by making my own mistakes but did not fail to let me know I'd made them!"

Barrington learned fast and worked hard. After several years as General Manager in collaboration with Russell, he was appointed Managing Director in 1956. One of Barrington's first moves was to relocate and provide a modern hotel kitchen. This was an ambitious project, especially since the inn was having to cope with higher taxes while post-war austerity had reduced its profits. The previous kitchen was transformed into a lounge, convertible to conference accommodation. At the same time, the guest rooms were redesigned and private bathrooms added, a major improvement and, in Barrington's estimation, a turning point in the Lygon's fortunes.

The large new conference area was fittingly named the Russell Room. Sir Gordon Russell personally carved the family name and the Lygon coat of arms in the stone plaque at the entrance to the room before it opened in 1957. The room gave renewed impetus to Barrington's sense that enlarged accommodation was needed for an ever-growing clientele.

At the official opening of the Russell Room on June 21, 1957, Sir Arthur Morse praised the Lygon's foresight in providing comfortable, modern facilities for its guests. "My chief concern...is to attract more overseas visitors to Britain," he told a large gathering. "But it is not a bit of good inducing more and more people to come here if we cannot provide them with the facilities they expect to find...The Lygon Arms gives human status to the guests in a way that is not always possible in large hotels in the big cities...while we talk of the dollar-earning capacity of the British hotel industry we do not often stress these human qualities..."[2]

Morse complimented the Russell brothers on the way in which their family had combined several centuries of history with modern design, which "would serve as a magnificent advertisement for British design and craftsmanship."

Douglas Barrington was acutely conscious of the role The Lygon Arms might play in advertising the best of Britain, and he pioneered personal visits to travel agents. He clearly perceived the importance of overseas visitors, especially Americans, and considered his trip to the United States in 1964 to have been one of his more productive accomplishments.

"It was the first time The Lygon Arms had wooed the travel agents and the effect was staggering," said Barrington of his marathon trip to 13 cities during which he saw 167 agents in just 26 days. "That year there was a marked increase in business through these agents. People were surprised that I would travel all that way to promote The Lygon Arms. We have benefitted ever since, directly and indirectly."

Since then, American visitors have continued to be one of the Lygon's largest sources of income, a tradition started by Sydney Russell in the early 1900's and strenuously continued by Barrington. Barrington's 1964 promotion was, in a sense, history repeating itself in a timely manner. Henry Ford first visited the inn in 1910 and returned again in 1929. The wave of American visitors first encouraged by Sydney Russell was attracted once more by Douglas Barrington half a century later, and has continued to return to the Lygon ever since. A British journalist observed in 1955: "If I were showing a party of critical Americans around England I would take them to The Lygon Arms so they might see what we can do in the way of country inns."[3]

Barrington's promotional campaign was so successful that even more accommodation was required. In 1960 the Garden Wing was built, and eight years later a second major addition, the Orchard Wing, went up. This wing included a conference room with sophisticated, up-to-date equipment. Both modern wings were designed by Richard Russell's partnership..

In the 1960's, parking space was already becoming a problem. As a result, anticipating the greater needs of later years, Barrington bought an adjoining property for a mere £300, pointing out that staff cars had to be allowed for as well as those of guests. Donald Russell replied, with his customary reluctance to spend: "If the staff can afford cars, you are paying them too much!"

Two different views, Victorian and twentieth century, collided head on, but peace was soon restored when Barrington ordered a new car with a radio for Russell. At first, Russell refused to consider driving it. Shortly after that he wrote Barrington a light-hearted letter in which he admitted: "This poor old sod who didn't want a car with a radio now doesn't know how he managed to live without it!"

Cordial disagreement between the old manager and the new one is a Lygon tradition, and has been one of its main strengths. In a previous generation, Sydney and Donald Russell often clashed over spending. In the same way, as he grew older and watched a young and progressive manager taking over, Don Russell sometimes argued heatedly in defence of the old ways. But compromise, in both cases, turned out to be good for the inn in the long-term.

One subject on which Douglas Barrington and Donald Russell did not, at first, agree, was the large amount of heavy furniture at the Lygon. Barrington did not realize the importance of these fine pieces, but was later grateful that Donald Russell was tolerant of some of his earlier prejudices, and patiently taught him to appreciate fine furniture. Barrington now considers the Russell family antique collection to be "one of the great attractions of the inn," and admits that it would have been a sad mistake to sell and scatter it.

Barrington did insist on brightening up the guest rooms with modern furniture and rugs, which were designed and built either by Gordon Russell or his brother Richard, and Richard's wife, the designer Marian Pepler. The skillful blending of the best of the old with best of the new was well summarised by a visiting British journalist: "Lygon Arms' owner Douglas J. Barrington has shaped this charming, cosy country inn, combining fine antiques, open fires, ancient chambers and public rooms dating from 1530 with sophisticated 20th century refinements..."[4]

The conference room in the Orchard Wing was first used in March, 1968, when The Lygon Arms was honoured by a visit from Prince Philip, Duke of Edinburgh. The Duke came to Broadway to tour the showrooms of Gordon Russell Ltd. because of his long-standing concern for high-quality production in British industry. This tour was followed by a reception and luncheon at The Lygon Arms. The Prince's secretary, in his letter of thanks, wrote:

"It would be worth visiting Broadway again if just for that excellent steak, kidney and mushroom pudding....I think one of the things that impressed me the most, leaving aside the actual production facilities you have there, was the atmosphere of a family business in which everybody knows everybody else—at its best."[5]

This accolade from Buckingham Palace was good for everyone's morale, especially since there had been a last-minute push to complete the Orchard Wing in time for the Prince's visit. Barrington complimented his entire staff for "rallying around" to meet the deadline, and the Orchard Wing came into full use a few weeks after the royal visit, with the conference room appropriately named the "Edinburgh Room."

In the late 1960's and throughout the 1970's The Lygon Arms was receiving more and more of this sort of national publicity. When the Lygon was the first country inn to receive the Queen's Award for Industry for Tourism, in July 1971, it was a banner occasion. It was marked by the cover story in *Caterer and Hotelkeeper* and the headline: "A Cotswold Inn Sends its Name Around the World." The entire staff was photographed in front of the inn, including such key members as Mrs. Roose, head housekeeper, Mr. Hollington, chef, and Mr. Ron Wagner, head porter. On the magazine cover is Douglas Barrington himself, "urbane and courtly," quoted as saying that the honour of the Queen's Award for Export Achievement is "public recognition of the valuable part the hotel industry is playing in the export field." The Lygon management also rewarded the staff by the purchase of a flat in Mallorca, which proved an extremely popular place for holidays.

Director Barrington, however, diplomatic as always, stressed the important role of the Lygon staff in making possible this unusual honour. "The success of the Lygon could not have been achieved without the help of the exceptionally devoted staff...this enables guests to enjoy a standard of personal service that is becoming increasingly rare."[6] Of this staff in 1971, 90 in number, 20 were "stalwarts" who had served for 15 years or more, and the men wore a special set of cufflinks to denote this fact. There is a Stalwarts Club to this day which in 1992, totals 29.

The appeal to overseas visitors was continued and increased. By 1971 Barrington had travelled as founder chairman of Prestige Hotels to Australia, Japan, Mexico, Denmark, France, Italy, Spain, Germany, Holland and Switzerland. Over 40 percent of The Lygon Arms's business in the 1970's came from overseas visitors. Barrington's role as international salesman and goodwill ambassador for The Lygon Arms was a milestone in the inn's history.

During his managing directorship of the Lygon, Barrington was appointed to the Board of the British Tourist Authority in 1971, reacting with "surprise but a determination to earn my keep," He was subsequently made chairman of the National Council for the British Hotel

Restaurants and Caterers Association (BHRCA), received the OBE in 1974 for services to tourism, and was one of only four British hoteliers to be made president of the International Hotel Association.

Meanwhile, in 1960, ten years before his death, Donald Russell gave Barrington a significant interest in The Lygon Arms, a firm mark of confidence in his chosen successor. Barrington was himself on the alert for promising new young blood at the management level. In 1975 he appointed a young man named Kirk Ritchie to become Food and Beverage Manager for the Lygon. Since then Ritchie has progressed to Managing Director.

As early as 1980 outside organizations had begun to express an interest in purchasing The Lygon Arms. At first this idea was resisted in deference to the tradition of the private Russell family inn. "DJB," as he is now affectionately called, looked upon the Lygon as a trust he had been given by the Russells and felt it was up to him to ensure that the Russell standards, and later his own, would be maintained. But when the shareholders, after careful consideration, sold outright to The Savoy Group of Hotels and Restaurants in 1986, "DJB" was confident that this transfer to a company of outstanding international repute would have had the approval of the Russell family.

Barrington considered his greatest achievement during his years at the helm of Britain's "most famous inn" to be the fact that he sensed, early on, that "if The Lygon Arms was to maintain its position as England's top country inn we had to be profitable. We could not be 'quaint' or a museum memorial to life in the past. Nor could we simply provide modern comfort in a country setting. We had to provide the best, most up-to-date comfort and convenience in a setting which yet retained all the excitement of an inn many hundreds of years old. This was not easy."

It may not have been easy, but this goal Barrington most superbly achieved. By slow stages, with persistence, and sometimes "like walking a tight-rope, alternating between elation and despair," he steered his way through old-fashioned attitudes, family politics and moments of conflict to make The Lygon Arms what it is now. Sixty-one bedrooms with private bathrooms. A quiet unostentatious atmosphere in which each guest feels like royalty. A tight ship, superbly run at all hours of the day or night, but with 'effortless superiority' that is not noticeable. This is the essence of the very best hospitality, old or new, and the two meet and mesh in perfect harmony at The Lygon Arms.

Epilogue

The Savoy Group: Towards the 21st Century

History was made at The Lygon Arms one summer afternoon in 1986, but it was not apparent to the casual visitor. Guests strolled in the formal gardens and sipped tea, unaware that for the first time in more than four centuries the ancient hostelry was owned by a public company—The Savoy Group of Hotels and Restaurants.

At a quiet gathering in London, the inn which Earl Beauchamp purchased for £1,280 in 1820, and which was then acquired by Sydney Russell in 1903 for £6,000, was transferred to The Savoy Group for £4.7 million. It was an historic moment, comparable to the signing of the ancient charter by King Eadgar that transferred Broadway lands to the Abbey of Pershore more than a thousand years before.

Like many historic moments, it passed quietly. The sale moved the old inn further towards the twenty-first century but changed the outward atmosphere very little. The Lygon's administrative style remained the same. Managing Director and General Manager Kirk Ritchie, who received his original training from The Savoy and was proud to be back "with the old firm," was encouraged to continue his policy of preserving old and much-loved Lygon traditions while enhancing them with modern comforts.

The Savoy itself is no stranger to tradition and history. On its present site in London once stood a Medieval palace owned by the Savoy family of France. The modern hotel was created in 1889 by the famous impresario, Richard D'Oyly Carte, to celebrate the success of his Gilbert and Sullivan operas, which have beguiled generations of music lovers. To this day, the crisp perfection of style that marks the operas also distinguishes the meticulous orchestration required by The Savoy Group.

This perfection of style, captured in the Savoy motto, "For Excellence We Strive," is exemplified by The Lygon Arms, just as it is by its London counterparts—Claridges, The Connaught, The Berkeley, and The Savoy itself.

The personal touch, cherished by generations of visitors, continues with new vigour. Guests of long standing find flowers and a handwritten card of welcome in their room and, in most cases, will receive a personal greeting in the lobby as well. Every return visit to the Lygon becomes a kind of homecoming.

The Lygon's style was described by a travel writer in 1981 as: "a very special ability to make a guest feel relaxed and at home...The Lygon Arms surrounds its guests with subtle refinements and unobtrusive service of a high standard...if they could bottle it and spray it on most of today's luxury hotels, they'd deserve the gratitude of all mankind...."[1]

Setting precedents is nothing new to Kirk Ritchie. When he fulfilled a life-long dream in becoming Managing Director of The Lygon Arms in 1979, he was one of the youngest managers in the history of English inns. He had first visited the Lygon with his Mickelton grandmother when he was twelve years old. Today he is dedicated to helping his guests experience for themselves the spell of the old inn that captured his boyhood imagination.

The Savoy Group training is often regarded as the finest in the world. Ritchie considers himself particularly fortunate to have been a Savoy management trainee. Accepted shortly after his first interview with the firm at the age of thirteen, he studied wines in France, simultaneously acquiring a command of the French language. After four years of management training at Claridges and The Savoy, where he was exposed to all sides of the hotel business, he spent three more years in London before joining The Lygon Arms as Food and Beverage Manager in 1975. Within eight years he had advanced to Managing Director.

The sale to The Savoy Group made funds available for improvements that would not have been possible for an independent hotel. The building was refurbished from cellar to attic under Ritchie's personal direction. "The Savoy is a remarkable company which allows each individual manager to run his own establishment in his own way," he explained. "So we have the best of both worlds—we are an individual unit but we have the additional support that a company can offer."

Despite its ever-growing popularity, the Lygon is not likely to become an "executive hotel." Only carefully selected conferences are accepted, either those that take over the entire inn or those that can be inconspicuously managed within the existing day-to-day framework.

The Lygon tradition of attracting overseas visitors continues and the management makes sure that their visits to the inn live up to expectations in unusual, even theatrical ways. One enthusiast from the other side of the Atlantic pronounced: "The Lygon Arms turns their guests into actors and their staff into supporting players. Indeed, the server and the served know their stay here is fantasy. It is easy to perform one's expected role...the staff know all the cues...it's on stage for everyone, and the play begins upon arrival...."[2] (Producer D'Oyly Carte would be delighted with these modern-day "Savoyards").

One of the most significant recent accomplishments is the creation of The Lygon Arms Country Club, which opened in March, 1990. Located in a redundant eighteenth-century abattoir, this modern facility is viewed not as a luxury but as a necessity in a time when everyone is concerned with keeping fit and healthy. The large cost and considerable risk of this venture, when first envisaged, were swiftly justified by the Club's popularity not only with guests, but with Broadway residents as well.

The Club is an inspired use of space. In half an acre one finds a spacious mosaic-floored swimming pool, a spa bath, saunas, and a roof garden for informal entertainment in the warm months. There are also Steam, Fitness and Billiard Rooms, and a Beauty-Therapy Salon. The colourful, colonnaded vistas, reminiscent of a Roman villa and suggesting Mediterranean ease of life, are a perfect antidote to business pressure. This provides yet another escape into the experience of being "Lygonized."

The Club, however, is invisible. One of the Lygon's secrets is the rare ability to provide the ultimate in luxury while managing to avoid self-conscious snobbery or a posh atmosphere. The Lygon today is welcoming, informal and thoroughly relaxed, just as it has been since the days of the Whytes and Sambaches.

Those people who savour the special quality of Lygon hospitality are fortunate that all four twentieth century innkeepers have had the courage and confidence to achieve much-needed changes but, at the same time, have preserved the traditions and manners which are the heritage of centuries.

Sit in your room and stir the fragrant pot-pourri. Sip the excellent glass of sherry that awaits you. Look from the casement window toward the "Bradway hills," and let your mind wander. Listen for a Drury hunting horn and the clatter of hoofbeats, the voices of the Lygon generals, and the bustle of the large Treavis family in the hallways. Overhear Thomas Whyte and his fellow merchants as they argue over the price of wool around the fire in the Inglenook. The halls of this old hostelry are peopled with friendly ghosts and an acute listener can hear their voices back through the ages of the Lygon's life. It is an old English hostelry at its best, and it is unique.

The Lygon Arms Country Club.
(Photo by Tim Curr)

Endnotes

Prologue
1. Harold John Massingham, *Shepherd's Country* (London: Chapman & Hall, 1938), 48.
2. Phillip Barrett, J.D. Chrichton, E.I. Johnston, and Marshall Wilson, eds., *Pershore, A Short History* (Worcester: Ebenezer Baylis & Son Ltd., 1972), 12-13.
3. Francis B. Andrews, *The Benedictine Abbey of SS Mary, Peter and Paul at Pershore, Worcestershire* (Pershore: Fernside & Martin; Birmingham Educational Group, 1901), 33-34; Thomas Nash, *Collections for the History of Worcestershire* ed. John Nichols, 1781, 243.
4. Nash, 144.
5. Barrett et al, 12-15.
6. H.C. Darby and I.B. Terrett, eds., *Domesday Geography of Midland England* (Cambridge: Cambridge University Press, 1954), 232.
7. Barrett et al, 15-18
8. Ibid., 17.
9. Frank and Caroline Thorn, Worcestershire eds., *Domesday Book*, gen. ed. John Morris (Chichester: Phillimore, 1982); Nash, 144
10. Barrett et al, 19.
11. Margaret Bramford, "The Monks of Pershore," in Philip Barrett, *The Book of Pershore,* (Buckingham: Barracuda Books, 1977), 11.
12. Lechmere Roll, 1275-1280, 28c, Worcester County Record Office (hereafter cited as WCRO). Transcribed by Elizabeth Howard, 1990.
13. Barrett et al, 27; Andrews, 13.
14. Sydney Bolton Russell and Gordon Russell, *The Story of an Old English Hostelry* (Broadway, 1914), 9; (hereafter cited as SBR); Gordon Russell, *Designers Trade* (London: George Allen & Unwin, 1968), 65. (hereafter cited as DT).
15. "Copy of Ancient Deed Relating to Broadway and Pershore Fairs," Prattinton Collection, 899: 15 BA343, Society of Antiquaries, London. Microfilm copy at WCRO.
16. J.J. Jusserand, *English Wayfaring Life in the Middle Ages,* trans. Lucy Toulmin Smith (New York: G.P. Putnam's Sons, 1939), 249-51.
17. Lechmere Roll, 1280, WCRO.
18. Algernon Gissing, *Broadway: A Village of Middle England* (London: J.M. Dent, 1934), 20-24; Rees Price, "The Church of St. Eadburgh in Broadway," 2, Barnard (Rees Price) Collection, Archives Division, Birmingham Library Services (hereafter cited as BLS); Andrews, 30.
19. Jusserand, 121-6.
20. Ibid., 150-52.
21. Eileen Power, *Medieval People* (London: Metheun, 1924), 111-14.
22. Edward Gregory and Henry Maskell, *Old Country Inns* (Boston: L.C. Page, 1911), 52-53.
23. Jusserand, 130-131.
24. Ibid., 126.
25. Ibid.
26. Ibid., 84.
27. Gregory and Maskell, 43-51.
28. Jusserand, 289.

29. J.D.T. Niblett and the Reverend William Bazeley, "Royal Badges in Gloucester Cathedral," *Records of Gloucester Cathedral* (Gloucester: 1882), I, 113-15. By courtesy of Canon David St. Z. Welander.
30. Ibid.
31. Anthony Steel, *Richard II* (Cambridge: Cambridge University Press, 1941), 223-24.

Chapter I

1. Barrett, 26-27.
2. G.M. Trevelyan, *English Social History* (London: Longmans, Green, 1934), I, 56-58.
3. Exemplification of a Decree 36 Henry VI, 6 February 1458, Prattinton Collection, 167-75, Society of Antiquaries, London. Microfilm copy at WCRO.
4. Trevelyan, I, 80.
5. Eileen Power, *The Wool Trade in English Medieval History* (Oxford: Oxford University Press, 1942), 86-103.
6. Ibid., 15-19.
7. *The Stonor Letters and Papers, 1290-1483*, ed. Charles Lethbridge Kingsford, (London: Royal Historical Society, 1919), 64.
8. Ibid., 64-65.
9. *The Cely Papers, 1475-1488* ed. Henry Elliot McLeen (London: Longmans, Green, 1900), 38.
10. Ibid.
11. Power, *Medieval People*, 140.
12. *Victoria History of the County of Worcester*, 4 vols., (*Victoria History of the Counties of England*), eds J.W. Willis-Bund and Arthur Doubleday, Vol. I; J. W. Willis-Bund and William Page, Vols. II-IV (London: A. Constable, 1900). Hereafter cited as VCH.
13. *Cely Papers*, 152-53.
14. Ibid., xliv.
15. Trevelyan, II 84-87.
16. Power, *Medieval People*, 130-39.
17. *Cely Papers*, xxxiv.
18. Ibid., 75.
19. SBR, 9.
20. Conventual Leases 278 (1490), Sheldon Miscellanea 5665, Barnard (Rees Price) Collection, #28, d/1, Archives Division, BLS.
21. Ibid.
22. Ibid., Conventual Leases 335 (October 1535).

Chapter II

1. William Harrison, "A Description of England," in *Holinshed's Chronicles*, ed. Lothrop Withington (London: Walter Scott, 1891), 35; Jusserand, 251.
2. Broadway Parish Registers, II, 1703-1812, BA 4869, 850, WCRO.
3. International Genealogical Index, Worcestershire. Hereafter cited as IGI.
4. Will of Thomas White, 8th August, 1556, 008.7, 1556/23, WCRO. Transcribed by Nicholas Harrison, Assistant Archivist.
5. Ibid., Inventory of Thomas White.
6. Conventual Leases 335 (1535), Barnard (Rees Price) Collection, BLS.
7. Sambache and Strelly Family Records, Barnard (Rees Price) Collection, BLS.

8. Ibid.
9. Deeds, White Hart Inn, 1620-1820, 705: 99, BA 3464, WCRO. Hereafter cited as WHD.
10. Penry Williams, *Life in Tudor England* (London: B.T. Batsford; New York: G.P. Putnam's Sons, 1964), 34.
11. Trevelyan, II, 9.
12. Harrison, 25-26.
13. Trevelyan, II, 7.
14. Harrison, 96.
15. Williams, 63-64.
16. Trevelyan, I, 303.
17. Williams, 39.
18. Conventual Leases 335 (1535), 308 (1538), 292 (1539), BLS.
19. *VCH*, II, 129; IV, 38-39; "The Manor of Broadway from the Dissolution," 16-27, Barnard (Rees Price) Collection, BLS.
20. *VCH*, II, 283.
21. Williams, 163.
22. *VCH*, II, 283.
23. Ibid.
24. Power, *Medieval People*, 158-60.
25. Trevelyan, II, 21-22.
26. Ibid.; Harrison, 28.
27. Sambache Family Records, 73 A-D, Barnard (Rees Price) Collection, BLS.

Chapter III

1. Williams, 1.
2. Lucy Toulmin Smith, ed., *The Itinerary of John Leland in or about the Years 1535-1543* (London: George Bell & Sons, 1908), I, viii-ix.
3. Ibid., II, 126.
4. Ibid., II, 129.
5. Ibid., V, 38.
6. Ibid., V, 91.
7. Ibid., V, 90.
8. Ibid., IV, 137.
9. Ibid., IV, 27.
10. Thomas Habington, *A Survey of Worcestershire 1560-1647,* ed. John Amphlett (Oxford: Parker for the Worcester Historical Society, 1895), I, 107.
11. Ibid., II, 334.
12. Ibid., I, 107.
13. Ibid.
14. Ibid., II, 36.
15. Ibid., I, 107.
16. Ibid., II, 34-35.

Chapter IV

1. *VCH*, II, 289; Nash, 320.
2. *VCH*, II, 290.
3. Ibid.

4. Daston Records, 5665 60D, Barnard (Rees Price) Collection, BLS; *VCH*, III, 339-40.
5. Edith Brill, *Cotswold Ways* (London: Robert Hale, 1985), 126.
6. SBR, 9; interview with Marian Pepler Russell, September, 1991.
7. Sambache Family Records, 8th May, 1578, Barnard (Rees Price) Collection; IGI, Worcestershire.

Chapter V
1. Mark Eccles, *Shakespeare in Warwickshire* (Madison: University of Wisconsin Press, 1961), 32.
2. Ibid., 36.
3. Ibid., 29.
4. E.K. Chambers, *William Shakespeare* (Oxford: Clarendon Press, 1930), II, 131.
5. Eccles, 102; 56 c, Barnard (Rees Price) Collection, BLS.
6. Eccles, 102; Chambers, II, 107-09.
7. Chambers, 119-22; Eccles, 104.
8. Eccles, 105.
9. E.A.B. Barnard, *New Links With Shakespeare* (Cambridge: Cambridge University Press, 1930), 61.
10. Eccles, 120; Chambers, 125.
11. Habington, II, 36.
12. Barnard, 98.
13. Broadway Parish Registers, I, 1610, WCRO.
14. Eccles, 99-100.
15. Ibid., 100.
16. Broadway Parish Registers, Sambache Family Records, 73 a-d, Barnard (Rees Price) Collection, BLS.
17. Ibid., 19 November, 1606.
18. Ibid., 10 September, 1612.
19. Eccles, 111-13.
20. Ibid., 47, 93-97, 100.
21. Ibid., 97.
22. Ibid., 95.
23. Stratford Birthplace Trust Records, Stratford Fires, 1594/95, ER 11-42-3.
24. Eccles, 139.
25. Christopher Whitfield, *Shakespeare's Gloucestershire Contemporaries* (Eton: Shakespeare Head Press, 1958), 27; Barnard, 68-69.
26. Eccles, 115.
27. Christopher Whitfield, *Robert Dover and the Cotswold Games* (London: Henry Sotheran, 1962), 17-25.
28. Ibid., 18.
29. Ibid., 21.
30. Ibid., 116-18.

Chapter VI
1. Manuscript account of Treavis family sent to S.B. Russell in early 1900's, no identification, no date, possibly from Richard Savage, archivist at Stratford-upon-Avon, Lygon Arms Archives [Hereafter cited as LAA].
2. Will of John Treavis the elder, 15 January, 1604 (probated 27 August, 1605), Public Record Office. [Hereafter cited as PRO].
3. WHD, WCRO.

4. Prattinton Collection, Society of Antiquaries, London.
5. IGI, Worcestershire
6. Prattinton Collection, Society of Antiquaries, London.
7. Manuscript account of Treavis family sent to S.B. Russell in early 1900s.
8. Will of John Treavis the elder, 15 January, 1604 (probated 27 August, 1605), PRO.
9. Ibid.
10. William Hebert, *History of the Twelve Great Livery Companies of London*, (London: published by the author, 1837).
11. Russell archivist, n.d., LAA
12. Herbert, II, 626.
13. LAA
14. IGI, Worcestershire.
15. Will of John Treavis the younger, 11 May, 1641 (probated 11 February, 1641/2), PRO.
16. WHD, December 18, 1863, WCRO.
17. Ibid.
18. Ibid.
19. Frances Parthenope Verney and Margaret M. Verney, eds., *Memoirs of the Verney Family During the Seventeenth Century* (London: Longmans, Green, 1925), I, 5.
20. Ibid., I, 1-14.
21. Gladys Thomson, *Life in a Noble Household*, 1641-1700 (London: Jonathan Cape, 1937), 253-54.
22. Verney, I, 8.
23. Quarter Sessions Records, 1633, 511, WCRO.
24. Ibid., 512.
25. Ibid., 49.
26. Ibid., 122
27. Ibid., 638.
28. John Noake, *Notes and Queries for Worcestershire* (London: Longman, 1856), 317; Barnard Collection, Evesham Library.
29. Verney, I, 277.

Chapter VII

1. J. Willis Bund, *The Civil War in Worcestershire 1642-1646 and the Scotch Invasion of 1641* (Birmingham and London: Simpkin, Marshall, Hamilton, Kent, 1905), 103.
2. Eva Scott, *Rupert Prince Palatine* (New York: Putnam's Sons, 1899), 120.
3. Edward Hyde, Earl of Clarendon, *History of the Great Rebellion*, ed. W. Dun Macray (Oxford: Clarendon Press, 1938), III, 354.
4. Richard Symonds, *Diary of the Marches of the Royal Army During the Great Civil War*, ed., from MS in the British Museum, Charles Edward Long (London: Camden Society, 1859), 8.
5. Ibid.
6. Ibid.
7. Ibid., 14.
8. Ibid., 15.
9. Letter from George Digby to Prince Rupert, Item 38 in catalogue *Civil War Papers of King Charles, Prince Rupert of the Rhine, and Sir Thomas Fairfax* (London: Sotheby's, 1980).

180 *The Story of The Lygon Arms*

10. Clarendon, III, 360.
11. Symonds, 25.
12. Ibid.
13. George May, *The History of Evesham* (London: Whittaker, Treacher, 1834), 232.
14. Symonds, 28-30.
15. Ibid., 164-66.
16. Bund, *Civil War*, 157-58.
17. Brill, 54-55.
18. *VCH*, IV, 34.
19. Bund, *Civil War*, 158.
20. Ibid., 159-61.
21. Clarendon, IV, 38.

Chapter VIII

1. The three surviving inventories describing rooms and furniture at The Lygon Arms in various centuries do not mention the "Cromwell Room." The Philip Hodges inventory of 1680 refers to the "Great Chamber," and the Giles Lawrence inventory of 1814 calls this same room the "Best Bed Chamber." The inventory taken in 1904, after Sydney Russell's purchase of the inn, but before alterations began, refers to "Bedroom # 5." In the year 1787, Viscount Torrington described his room as the "grand bedchamber of an old family seat," detailing the cornice and fireplace but without mention of Cromwell. The first surviving reference to the possibility that a bedroom was "said to have been occupied" by Cromwell was made by J.J. Hissey in his account of a visit to the inn in 1891. The idea that this room was known "through generations" as the "Cromwell Room" is therefore open to considerable question. It apparently took that name some time after 1904.
2. Bund, *Civil War*, 229.
3. J. Allanson Picton, *Oliver Cromwell: The Man and His Mission* (New York: Cassell, Petter Galpin, 1882), 352.
4. Lieut. Col. T.S. Baldock, *Cromwell as a Soldier* (London: Kegan Paul, Trench, Trubner, 1899), 502.
5. Wilbur Cortez Abbott, ed. *Writings and Speeches of Oliver Cromwell*, 1649-53 (Cambridge, Mass.: Harvard University Press, 1929), 452.
6. Ibid., 453; *Oliver Cromwell, Letters and Speeches of Oliver Cromwell*, ed. Thomas Carlyle (London: Methuen, 1904), II, 219-32.
7. Abbott, 454; Peter Gaunt, *The Cromwellian Gazetteer* (Stroud, Gloucestershire: Alan Sutton and the Cromwell Association, 1987), 80.
8. Maurice Ashley, *Cromwell's Generals* (New York: St. Martins Press, 1955), 256-58.
9. Bund, *Civil War*, 236-38; Gaunt, 85.
10. Abbott, 457; Gaunt, 85.
11. Abbott, 457.
12. Picton, 353-54.
13. *VCH*, II, 119-21.
14. Abbott, 461.
15. Baldock, 509-10.
16. Abbott, 462-63.
17. Ibid., 466.
18. John Buchan, *Oliver Cromwell* (Boston: Houghton, Mifflin, 1934), 329.

19. Abbott, 468.
20. Ibid., 470.
21. Ibid., 471.
22. Picton, 213.

Chapter IX

1. Inventory of Phillip Hodges, October 25, 1680, Wills and Inventories, 008.7, BA 3686, 234, WCRO.
2. WHD, 1683-1700. WCRO.
3. Inventory of Phillip Hodges, WCRO.
4. Thomson, 249-50.
5. Ibid., 221.
6. Ibid., 218-19.
7. Ibid., 213-14.
8. Noake, 98-99.
9. Thomson, 213-14.
10. SBR, 9-10, LAA.
11. Overseers Accounts, 1691, Broadway Papers, WCRO.
12. WHD, 1700, WCRO.
13. Will of Phillip Hodges, 1680, WCRO.

Chapter X

1. Oliver Goldsmith, *She Stoops to Conquer*, (New York: Barrons Educational Services, 1958).
2. Joseph Addison and Richard Steele, *Sir Roger de Coverley and Other Essays from the Spectator*, ed. Zelma Gray (New York: Macmillan, 1930), 169, 75.
3. Acts of Parliament Relating to the County of Worcester, 33, WCRO.
4. Ibid.
5. WHD, 1700, WCRO.
6. Inventory of the Angel Inn, WCRO.
7. IGI, Worcestershire.
8. Will of Francis Phipps, 15th March, 1712 (proved 14 November, 1713), WCRO.
9. WHD, 1734, WCRO.
10. Birth of John Cormell, 22 May, 1687; marriage of John Cormell to Ann Smallman at Willersey, 3 July 1706, IGI, Gloucestershire.
11. WHD, 1790, WCRO.
12. *Berrows' Worcester Journal*, 1 April, 1736 (at WCRO).
13. Constables Expenses, Broadway Parish Papers, 1092, Barnard Collection, Evesham Library.
14. Newspaper clipping sent to S.B. Russell, n.d., LAA.
15. Ibid.
16. Court Leet in Broadway, Broadway Parish Papers, Barnard Collection, Evesham Library.
17. Tax records, 1787 land tax, Broadway Parish Registers, WCRO.
18. SBR, 9.
19. Barnard (Rees Price) Collection, BLS; LAA.
20. Trevelyan, III, 23.
21. Ibid., III, 112.

22. James Woodforde, *The Diary of a Country Parson*, ed. John Beresford (London: Oxford University Press, 1926), 19.
23. Trevelyan, III, 114.
24. Goldsmith, 78-9.
25. Ibid., 70.
26. Trevelyan, III, 87-88.
27. Thomson, 207.
28. *VCH*, IV, 37.
29. Toll Book, Broadway Parish Papers, 1224, Barnard Collection, Evesham Library.

Chapter XI
1. *The Torrington Diaries: Containing the Tours through England and Wales of the Hon. John Byng (later Viscount Torrington) between the Years 1782 and 1794*, ed. C. Bruyn Andrews (London: Eyre & Spottiswoode, 1934), I. li.
2. Ibid., I xvii.
3. Ibid., I xvi.
4. Ibid., I, 190-91.
5. Ibid., I, 318-20.
6. Ibid., I, 179.
7. Ibid., II, 182.
8. Ibid., I, 106.
9. Ibid., I, 372.
10. Ibid II, 201.
11. Ibid., III, 5-6.
12. Ibid., IV, 33.
13. Ibid., I, xi.
14. Ibid., I, xii, xv, xvi.
15. Ibid., I, xxxi.
16. Ibid., I, lii.

Chapter XII
1. Broadway Census, 1841, WCRO.
2. Catalogue of the Topgraphical Collections and of the Correspondence and Papers of Sir Thomas Phillipps, Bart., 1792-1872, given to the Bodleian Library, Oxford, by Lionel and Philip Robinson, 1958, b. 94, fol. 22; b. 97, fol. 26. Hereafter cited as PC.
3. WHD, 1809, WCRO.
4. *Baileys Monthly Magazine*, 1808 (reprinted December 1872), LAA.
5. Inventory of the Contents of the White Hart Inn, for Giles Lawrence, 21-24 March 1814, by Handy & Moore, Wills and Inventories D2080/151, Gloucester County Record Office [Hereafter cited as GCRO].
6. Ibid.
7. Trevelyan, IV, 35.
8. John Morris, *The History and Traditions of Middle Hill* (Rotherham: W. Ball. n.d.).
9. PC, c. 405, fols. 185-86.
10. Ibid.
11. Ibid.
12. Ibid., c.233, fol. 71.
13. Ibid., c.422, fols. 239-43.

14. Ibid., b.112, fols. 234-35.
15. WHD, 15 June, 1820, WCRO.
16. Prattinton Collection, 142, Society of Antiquaries, London.
17. PC, c.415, fol.64.
18. *VCH*, IV, 118-21.
19. Military records of the 13th Light Dragoons, now held by the 13th/18th Royal Hussars, 3 Tower Street, York, courtesy of Captain G.E. Locker; *Berrows' Worcester Journal*, 17 November, 1860 (obituary of E.P. Lygon).
20. J.P. Nelson, *Chipping Campden*, GCRO, 97.
21. *Berrows' Worcester Journal*, 10 March, 1863.
22. Ibid.
23. PC, c.420, fols. 114-24.
24. Ibid., c.422, fols. 239-43; c.426, fols. 54-56.
25. Ibid., c.482, fols. 62-65.
26. Ibid., e.375, fols. 63-64.
27. Ibid., c.491, fols. 75-76.
28. Ibid., c.527.
29. "Particulars of an Eligible Family residence called Spring Hill in the Parish of Broadway, Worcestershire, to be Let with Immediate Posession," Thomas Denton, Land Surveyor, Ashford, 1819, WCRO.
30. Wills of Edward P. Lygon, 12 December, 1860, and Henry Lygon, 8 September, 1863, PRO.
31. *Pigot's Directory*, 1825-29, LAA.
32. Ibid.
33. PC, c.491.

Chapter XIII

1. Interview with Mr. and Mrs. A. V. Freeman of Broadway, April, 1991.
2. 31 May, 1801, Gloucestershire, IGI.
3. Marriage record, Saint George's Hanover Square, 7 March 1839, PRO.
4. Marriages and Baptisms 6 September, 1840, Broadway Parish Registers, WCRO.
5. *M. Billings Directory and Gazetteer of the City of Worcester* (Birmingham: M. Billings, 1855); *Cassey's Directory*, 1860.
6. Broadway Census, 1855, WCRO.
7. PC, d.164, fols. 55-65.
8. Notice of Auction, 23 October, 1867 (copy), LAA.
9. Estimate of costs for adding a room for Charles Drury, Lygon Arms Hotel, 6 April, 1869, by Christopher Hensley, Land Surveyor and Agent, 899: 933, BA: 1035/1, WCRO.
10. *Evesham Journal*, n.d., February, 1871.
11. Ibid., 1 February, 1879.
12. Receipt in Lygon Arms scrapbook, LAA.
13. Obituary of Charles Drury the younger, *Evesham Journal*, 18 May, 1900.
14. *The Antiquary*, October 1881 (copy), LAA.
15. J.J. Hissey, *Across England in a Dog Cart from London to St. David's and Back* (London: Bentley and Son, 1891), 96-110.
16. Charles R. Drury, *Picturesque Broadway* (Cheltenham: S.H. Brookes, 1885), LAA.
17. Reverend J.S. Stone, "Over the Hills to Broadway," 1893, LAA.

18. *Evesham Journal*, 18 August, 1900.
19. Ibid.
20. Richard Kenin, *Return to Albion: Americans in England 1760-1940* (New York: Holt, Rinehart & Winston, 1979), 108-120.
21. J. M. Barrie, *Allahakbarries*, ed. Don Bradman (London: J. Barrie's Publishers, 1899), xi-xiv.
22. *Evesham Journal*, 18 August, 1900.
23. Interview with Stuart Lloyd Drury, April, 1991.
24. Ibid.
25. *Kelly's Directory*, 1896 and 1904.

Chapter XIV
1. Interview with Jack Hodge of Snowshill, April 1990.
2. SBR, 7.
3. Interview with Mr. and Mrs. A.V. Freeman of Broadway, March, 1990.
4. *DT*, 27.
5. Ibid., 28.
6. Ibid., 64-65.
7. Ibid., 64-66.
8. Ibid., 69-70.
9. SBR, 11.
10. DT, 68.
11. *The Car*, 6 July, 1910, LAA.
12. Ibid., *The Car*, 29 December, 1915.
13. Interview with Douglas J. Barrington, April, 1991.
14. Ibid.
15. DT, 136-7.
16. *Christian Science Monitor*, 28 September, 1920, LAA.
17. *Evesham Journal*, 15 July, 1905, LAA.
18. Handwritten letter to Sydney B. Russell and his reply, 1913, LAA.
19. "Defence of the Realm," April 1917, LAA.
20. *Caterer and Hotel Keeper's Gazette*, 16 July, 1917, LAA.
21. Interviews with Jack Hodge and A.V. Freeman, April, 1991.
22. Interview with Jack Hodge, March, 1990.
23. Treavis family tree sent to Sydney B. Russell, LAA.
24. *DT*, 160.
25. Ibid., 160-161.

Chapter XV
1. Speech by Sir Arthur Morse, President, British Tourist and Hotels Association, 21 June, 1957, LAA.
2. *DT*, 112-17.
3. Ibid., 118-21.
4. Ibid., 116.
5. Ibid., 125.
6. Interview with A.V. Freeman, April, 1991.
7. *DT*, 128, 133-34.

8. Ibid., 135-39.
9. Interview with A.V. Freeman, April, 1991.
10. DT 182-83.
11. Ibid., 178.
12. Ibid., 221-23.
13. Ibid., 248.
14. Conversations with Sir Gordon and Lady Russell in 1946, 1957, 1972 and 1974 at Kingcombe.

Chapter XVI

Much of the information in this chapter is based on extensive interviews with Douglas J. Barrington between 1989 and 1991, and on material from his scrapbook which he generously made available to the authors.

1. *Western Daily Mail*, 1971.
2. Speech by Sir Arthur Morse, 21 June, 1975, LAA.
3. *Country Life*, December 1955.
4. *Birmingham Post*, 24 April, 1987, LAA.
5. Letter from David Gallagher, Buckingham Palace, to Sir Gordon Russell, 19 May, 1968.
6. *Caterer and Hotel Keeper*, July, 1971.

Epilogue

Much of the information in this chapter was provided by several interviews with Kirk Ritchie, Managing Director of The Lygon Arms, between 1989 and 1992.

1. The *Waterbury Sunday Republican*, 5 April, 1981, LAA.
2. *Travel Talk*, May, 1985.

ABBREVIATIONS

BLS	Archives Division, Birmingham Central Library, Birmingham Library Services
DT	*Designer's Trade* (Autobiography of Sir Gordon Russell)
GCRO	Gloucester County Record Office
IGI	International Genealogical Index
LAA	Lygon Arms Archives
PC	Phillipps Robinson Collection, Bodleian Library, Oxford
PRO	Public Record Office, London
SBR	*The Story of An Old English Hostelry* by Sydney B. Russell and Gordon Russell
VCH	*Victoria History of the Counties of England* (Victoria History of the County of Worcester)
WHD	White Hart Deeds, 1620-1820
WCRO	Worcester County Record Office

Whyte Hart. Drawn by Gordon Russell.

Appendix A
The White Hart and Richard II

The association of King Richard II and other Plantagenet kings with the symbol of the white hart is an ancient and well-founded one. How far this influenced the name of the first Broadway village inn in the twelfth, thirteenth or fourteenth centuries is a matter of conjecture.

King Richard II was linked to the white hart not only through his paternal ancestor, Richard the Lion-Heart (1189-1199), who used the symbol in one of his seal rings, and through his immediate predecessors Kings Edwards I, II and III, all of whom used the hart, but also through his mother, Joan, the "Fair Maid of Kent." Joan, first the wife and then the widow of Edward, the Black Prince, came from Macclesfield in Cheshire where wild white deer abounded in the forests. It was from this county that Richard later recruited his personal bodyguard of archers who wore the white hart livery.

The white hart itself is a much older symbol. An ancient legend dating back to the Greeks maintains that the white stag was sacred and could not be killed except by one who had conquered the whole world. The Roman historian, Pliny the Elder, cited Alexander the Great and later Julius Caesar and Charlemagne as emperors who captured the white stag, decorated it with a golden collar and released it.

Many years ago on the Dorchester road, near Stowminster, there was an inn with a kingly stag painted on the sign with, underneath, words from a medieval quatrain, roughly translated:

> When Julius Caesar landed here
> I was then a little deer,
> When Julius Caesar reigned King,
> Round my neck he put this ring;
> Whoever shall me overtake,
> Spare my life for Caesar's sake!

Though more fanciful than historical, the passage does suggest that the white stag or deer was of ancient origin and had the sort of mystique which would have appealed to a sensitive, artistic and somewhat fearful young King. He might have thought of himself as the white deer, hoping to be protected by Providence and centuries of sacred tradition: Since it was unlucky to kill the stag, therefore he, Richard, would be safe.

His great-grandfather had been horribly murdered. His grandfather had been forced to fight all his life; his own father had been in the forefront of battles as a teen-ager, was famous for his courage, and died young. Death must have looked over Richard's shoulder all the time as a boy and as a young man. After his beloved wife, Anne of Bohemia, who was also his best friend and counsellor, died in 1394, he would have been more lonely and fearful than ever. It is not surprising that he should have adopted as his personal badge a sacred emblem of peace and blessed forest groves, in essence, a "protected species." The famous Wilton Diptych in the National Gallery depicts angels hovering around the king dressed in robes adorned with white harts. It is not surprising that when real threats loomed towards the end of his reign, King Richard fell back on the white hart: "God for his Richard hath in heavenly pay a glorious angel; then, if angels fight, weak men must fall, for heaven still guards the right...."

When Richard became King in 1377 at the age of eleven there were no threats and he was hailed as the young saviour of the realm. Despite celebrations touched off by the King's youth, discontent among members of the peasant class grew. This was aggravated by rabble-rousing preachers like John Ball, who, according to Froissart, suggested: "When Adam delved and Eve span, who was then the gentleman?...Ah, ye good people, the maters gothe nat well to passe in England...what have we deserved or why shulde we be kept thus in servage?....They dwell in fayre houses and we have the payne and travail, rayne and wyndes in the fieldes...from our labours they kepe and maynteyne their estates...Lette us go to the kynge, he is younge, and shewn him what servage we be in...."

"Thus John sayd on sondayes when the people issued out of the churches in the vyllages and so they would murmure one with another in the fieldes and in the wayes as they went togyder affermyng how John Ball say trouthe...." (Jusserand, 289)

Disgruntled landless labourers, already disgusted with a diet that consisted at best of cold bacon and stale cabbage, listened alertly to this sort of propaganda, their dissatisfaction culminating in the Peasants Revolt of 1381. When a large army of labourers, peasants and others recruited as they marched, invaded and captured London, the young King behaved with great bravery, especially for a boy of fifteen years. He rode out to meet the revolutionaries in person. (Steel 77)

This confrontation with the rebels at Mile End is undoubtedly one of Richard's finest hours. Unfortunately the defeat of the rebellion was accomplished by a mixture of courage and fraud. The crowd cheered as the young King rode out boldly to face the army that had gathered strength as it marched from Kent and was strong enough to have massacred the king and all his retainers. He shouted loudly: "I am your King—follow me!" and successfully led the insurgents away with promises of pardon and the commutation of servile dues on the land to fourpence a year. Deplorably, after the immediate danger was over, Parliament refused to honour the young king's pledges to his subjects. (Steel, 70-77); (Oman, 200-202)

As his reign progressed, Richard had to deal not only with peasant discontent, but also with revolts organised by his more powerful nobles. Some of these skirmishes brought him into close contact with the Cotswold counties. In 1387 the Earls of Warwick, Gloucester and Arundel "raised a small, private army to oppose him." After this uprising was quelled, the King "took in hand Warwick's hereditary shrievalty* of Worcestershire, leaving the chattels of the fallen lords to be sold...the proceeds are recorded in the receipt rolls of the time...." The King, in effect, confiscated a vast quantity of land. He also made Thomas Percy, one of his supporters, Earl of Worcester. (Steel, 240) Another loyal follower was Sir William Bagot, a Warwickshire knight, who had acquired the Castle of Baginton near Coventry. He

*Area of jurisdiction

was Sheriff of Warwickshire as early as 1382 and represented the county continuously in Parliament from 1388 to the end of King Richard's reign.

It is possible that either of these two powerful men, or one of their adherents, could have named an existing inn after their leader in the years between 1382 and 1399. Another of Richard's close friends was Tydeman, the "Courtier Bishop" of Worcester. He was a former Cistercian monk of Winchcombe, a man of power and influence, who had been the King's personal physician. (Steel, 226) He also could have named any number of inns for his royal master.

How the White Hart badge became part of the royal livery is not entirely clear. Early in his reign, Richard, like other kings before him, had passed ordinances against liveried followers of noblemen, because these easily evolved into small, private armies capable of challenging royal authority. After certain noblemen revolted in 1387, however, Richard was very much on his guard against repeated uprisings and was forced to fall back on liveried retainers, his Cheshire archers, in pure self defense. (Steel, 169)

After Richard II was assassinated in 1399, the name of the inn may have been changed to the Swan for King Henry IV, who replaced his cousin. It may have remained the Swan until John Treavis purchased it under that name in 1620, or it may have been re-named several other times in the two intervening centuries. Popular young King Henry V used both the hart and swan as symbols, which opens up a clear field for either or both of these signboards between 1413 and 1422 when Henry V died.

The inn may have had other names in the Tudor period. When John Treavis purchased the property from the descendants of Elizabeth White Sambache in 1620, it was called or known "by the name or sign of the Swan." By 1641 it had been named or re-named "by the name and sign of the White Hart," and so referred to in all later deeds. Why is this? One possible explanation is that the year 1620 is, as the deed notes, "the seventeenth year of the raigne of King James."

King James I of England was King James VI of Scotland and the son of Mary, Queen of Scots. His mother had been educated at the French Court, married the young Dauphin, and was devoted to French customs and thinking. James believed strongly in the divine right of kings which eventually was his family's undoing. The sacred white hart and its connection with Richard of Bordeaux and other ancient kings of France would have appealed to him vastly.

It is possible that John Treavis, who extensively rebuilt and added to the Swan, was astute enough to change the name back to what he knew from hearsay had been its much older name. More than two hundred years had passed but the new scion of the House of Stuart and the ghost of the young Plantagenet king were linked in their devotion to ancient, sacred royal symbols. Would it have been good for future business if the White Hart swung once more in the village thoroughfare?

Appendix B
The Stonor Letters and Papers 1293-1483, and *The Cely Papers, 1475-1488*

These are the most valuable first-hand sources for the wool trade in the thirteenth and fourteenth centuries in England. We owe the preservation of both these unique collections to legal actions taken later. In the first case, Sir William Stonor, who was a prosperous sheep grazier in Oxfordshire, Buckinghamshire, Gloucestershire and other counties, and married to a Dame Elizabeth, joined the Duke of Buckingham's ill-fated revolt against King Richard III in 1484 and all his papers were confiscated and taken to London.

Sir William was charged and convicted and although he was eventually pardoned, the family papers were never returned; thus an incomparable record of the early years of the sheep and wool business was preserved for all time.

One of Stonor's principal agents was a merchant named Thomas Betson. A merchant of the Staple, he spent most of his life travelling for Sir William and Dame Elizabeth between the Cotswold wool country and Calais. He was first engaged and later married to young Katharine Riche, Dame Elizabeth's daughter by her first marriage. He corresponded both with the Stonors and with Katharine and his letters are full of endearing gossip and the details of his journeys.

In the second instance, the Cely family, sometime after 1488, were involved in a lawsuit about a will and, as a result, their records were similarly summoned to London, where, after the conclusion of the lawsuit, they remained.

The Cely family had vast holdings of land in many parts of England. At one point they had twenty-one boats plying between London and Calais. There are five family members who figure in the letters: William Cely, the Elder, who started the family business; his three sons, Richard, George and Robert; and, a cousin and faithful agent, William. Most of the letters are between the two older brothers, Richard and George and this family agent William.

Both the Stonors and the Celys dealt extensively in Cotswold wool and were continually going into or coming out of 'Cottyswolde.' Therefore their letters give us a fair picture not only of the life of a Merchant Stapler, his packmen and carriers to the coast and his dealings in the port of Calais, but also of what must have been happening in the life of the sheep farmer in Broadway and the Cotswold country.

The Merchants of the Staple, of whom Betson was one, were the most powerful group of businessmen in England for much of the thirteenth, fourteenth and fifteenth centuries. From the time of King Henry III, the monarch had collaborated with them and made use of their wealth for his own purposes.

By the end of the 14th century the Staple had become compulsory, due to King Edward III's manoeuverings. He could not do without a compulsory wool tax. The Staple was two things at once: a "fixed place through which the wool was compulsorily directed and a corporate company of merchants handling the wool. It was a "compromise...by which the King was left in possession of a very high subsidy on wool, Parliament was left in possession of control of taxation and a body of English merchants, known as the Company of the Staple, was left in possession of a quasi-monopoly of the wool trade..." The wool tax was the source of royal revenue and almost coincident with the appearance of the Commons..." (Power, *Wool Trade,* 19)

Appendix C
Christopher Westerdale, Bailiff of Broadway, and Broadway tenants v. Abbot John Stoneywell of Pershore, 1535-154—.

The well-documented dispute between Christopher Westerdale, Bailiff of Broadway, and Abbot John Stoneywell of Pershore, was the harbinger of a longer contest over control of Abbey lands among four other lessees—Ralph Sheldon, Anthony Darston/Daston, Philip Hoby and Walter Welche. The case lasted for more than ten years.

Old Westerdale accused the abbot, who was also the Bishop of Polizzi in Italy, of having impoverished him with suits, taking from him a parcel of ground he used as his bailiff's office, called the Play-hey, "refusing to pay him money due for butter, cheese and calves delivered to his predecessor, Abbot Compton, and for steers, capons, butter, milk and cream bought for the present Abbot's household." He also protested the fact that he had been dismissed by Abbot Stoneywell from the lucrative Bailliewick of Collectorship, granted by Abbot Compton.

Abbot Stoneywell replied vigorously, claiming that Westerdale had not performed the office of bailiff properly and stating his belief that all debts had been paid. Then he brought a countersuit in which he said craftily: "If the said Christopher will have it otherwise then this defendant sayeth that he, said Westerdale, bearing the office of Portership of his Monastary, and his wife Elizabeth, by reason of unlawful familiarity with my predecessor, as the common fame is, conveyed out of the Monastery plate of silver, pots, flagatts, spoons and other goods to the value of £80 or more...and £100 of jewels which he prayeth to be restored..."

Stoneywell's meaning was clear—withdraw the suit or face a scandal—and be accused of theft and possibly an illicit relationship between Westerdale's wife and Abbot Compton, whose regime had been notably lax in morals as well as in administrative skill.

This suit and countersuit caused an uproar and many of Westerdale's friends and neighbours jumped into the fray. Some villagers must have been adversely affected by the Abbot's land management policy even if Daston was not, because the Abbot was charged with denying them the ancient right of common pasture, "common of shippe..." by refusing to accept rents of ten shillings a year and forty shillings in arrears.

Matters were further inflamed by the case of Agnes Walker, "a very poor woman" who complained to the King* that she "engaged a neighbour last harvest to carry her corn, who chanced to carry away one sheaf from John, Abbot of the Monastery of our Lady and St. Eadburgh of Pershore, thinking it was your poor subject's...." Agnes offered to make reasonable amends but the Abbot had cruelly insisted on citing her in court. Ex-Bailiff Westerdale was old and well-liked. Agnes Walker was

* Villagers all over England were in the habit of appealing directly to King Henry VIII as did Agnes Walker.

poor and wronged. Abbot Stoneywell was not popular and the upshot was that Squire Ralph Sheldon, with the largest lease from the Abbey and the most money at his command, made common cause with the poorer tenants.

This case is typical of the times since it involved not only the most powerful local churchman in a dispute but also, indirectly, the King. Stoneywell's financial policy for getting out of debt was to consolidate the Abbey income in three long-term leases—to Daston, to Sheldon and to one Walter Welche, the combined income of which was £169-18s. 4d in 1539. Soon after the dissolution of the monasteries, Daston's lease became a matter of controversy. Walter Welche died. Henry VIII became embroiled in this dispute when a gentleman of the King's household, Philip Hoby, who had married Welche's widow, claimed that Welche's lands were his by marriage right. He also claimed that Welche's lease had preceded Daston's, due to the fact that King Henry had granted lands to a certain Sir William Compton and his wife Dame Elizabeth, first in 1511 and by reconfirmation in 1523.

Dame Elizabeth was the source of all the trouble. She married three times, first Sir William Compton, then Walter Welche, groom of the Privy Chamber to the King, and, after Welche's death, Philip Hoby. Hoby began suit against the Abbey of Pershore. A long inquiry followed. Ralph Sheldon and other principal inhabitants of Broadway were summoned as witnesses. Old Abbot Stoneywell, who must have been sorely embarrassed by the whole thing, sent his lawyer, claiming that he himself was afflicted with "such infirmities of age than can scarsely keepe my lyfe without any walkynge or riding out of my house..."

Whatever else Stoneywell may have been he had a good head for business. When he took over the Abbey from Compton in 1527, It was more than £1,000 In debt. When he retired In 1539 it was debt-free. As he wrote pathetically to Thomas Cromwell that year: "No doubt the benefice has been sweet to me, as your lordship says, but remember what I left when I came to this...I desire you to deliver my age from vexation, of which I have long been weary..."

No outcome of the suits is recorded and it may well be that Stoneywell was in the right, especially considering the lax administration of his predecessor. But ultimately it was Daston, who kept quiet but refused to allow Hoby on the land, who emerged as the winner. He leased the lands in 1535 and kept them until 1558, seeing no need to be cowed by distant courtiers who claimed land rights through a woman. He went on sheep farming, employed local people and kept on good terms with fellow tenant Ralph Sheldon, hoping that matters would eventually sort themselves out, as indeed they did. Daston's wife, Anne Sheldon Savage Daston, later became the largest landowner in the surrounding area.

Sources for the Westerdale case
BLS:BRPC, Conventual Leases 1535-1539, 28 d/i #292,308,335
Ibid, Rees Price, 28 a/i. *The Manor of Broadway from the Dissolution*, 16-21
VCH, IV, 37-38

Appendix D
Owners and Tenants of The White Hart, 1740-1790

1740
Sometime before her death Ann Cormell borrowed £220.12s.6d. from Isaac Averill with the White Hart as security. Isaac Averill paid off William Corbett's mortgage of £100.00, and therefore had a total mortgage secured on the White Hart of £325.00. Ann Cormell died intestate in 1740, and her estate was administered by letters of administration.

1761
Isaac Averill died. His executrices, Sarah Stephens (m. to Parry) and Mary Whinney (m. to John), transferred the benefit of the £325 mortgage to John Ricketts. The Cormell heirs still owned the property.

November 1778
John Ricketts transferred the benefit of the mortgage to Daniel Clemens for a loan of £162 12s. Ricketts defaulted on the loan, and the White Hart property was held by Clemens.

11 March 1786
Charles Ellison and Sophia Teresa Ellison (Sophia Teresa Purser, grand-daughter of Ann Cormell) had become entitled to a quarter share in the White Hart Inn. They transferred their share in the inn to John Scott, wine merchant, for the sum of £50.00

30-31 August 1790
Shortly before this date Daniel Clemens died intestate, leaving Ann Spencer as his personal representative. At this point six different parties with a financial interest in the inn transferred the White Hart, its houses and outbuildings, to three other parties. On the selling side were Ann Spencer, Charles Ellison and Sophia Teresa Ellison (grand-daughter of Ann Cormell); Joseph Harris and Sophia Touch Harris (grand-daughter of Ann Cormell by her third daughter, Elizabeth); Sarah Baylis and John Baylis (great-grandson of Ann Cormell and grandson of Elizabeth Cormell Touch); John and Lillies Scott (wine merchant and wife). The buyers in this complex transaction were Theophilous Knowles, John Knowles and Christopher Holmes.

John Knowles paid Ann Spencer £162. 12s. for Daniel Clemens's mortgage, Christopher Holmes paid the shareholders £500 for the inn with its houses and outbuildings, and put the inn first in the name of Theophilous and then in his own name and that of John Knowles. Holmes and John Knowles became joint owners.
WCRO. #705:99 VA3464. White Hart Deeds 1620-1820.

Appendix E

The Lygon Letters:

Letters exchanged between General Edward P. Lygon and M.P. Henry Lygon of Spring Hill, and Sir Thomas Phillipps of Middle Hill in the years 1820-1860.

On the death of King George III, February 1820, Henry Lygon, M.P. to Sir Thomas Phillipps:

Madresfield February 15, 1820
My Dear Sir:
As the late melancholy event of his Maj.'s death must consequently produce a dissolution of Parliament allow me to submit a repetition of your kind support and interest whenever that period may arise.
With a grateful remembrance of former favours.
Believe me my dear sir
Your obedient and faithful, H.B. Lygon (w. seal)   (c. 405)

On book collecting, Henry Lygon to Sir Thomas Phillipps March 2, 1822:
My Dear Sir Thomas:
I was requested by Mr. P._____ on whom I called the other day to take charge of the accompanying book and leave it at your door. I hope you are all well and believe me yours very truly,
Henry Lygon
(c.482 ff 66-67)

Regarding a Petition to which Sir Thomas Phillipps has alluded in a letter to M.P. Henry Lygon:
St. James Square. March 2, 1822
"The Petition you allude to in your letter which I have just received was given to me to present. Neither of the Evesham members being present, I knew no more of it. I hope for the pleasure of meeting you at our Assizes the week after next, when we will talk the subject over and I will take care in the meantime that if the Bill is printed you shall be furnished with a copy. My best regards to Lady Phillipps and believe me my dear sir, yours very truly, Henry Lygon.   (c. 460 ff24-25)

There is a protracted correspondence about the possibility of the Lygon brothers renting Sir Thomas Phillipps' lands for hunting in the winters of 1826 and 1827. Sir Thomas tried to charge too much for the Lygons' liking and literary skirmishing continued:

St. James Sq. Aug. 28, 1826
My Dear Sir:
In my brother's name and my own I have to send you our best thanks for your very kind offer cont. in your letter of the 23rd forwarded from Spring Hill. Neither of us are great performers with the gun and tho' it would be a

great object to keep our neighbouring county quiet, yet from my frequent absences from home I fear the undertaking would be too considerable and under these circumstances I am obliged to decline the offer. With my best compliments to Lady Phillipps I remain very faithfully yours.
Edward P. Lygon

Sept. 11, 1826 St. James Square
I regret that I had not the pleasure of meeting you during my short stay at Spring Hill. Having considered your kind offer of renting your manors for which I feel greatly obliged, I wished to ask if you would object to include Buckland with Middle Hill at one hundred pounds per annum. I mention this as possibly you may not have entered into any engagement and it will be a considerable accommodation to me. Should this at all meet your views you will have the goodness to mention the period you will allow me to rent those manors. As the first of Oct. is not far distant and the commencement of feeding fast approaching you will perhaps oblige me with an answer as early as convenient.
I remain...E.P. Lygon

Phillipps scrawled a note of reminder to himself at the bottom of this page: "Offered the two manors at £150 per annum for three years but reserved the liberty of killing rabbits on the hill...in order to keep them down...."

The mail coaches must have been operating on time and swiftly because a reply came from Edward Lygon the next day:

St. James Sq. Sept. 13, 1826
I beg to apologise for giving you so much trouble but I was obliged to take into consideration the situation...on Middle Hill and Buckland manors which makes the feeding very expensive. Not being a keen shot myself and being generally fully occupied with my hounds it would not meet my views to incur a further charge than that I have named which I have to regret does not quite meet your approbation.
My brother feels much obliged by your kind congratulation and I am happy to say Lady Susan and her child are doing extremely well.
I remain, my dear Sir, very faithfully yrs. E.P. Lygon

Evidently Phillipps must have lowered his offer too little, too late, because Edward Lygon's next letter states:

Hyde Park. Oct. 17, 1826
My Dear Sir
I feel very much obliged to you for your letter and I have only to regret we did not establish a better understanding a little earlier. As circumstances now are I am obliged to decline this offer of renting your manors and I beg to return you my best thanks for your kind consideration.
I remain etc. E.P. Lygon.

A social incident, probably connected with the tax case, Lady Louisa Lygon to Sir Thomas:

> I will be very happy to see you tomorrow morning at Spring Hill...the accounts that reached me were greatly exaggerated...I was, however, soon satisfied that my fears were unnecessary and I was under alarm.

About the high cost of lawyers to the poor, Sir Thomas Phillipps to Henry Lygon: 23 April 1843:

> My dear General:
> I have no doubt you are aware of the great expense it will be to the voters among the tradesmen and farmers if they were obliged to write to London and pay lawyers every time they might wish to discuss their relatives wills...if your exertions and those of your fellow members on their behalf...about this expense...it will tell well with your voters at the next election...
> Thomas Phillipps.   (c. 483 ff94-95)

Regarding the outcome of Sir Thomas Phillipps's tax case, to Henry Lygon:

> Middle Hill 15 July 1843
> My dear General:
> The business is over and I am condemned to pay £10, just twice as much as I expected to be fined...this man Cooper actually nominated himself...disgraceful conduct of the fellow before the magistrates in Court...it is essential to the government to have respectable persons as collectors of taxes and not add to the odium of the office by employing disreputable characters...this Cooper has rendered himself so odious to the village that they burnt him in effigy last spring....
> T.P.

The reply to an appeal from Thomas Phillipps to Henry Lygon for help to a friend seeking a seat on the Bench:

> 3 February, 1844
> My dear Sir Thomas:
> Your letter has followed me here. I have the greatest sympathy with your discussion but without knowing who the party is I cannot answer your question as his seat must depend on the gentleman's fitness and not on my interest. There is a gentleman living not far from you who thinks he would be an addition to our Bench about whom I finally heard there would not be much difficulty, but we may not mean the same. I have not heard from him these last few days....
> I am, yours faithfully,
> Henry Lygon
> (c. 484)

Catalogue of the Topographical Collections and of the Correspondence and Papers of Sir Thomas Phillipps Bart. 1792-1872, given to the Bodleian Library, Oxford by Lionel and Philip Robinson, 1958. (PRC)

Appendix F
Excerpts from
Across England in a Dog Cart
J. J. Hissey, 1891

This rare book, now hard to obtain, which inspired Sydney B. Russell to purchase The Lygon Arms in 1903, is thought to be of sufficient interest to include all the references to The Lygon Arms contained in Hissey's visit to Broadway:

Soon now we reached the top of Broadway Hill. Here a wonderfully extensive panorama over the rich and fruitful vale of Evesham was spread out before us; it was as though the world in front of us had suddenly dropped down, and we gazed upon a miniature kingdom, with its cities, towns and villages, its mountains, hills and rivers. It would have been worth the whole drive if only to have had that one revelation of scenery. The superb view from this spot, one of the finest in England, was far famed in the days of road-travel, even the coaches used to stop here a short time that the passengers might enjoy the prospect; but now, when everybody is conveyed by railway, few possibly know of its existence....

Now a long, winding and steep descent took us into the quaint and charming village of Broadway. Here we pulled up at the Lygon Arms, one of the finest and most interesting of old coaching inns imaginable, and but little altered or spoilt though it bears the date of 1620 on its carved stone doorway, and must therefore have existed for over two centuries. An ideal old hostel, a romance in stone, more like what one would expect to find in a painting, or described in a novel, than to meet with actually existing by the roadside in these present prosaic times.

The village of Broadway is unique; it consists of a wide thoroughfare with a bit of triangular green at one end. This thoroughfare is bounded on either side by the most charmingly quaint old stone-built houses conceivable, many dating from the 16th century, when men knew how to build both well and picturesquely.

It was as though we had driven back two centuries or more, even into a bit of England of Shakespeare's day. There are few if any spots remaining now that so thoroughly bring before one the picturesque aspect of times departed.

Our inn, as I have said, was a romance in stone, an ideal hostelry, and the landlord too was an ideal one, in true sympathy with his romantic surroundings. Seeing the great interest we took in his delightful old-time inn, he kindly showed us all over it; and fortunate indeed is the chance that has given to such a rare old building a proprietor who so highly prizes its possession.

The interior of the Lygon Arms is very interesting to antiquaries and lovers of the picturesque; it abounds in suggestive bits of architectural detail, with its ancient panelling, half-timber stairway (formerly hidden by plaster which the estimable landlord promptly removed on coming into possession), its oaken doors, mouldings, carved spandrels, and quaint ironwork, such as curiously shaped hinges, bell pulls., locks, casement fastenings and the like.

Mine host also showed me an old oak-panelled room, his especial "den," a most charming room with a little staircase all to itself and that opened into it through a corner of the panelling, though there was another way of reaching it. This reminds me that after ascending to our bedroom we went down some steps into it in the most quaint fashion. We were also shown a very fine sitting-room with an enriched plaster ceiling and a decorative frieze running round the walls. The room also possessed a grand carved mantlepiece. This and the bedroom adjoining are said to have been occupied by Cromwell when staying here shortly before the battle of Worcester.

At the time of our visit these apartments were engaged by a famous architect, doubtless making studies and taking notes in the village and around. Architects in search of motives and fresh ideas might well come to Broadway; the buildings here are thoroughly English, abound in suggestive detail, and, if I may use such an expression, are racy of the soil from which they spring.

To return to our inn. This, we learnt from our landlord, was originally called the White Hart, but having been some time ago purchased by the Lygon family, whose name it had borne so long was thereupon changed for that of the Lygon Arms. My *Paterson's Roads*, last edition of 1829, gives the inn here as the White Hart. The old inn now belongs to its present occupier, and we tried our best to persuade him to re-christen it with the ancient title so familiar to all travellers by road, and second only in popularity to the Red Lion. It appears that as far back as 1549 the White Hart here was in the possession of one John Treavis. In view of the date 1620 over the doorway, we concluded that this must have been an earlier building possibly pulled down to make room for the present structure. The landlord, however, appeared to think otherwise, and considered that the date 1620 related only to the doorway as being added at that time.

Not far from the [Abbot's] grange stands a substantial stone-built barn. This has been converted into a grand studio; for certain fortunate artists have discovered Broadway, and besides converting a barn into a studio, have, I believe, converted an old farmhouse into a delightful country abode. Only the other day I came upon the engraving of a drawing in which the picturesque old Lygon Arms was the chief feature, though the name of the place was not given—perhaps wisely not, for having found a good thing it does not always do to make it public and thus perchance have it spoilt.

And this reminds me that I may be doing so myself. But the charms of Broadway are of the quiet unassuming kind, not such as attract the cheap tripper or noisy excursionist; and besides there is no railway within miles, and the tripper likes to be within hail of a station.

Once more we found ourselves beneath the sign of The Lygon Arms, pleasantly tired after our day's wanderings, with many charming additions to our sketch book, and we trusted not a few interesting photographs, but these were an unknown quantity, for we were not in a mood to develop our negatives just then.

And whilst my wife put the finishing touch to her sketches, I sought out mine worthy host in the bar who entertained me with pleasant gossip and local information over a glass of whisky and a friendly pipe.

OPINIONS ABOUT THE ARCHITECTURE OF THE LYGON ARMS, 1924-1992

Twentieth century architects, designers, and archaeologists who have examined The Lygon Arms disagree on the precise age of the main building, but concur that the extensive and skillful renovations carried out by Sydney Russell in the early 1900's make it very difficult to determine exactly when the first inn was built.

Because professional opinions differ widely about specific dates, we have thought it best to allow readers to study these views for themselves, bearing in mind that the architecture of a building, like deeds, wills, inventories, journals and other written documents, is a strong clue, but only one indication among many about the history of a place such as The Lygon Arms.

We include below the findings of five experts from different periods of the twentieth century. Sir Gordon Russell, who observed firsthand the alterations his father made to the inn between 1903 and 1927, and recorded them in the 1929 edition of *The Story of An Old English Hostelry*, is the first to be quoted. He describes how his father frequently salvaged building materials and sometimes entire fireplaces from other nearby old buildings. Russell is followed by the noted architectural author, Sir Nikolaus Pevsner, in 1968, and then by three present-day architectural historians. All statements and opinions are presented without editorial comment. We have included a short glossary of the more common architectural terms at the end of this section.

Gordon Russell, *The Story of an Old English Hostelry*, 1929:

Early History

Broadway...was liberally endowed with inns, most of them interesting buildings but one, The Lygon Arms, stands apart. It is not only remarkable for its size as an inn, but as an example of a Cotswold house of the XVIth century it holds a high place in a district celebrated for its early domestic architecture. It seems, as Mr. Cecil Aldin says, to dominate the village, it is Broadway....Unfortunately, very little is known of the early history of the Inn. The name of the original builder has not survived, but the main block of the building with its four great gables, dates from the middle of the XVIth century, and it is said to have held a licence continuously from that date, being known as the "White Hart." This was one of Richard II's badges, so possibly it stands on the site of a yet older house, and the great thickness of some of the back walls, in one of which a XIVth century fireplace was discovered, lends some colour to this view...

Repair Work 1904-1929

The result of twenty five years' work can be seen in "The Lygon Arms" of today. Or rather, it can to some extent be gauged, for no one who did not see in 1903 the tawdry furniture and appointments, the garish, dirty wall papers, the inconvenience and squalor of the kitchen and back premises and the stark ugliness of the

"Assembly Room" can really appreciate the magnitude of the accomplishment. The first work was, of course, to ensure the stability of the fabric, which in places showed signs of settlement. Then, room by room, wallpapers were stripped, rotten sash windows were replaced by stone mullions, beautiful fireplaces uncovered, and the furniture, which was nearly all both cheap and nasty, was replaced by pieces of the same date as the house. The work involved most careful supervision and took many years.

Rebuilding Work and Additions 1907-1929
Meantime there were other pressing problems, such as the replacement of the terrible Assembly Room by a room which harmonised with the Inn and could be used for meals in summer and dances in winter, the complete rebuilding of kitchens and offices, and the addition of bathrooms and bedrooms, the provision of garage accommodation on an extensive scale, with rooms for staff over; the laying out of pleasure gardens, kitchen gardens and orchards, the building and repair of cottages for staff, of a laundry, of pigsties and outbuildings, the installation of electric light, bells and central heating, the running of a home farm, and the establishment of a joinery shop, to enable much of the repair work to be tackled on the premises. Each year brought its own particular problems, and each year saw a definite advance towards the completion of the plan which had been visualised from the beginning.

The Jacobean Doorway
From whatever point the Inn be viewed, from the village street the effect is one of great dignity and simplicity; the splendid gables, weathered to an indescribable mixture of greys, browns and greens by more than three centuries of sun, wind and rain, rise sheer from the little parapetted terrace which gives access to the fine doorway. This...was added by John Treavis and bears his name, together with that of his wife, Ursula, with the date 1620. Traditions die hard in outlying country districts and the rounded Tudor arch, with its unusually large carved spandrels, has a distinctly Gothic flavour, although the Ionic pilasters, architrave, strip-carved frieze and bold cornice, surmounted by the scrolled and fretted finials typical of early Jacobean work, prove the date to be correct, 1620.

The Interior
The visitor will be agreeably surprised that, unlike so many old houses, and particularly old inns, the charm of The Lygon Arms is not confined to the exterior. The oak ceilings, deeply recessed mullion windows with leaded lights, the timber-framed corridors and moulded oak doorways with richly carved spandrels, the oak panelling and huge open fireplaces combine to make an admirable setting for the collection of old English furniture and domestic objects, which cannot fail to appeal to those who have an eye for the beautiful.

Mediaeval Back Door
Immediately opposite the front door is another huge arch-headed doorway, still retaining its original oak door with its gigantic pair of strap hinges. This was once the back door of the Inn, and led to the courtyard. On the right of the entrance door

is a small lounge with a well proportioned open stone fireplace. This was probably originally part of the hall. A corner cabinet here contains an interesting collection of old English jugs, and in another cabinet are placed all the articles which have been discovered during repairs to the Inn: silver coins of Edward the First, 1273-1307; Elizabeth, 1573-1576; James the First, 1604; Charles the First 164—; and copper coins of all the Georges; numbers of clay tobacco pipes from the early part of the XVIIth century onwards; old black wine bottles, one of which still retains its worm-eaten cork. These were discovered between the joists of a ceiling and could perhaps unfold a tale of midnight revels. [This old cabinet, with its "group of Finds," is unfortunately no longer in evidence].

The Dining Room

One next enters the smaller dining room—a large, square parlour facing south. Its walls are wainscotted with old oak panelling from Babington Hall, Derby, demolished some years ago. The large open fireplace is quite simple, but originally had carved pilasters and entablature like that in the Cromwell Room immediately above. The ceiling also was enriched with modelled plaster, but all this has gone. There is a very interesting Gothic cupboard here with pierced front panels and sides carved with a simple linenfold pattern and an "Act of Parliament" clock. The mediaeval fireback with a primitive design cast on it—possibly intended for the Tree of Life—is worthy of note.

Notes on the building of the Great Hall

The new Great Hall is entered from this room, but it may be as well, before describing the Hall itself, to give some idea of the causes which led to its building.

Until 1869 the ground on which most of the Great Hall stands was not built over, and formed part of the garden belonging to the Inn. But in that year the owner decided to erect a room in which the annual ball of the newly formed North Cotswold Hunt, of which the Inn has always been the headquarters, could be held. Unfortunately, this room was built with great sash windows—a kind of enlarged railway waiting room—and even the most drastic alterations could never have made it harmonise with the old Inn....

It was therefore decided in 1909 to clear the site of the Assembly Room and also of Spencer House, an adjoining property with a modern shop front, recently acquired. The work of designing the new room was entrusted to Mr. C.E. Bateman...the building runs parallel to the street, facing south and there is a flagged terrace in front with a dwarf stone wall....this arrangement not only linked up the Inn with Spencer Cottage, which bounds the property on the east, but gave space for a secluded garden at the rear.

The Great Hall is 56 feet long and 24 feet wide. The floor is of oak, the ceiling barrel-shaped and enriched with modelled plaster bands in low relief. The fine old open fireplace of local stone, richly moulded, was rescued from a dilapidated Tudor house near the Abbey Church in Winchcombe. In its removal—a somewhat hazardous enterprise since the floors had already fallen in and the chimney stack was fast falling—a curious hiding hole was discovered, but it was found impossible to incorporate this in the new building.

The Sussex iron fireback is an exceptionally fine one, weighing more than a quarter of a ton, with the arms of Hyde, Earl of Rochester, cast upon it; and came from Bromley Palace, Kent....The Great Hall is panelled to the line of the window transoms, and above the panelling are placed the coats-of-arms of the men of note who have visited the Inn, forming a continuous line of glowing colour round the walls. The shields of arms reading from left to right are Earl of Gainsborough, Duke of Portland, Earl de la Warr, H.R.H. the Prince of Wales, Lord Montagu of Beaulieu, the See of Worcester and Sir James Stirling. These have been painted by the Rev. E.E. Forling, M.A., whose vigorous work is known to all students of heraldry.

The Inglenook
On the left of the entrance door is the Inglenook, which as its name implies, contains a huge fireplace spanned by a single beam. This...room is of fine proportions, lighted by two mullioned windows and with an old spiral staircase leading up from one corner. Ranged along the mantel are a number of early culinary utensils, including a series of steel spits, the cobirons for which stand below. There are also some fine pieces of old ironwork in the chimney corner, among which may be mentioned a beautiful XVIIth century pot-hook sway and a cast fireback dated 1620. In this room is a fine English hutch of the middle of the XVth century. The front is panelled and contains three doors, on either side of which are panels boldly carved in geometrical designs, and the ends are composed of solid planks.

The South Parlour
A doorway in the southwest corner leads to the South Parlour. This large room, for many years the Bar, has been remodelled and now makes a most comfortable reading and writing room, well supplied with modern easy chairs. The fireplace originally came from Merton Abbey, the home of Lady Hamilton. [This room is now the Gift Shop]

The two Smoking Rooms
At the back of this room is the small smoking room [now Gin Corner] with its great open fireplace, from which a doorway leads across the entrance to the inn-yard under the bridge to the public smoking room This is a delightful room, with two little bay windows looking onto the street. [Now Goblets and Wine Bar].

First Floor Rooms
The Cromwell Room and the oak-panelled room are situated on the first floor, approached by the original Elizabethan staircase of easy flights. The Cromwell Room is generally admitted to be the finest apartment in the house.... The fireplace is a very good example of Elizabethan craftsmanship—quite one of the best in the county. The opening is of large size, with a depressed Tudor arched head, simply chamfered. It is flanked by Corinthian pilasters decorated with strap carving in low relief, which support an architrave, frieze and cornice with three projections. The frieze is carved with a delicate interlacing strapwork design, and the whole composition is further enriched by the very beautiful plaster frieze which surmounts the ceiling.

The East Wing and Lounge
In 1927 further alterations were commenced at the east boundary of the property. Spencer Cottage, which had previously been used as an Antique Shop, was rearranged, and access is now gained through the Great Hall. The ground floor provides a spacious lounge, reserved for guests staying in the Inn....The first floor of this building presented a real problem, as in the XVIIIth century the front of the Elizabethan cottage had been extended to give more rooms; however the waste of space has been the means of making a landing of two large rooms, with delightful exposed timber roof construction. The visitor can see that the XVIth and XVIIth century builders used timber of ample dimensions....

Sir Nikolaus Pevsner, *The Buildings of England*;
Worcestershire, (Penguin Books, 1968) 105-6.

...The Lygon Arms, formerly the White Hart, and yet earlier a private house is by far the best house of the Cotswold type in Broadway.... Lord Torrington in 1787 saw in the White Hart still "all the marks of having been a manor house," and so can we. Recessed centre and two projecting wings. They have their gables, the centre two two-storied dormers. The windows in the l. wing are mullioned and transommed; in the centre they are all of the cross-type. Door surround with tapering pilasters, a strapwork top and the date 1620. Inside the small doorway between centre and l. wing is C16 and was once an outer doorway. The place where it probably was is still visible in the outer wall of the room in which it now is, looking toward the main entrance. The chimneypiece in the room into which it leads must be as early as the time of Henry VIII. Is it ex situ? It has a leaf and an animal in the spandrels. A monumental late C17 fireplace in another of the ground floor rooms comes from a house at Winchcombe.... One upstairs room of the old part [the Cromwell Room] has an ornamental plaster frieze and ceiling and a large Jacobean chimneypiece.

Nicholas J. Moore, Architectural Historian
Preliminary Notes, November, 1991

The original build of The Lygon Arms is that part constructed of stone with an approximately symmetrical frontage facing south, with four main gables. It is a wholly new building dating from 1620. If there was an inn on this site earlier than 1620, it is possible that John Treavis demolished it and rebuilt.

The only parts of the original build that are older than 1620 have been introduced later, probably during the ownership of the Russell family earlier in the present century. These include the early 16th-century fireplace in the [gift] shop, and a handsome moulded ceiling beam and chimney bressummer in the Snuggery, both also 16th century, and perhaps much of the oak wainscot.

None of the 17th century oak wainscot in the inn is both original to the building and in its original position; Russell does not mention any panelling in the Cromwell

Room in 1929, and that in the Oak Room, which he says is original, is of two different patterns. It cannot easily be said which wainscot might have been moved within the inn and which brought from elsewhere, although Russell says that that in the small dining room came from Babington Hall, Derbyshire. The 'mediaeval door' opposite the front entrance and the slightly ogee-shaped stone chimneypiece in Bedroom 7 are both good original features dating from 1620.

The major periods of addition are relatively few. The only significant one before the present century is that part at the rear which contains a first-floor reception room, dating from about 1790-1800. This is built of brick as a drawing room, with a domed ceiling and handsome chimneypiece [its lower storey has been gutted]....

The pre-1900 periods of alteration to the old building are now difficult to detect. They were probably not substantial and have mostly been deliberately reversed earlier this century. Among them are the replacement of original mullioned windows on the main elevation with sashed ones (which can be seen in early photographs). No accurate date can now be assigned to them, but they may have been part of an attempt to modernise the Inn in about 1800, when the drawing room was added.

Minor alterations are also apparent on the top floor in the wings. For example, the west wing [the 'great chamber,' room 20] is now open to the roof, and this is unlikely to be an early 20th-century change....

Two 16th century cottages at either end are now incorporated in The Lygon Arms. The East wing, formerly Spencer Cottage, dates from the second half of the century....The western cottage, now Goblets Wine Bar is also late 16th century and retains original features.

Richard K. Morriss, City of Hereford Archaeology Unit
Preliminary Notes September, 1991

Pevsner quotes Lord Torrington as writing in 1787 that the White Hart, now The Lygon Arms, showed "all the marks of having been a manor house." Certainly, Pevsner himself seemed to agree with Lord Torrington and the initial overall impression is that it was not built as an inn. In 1903, S.B. Russell set about restoring the old portions of the inn and began a programme of sympathetic enlargements that still continues today. The work involved the restoration of surviving features and the importing of materials including fireplaces and furniture from other buildings in the area.

The sheer scale of the renovation and restoration work and the skill with which much of it was carried out actually makes the job of understanding the development of The Lygon Arms more difficult than would otherwise have been the case. The quality of Cotswold stone helped preserve architectural features, such as hood moulds, mullioned and transommed windows and the four-centered arch to doorways and fireplaces, long after they had gone out of fashion elsewhere. Cotswold stone buildings can be very difficult to date.

The Exterior

The main portion of the present hotel, and possibly the extent of the original inn, is the central block which is essentially 'H' shaped. It is built of the local Cotswold stone, ashlared on the facade but coursed partly-worked rubble to the sides and rear apart from the quoins. Cotswold stone is a good quality and easily worked oolitic limestone.

* * *

It is difficult to date the building simply by the evidence of the facade, especially as many of its motifs are fairly common and long-lasting. Only a general date range between the late-16th and early-17th centuries can be given. One of the windows in the building has graffiti on its mullions, with dates, the earliest apparently being carved by Richard Jervis in 1586. However, the credibility of such evidence is open to considerable doubt.

Several of the chimney stacks are diamond-set with simple moulded caps. There are also two examples of paired stacks beneath the same moulded caps, one between the central portion and west wing, the other in a side-extension at the rear of the east wing. These stacks may belong to the early 17th century.

Ground Floor

The main door leads into a cross-passage, which originally ended in a large doorway to, presumably, a courtyard between the projecting rear wings. This doorway is rebated internally to take the door, and has chamfers on the former outer edge of its jambs. It has a four-centred head but the door it took was clearly square headed. There is no suggestion that the back of the door head was ever rebated [notched] to take a door with an arched head. The present door, nail-studded with upright planking on one face and lateral planks on the other, has large strap hinges, and could be original. Stylistically, the doorway could date from the early-16th to the late-17th century or could be contemporary with the Jacobean front door itself....

To the east of the passage is a small room within the confines of the central block, called the Small Lounge by Russell in 1929. It has a small fireplace of late-16th or early-17th date. On the opposite side of the passage is a much larger room, known as the Inglenook because of its huge fireplace. In one corner a timber-framed closed stair tower could be original or a very early insertion, unlikely to be later than the early-17th century in date. It has a spiral staircase with chamfered newel.

First Floor

The stair tower in the Inglenook leads up to the first floor and into the oak-panelled room known as the Oak Room. The square panels on the walls of both the tower and the room itself are not all of the same design and the pattern is asymmetric. The panelling also stops at an almost neo-classical cornice at picture rail height, the moulding of which is not consistent all round the room, and does not respect the wide late-16th or early-17th century fireplace with its four-centred head. To the west of the Oak Room, in the west wing, there is a very large room now called the King Charles Room, divided into three `bays' by its wide-chamfered ceiling beams. These beams could be of the late-16th century, as could the fireplace.

In the east wing is the Cromwell Room, possibly the best in the hotel. It has a plaster ceiling with delicate strap-work that is almost Italian in feel, but probably derived from French or Flemish work. This room also has a delicate plasterwork frieze around the tops of the walls. Its fireplace is magnificent, with pilasters and strap work echoing the style of the front door case. All this work appears to be of early 17th century date.

* * *

Second Floor
None of the upper rooms is large and none appears to have been grand. In the west wing there is the so-called Great Chamber, which is two storeys high and open to the apex of the roof. However, it is quite clear that this height has been achieved by the simple expedient of removing the attic floor. The timber-work of the roof shows that a considerable degree of reconstruction has taken place.

The stair tower was lit by small square-headed loops in the masonry of the rear wall, a further indication that this was probably an original feature of the building. It is possible that there may have been another staircase in the eastern part of the hotel, where there are odd changes of level in doorways, both past and present, that might be explained by such a feature.

The West Extension
The main part of the old inn is linked by a modern bridge at first floor level over the driveway into the rear courtyard. This was built in 1922 and was associated with work that had incorporated a 17th century stone building.

Bruce Watson, Architectural Historian, February, 1992

Facade
The imposing facade of The Lygon Arms, constructed of oolitic limestone ashlar, consists of two projecting gable wings, with two other gables occupying the central portion of the building. It is two and a half storeys high, with a slate clad roof and a disused attic storey which was originally intended for storage and servants' accommodation.

All the facade windows are stone-framed. The windows of the lower two floors are all 17th C style, rectangular in shape, with mullions and transoms, while the attic has much smaller mullioned windows. A photograph of c. 1895 shows that the lower two storeys had Georgian style sash windows. Presumably the windows were replaced during the Russell restoration, which would explain the vertical breaks in the ashlar around the present windows.

Interior: Ground Storey
Clearly the interior was altered considerably during the Russell restoration. Subsequent alterations, such as the insertion of bathrooms, make architectural history difficult to interpret. The front door leads across a short passageway to a stone-framed, four centred arch door, with a rebate on the south side. Such a door cannot be dated precisely but is probably 16th or early 17th C. In the room to the west of the passageway (known as the Inglenook) is a large open hearth late 16th or early 17th C fireplace. An enclosed spiral staircase (for the servants) leads out from the west side of the Inglenook room.

Interior: First Storey
A number of first floor bedrooms contain historic features, such as internal timber-framed partitions or exposed rafters and chamfered ceiling beams. The rear of the building contains a number of small, stone mullioned, windows of late 16th or 17th C.
The following rooms contain features of special interest:
Room 3. On the window mullions are carved initials of uncertain date.
Room 5. Has a moulded plaster ceiling beam decorated with vine leaves and grapes.
The Cromwell Room in the east wing has a fine moulded plaster ceiling and frieze around the top of the walls. The stone fireplace in this room is magnificent; it is reminiscent of the front door with its Corinthian style pilasters and strapwork ornament on the lintel. The grandeur of this room indicates that it was intended as a sitting room or parlour. The Jacobean timber panelling in this room looks like a modern addition of old material, probably from another building. Room 15, the Charles I Suite, is a fine Jacobean timber panelled room. The panelling is of two slightly different styles and contains several reused timbers, which suggest that most or possibly all of it is a modern addition.

* * *

On the east side of the Great Hall is another stone-built, former dwelling house known as Spencer Cottage....The rear wing appears to be of late 16th or 17th C date, judging by the internal timber-framing and small stone mullioned windows. A number of tree trunk purlins have been exposed.....

Discussion
The deed of 1620 mentions a house or Inn, presumably on the site of the present building. No visible part of the building as it now stands can be safely dated before 1620; however there are some features, such as the open hearth fireplace, which have quite a broad date range, and possibly could be earlier than 1620. The earliest fabric is most likely to survive in the cellars (mentioned in the inventory of 1814) which are sealed today.

It is very probable that the front door (dated 1620) commemorates either a very extensive or perhaps a total rebuilding of the property, as there is no sign that the front door has been inserted in the facade. Certainly the height and design of the facade suggests a 17th C date.

My impression is that earlier this century S.B. Russell sought to restore The Lygon Arms as an Elizabethan style country house hotel and did so very successfully by removing a number of later, disfiguring features, such as sash windows. He carefully restored the internal timber framing, replaced doors and inserted new features such as the first floor fireplaces, all with the highest standards of craftsmanship and materials. All of this has resulted in a truly splendid edifice.

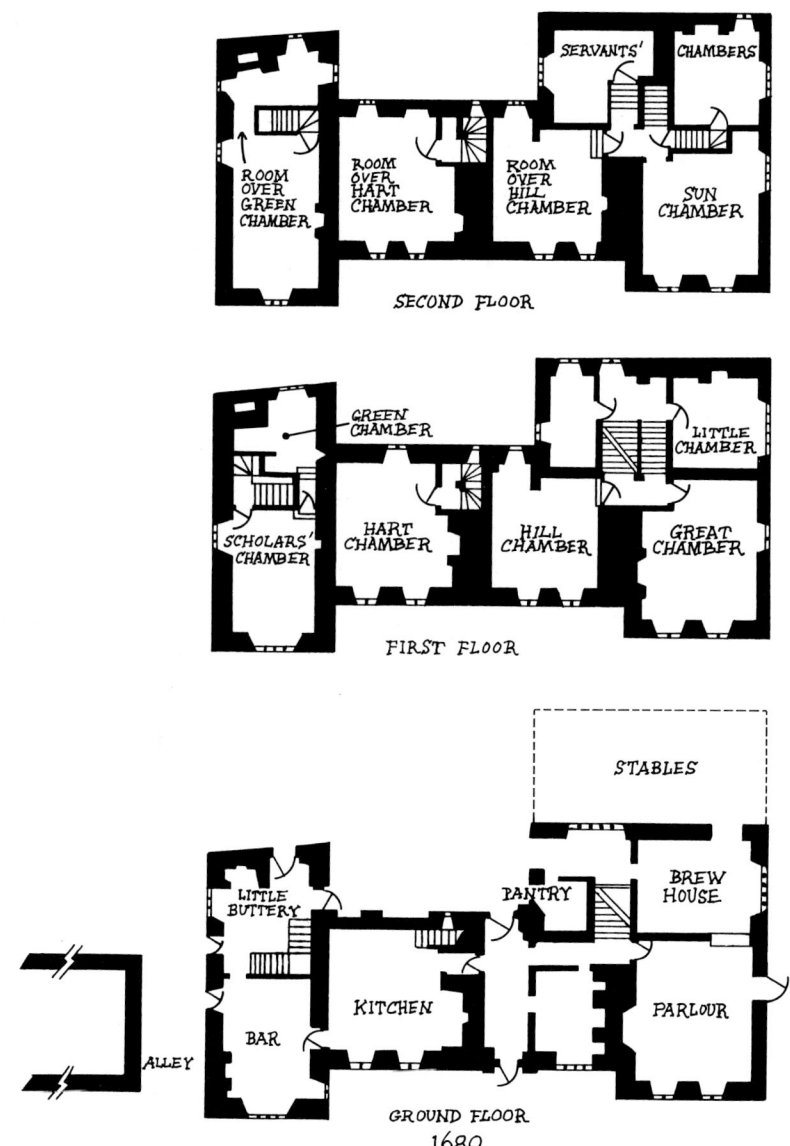

An artist's interpretation based on inventories and structural observations.

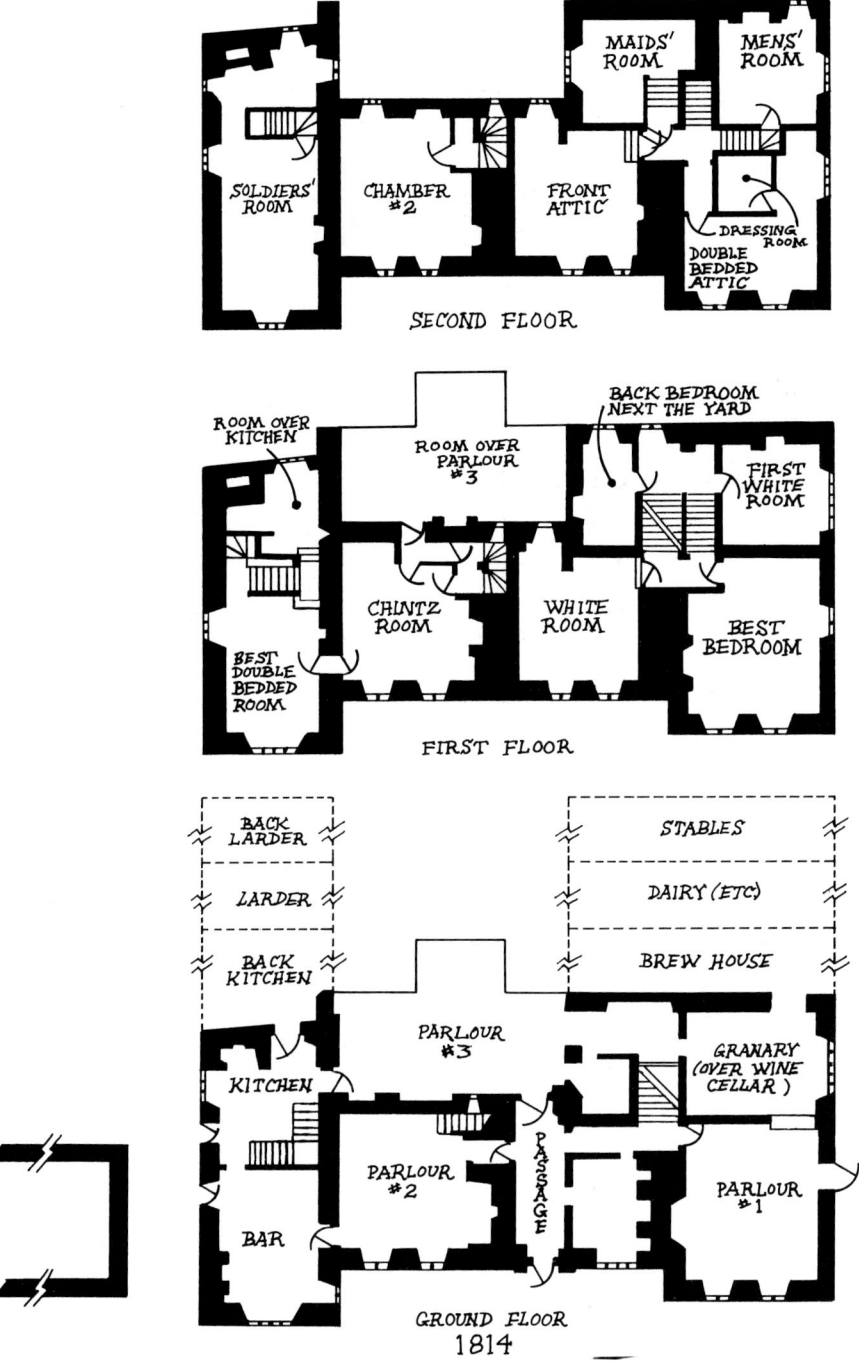

An artist's interpretation based on inventories and structural observations.

Glossary of Architectural Terms

Ashlar: Masonry of large blocks wrought to even faces and square edges.
Bays: Internal compartments of a building each divided from the other not by solid walls but by divisions only marked on the side walls.
Bressumer: Beam in a timber-framed building to support the usually projecting superstructure.
Chamfer: Surface made by cutting across the square angle of a stone block or piece of wood at an angle of 45 degrees to the other two surfaces.
Cross window: Windows with one mullion and one transom.
Cruck: A big curved beam supporting both walls and roof of a cottage.
Dripstone: See Hood Mould.
Finial: Top of a canopy, gable or pinnacle.
Hood Mould: Protecting moulding above an arch or a lintel to throw off water (also called dripstone or label).
Inglenook: Bench or seat built in beside a fireplace, sometimes covered by the chimneybreast.
Lintel: Horizontal beam or stone bridging an opening.
Mullion: Vertical post or upright dividing a window into two "lights."
Pier: Strong solid support, frequently square in section.
Pilaster: Shallow pier attached to a wall.
Quoins: Dressed stones at the angles of a building.
Rebate: Continuous rectangular notch cut on an edge.
Spandrel: Triangular surface between one side of an arch and a wall or between two arches.
Strapwork: Sixteenth century decoration consisting of interlaced bands similar to fretwork or cut and bent leather.
Transom: Horizontal bar across the openings of a window.
Wainscot: Timber lining to walls.

Bibliography

Abbott, Wilbur Cortez, ed. *Writings and Speeches of Oliver Cromwell, 1649-53.* Cambridge, Mass.: Harvard University Press, 1929.

Addison, Joseph, and Richard Steele. *Sir Roger de Coverley and Other Essays from The Spectator.* Ed. Zelma Gray. New York: Macmillan, 1899.

Andrews, Francis B. *The Benedictine Abbey of SS Mary, Peter and Paul at Pershore, Worcestershire. Pershore:* Fernside & Martin; Birmingham: Midland Educational Group, 1801.

Ashley, Maurice. *Cromwell's Generals.* New York: St. Martin's Press, 1955.

Baldock, Lieut. Col. T.S. *Cromwell as a Soldier.* London: Kegan Paul, Trench, Trubner, 1899.

Barnard E.A.B. *New Links With Shakespeare.* Cambridge: Cambridge University Press, 1930.

_____. *Notes and Queries Concerning Evesham and the Four Shires.* Evesham: W..Smith, The Journal Press, 1911.

Barrett, Philip, Chrichton, J.D. Johnston, E.I., and Wilson, Marshall, eds. *Pershore, A Short History.* Worcester: Ebenezer Baylis & Son, Ltd., and Trinity Press, 1972.

Barrett, Philip. *The Book of Pershore.* Buckingham: Barracuda Books, 1977.

Barrie, J.M. *Allahakbarries.* Ed. Don Bradman. London: J. Barrie's Publishers, 1899.

Brill, Edith. *Cotswold Ways.* London: Robert Hale, 1985.

Buchan, John. *Oliver Cromwell.* Boston: Houghton, Mifflin, 1934.

Bund, J. Willis. *The Civil War in Worcestershire 1642-1646 and the Scotch Invasion of 1641.* Birmingham and London: Simpkin, Marshall, Hamilton, Kent, 1905.

The Cely Papers. Ed. Henry Elliot McLeen. London: Longmans, Green, 1900.

Chambers, E.K. *William Shakespeare.* 2 vols. Oxford: Clarendon Press, 1930.

Civil War Papers of King Charles, Prince Rupert of the Rhine, and Sir Thomas Fairfax. London: Sotheby's, 1980.

Clarendon, Edward Hyde, Earl. *History of the Great Rebellion.* Ed. W. Dun Macray. 6 vols. Oxford: Clarendon Press, 1938.

Cobbett, William. *Rural Rides.* London: Dent and Sons, 1912.

Cox, David C. *Chronicle of Evesham Abbey.* Evesham: Vale of Evesham Historical Society, 1964.

Cromwell, Oliver. *Letters and Speeches of Oliver Cromwell.* Ed. Thomas Carlyle. 3 vols. London: Methuen and Company, 1904.

Darby H.C. and I.B. Terrett, eds. *The Domesday Geography of Midland England.* Cambridge: Cambridge University Press, 1954.

Drury, Charles R. *Picturesque Broadway.* Cheltenham: S.H. Brookes, 1885.

Eccles, Mark. *Shakespeare in Warwickshire.* Madison: University of Wisconsin Press, 1961.

Evans, Herbert A. *Highways and Byways in Oxford and the Cotswolds.* London: Macmillan & Co. 1900.

Firth, C.H. *Oliver Cromwell.* Boston: Houghton Mifflin, 1934.

Fraser, Antonia. *Cromwell the Lord Protector.* New York: Knopf, 1973.

Gaunt, Peter. *The Cromwellian Gazetteer.* Stroud, Gloucestershire: Alan Sutton and the Cromwell Association, 1987.

Gissing, Algernon. *Broadway: A Village of Middle England.* London: J.M. Dent, 1934.

Goldsmith, Oliver. *The Collected Works.* Ed. Arthur Friedman. 5 vols. Oxford: Oxford University Press, 1966.

Gregory, Edward and Henry Maskell. *Old Country Inns.* Boston: L.C. Page, 1911.

Habington, Thomas. *A Survey of Worcestershire 1560-1647.* Ed. John Amphlett. 2 vols. Oxford: Parker, for the Worcester Historical Society, 1895.

Harrison, William. "A Descripton of England," in *Holinshed's Chronicles.* Ed. Lothrop Withington. Intro. F.J. Furnivall. London: Walter Scott, 1891.

Harnett, Cynthia. *The Wool-Pack.* London: Methuen & Co. 1951.

Herbert, William. *History of the Twelve Great Livery Companies of London.* 2 vols. London: published by the author, 1837.

Hill, Christopher. *God's Englishman.* Weidenfeld and Nicolson, 1970.

————————. *The Century of Revolution.* Wokingham, Van Nostrand Reinhold Co. Ltd. 1980.

————————. *The English Revolution, 1640.* London: Lawrence & Wishart Ltd. 1955.

Hissey, J.J. *Across England in a Dog Cart from London to St. David's and Back.* London: Bentley & Son, 1891.

Houghton, Colin. *A Walk About Broadway.* London: Ian Allen Ltd. 1980.

Jusserand, J.J. *English Wayfaring Life in the Middle Ages.* Trans. Lucy Toulmin Smith. New York: G.P. Putnam's Sons, 1939.

Kenin, Richard. *Return to Albion: Americans in England 1760-1940.* New York: Holt, Rinehart, and Winston, 1979.

Kenyon, M.P. *The Civil Wars of England.* New York: Alfred Knopf, 1988.

Kingsford, Charles Lethbridge, ed. *The Stonor Letters and Papers 1290-1483.* London: Royal Historical Society, 1919.

Leland, John. *The Itinerary of John Leland in or about the Years 1535-1543.* Ed. Lucy Toulmin Smith. London: George Bell & Sons, 1908.

Mason, Carolyn. *Snowshill, a Gloucestershire Village.* Cheltenham: Thornhill Press, 1987.

Massingham, Harold John. *Shepherd's Country.* London: Chapman & Hall, 1938.

May, George. *The History of Evesham.* London: Whittaker, Treacher, 1834.

Morris, John. *The History and Traditions of Middle Hill.* Rotherham: W. Ball, n.d.

Nash, Thomas. *Collections for the History of Worcestershire.* Ed. John Nichols. 2 vols. 1781.

Niblett, J.D.T., and the Rev. William Bazeley. "Royal Badges in Gloucester Cathedral." *Records of Gloucester Cathedral*. Gloucester: 1882. Courtesy of Canon David St. Z. Welander.

Noake, John. *Notes and Queries for Worcestershire*. London: Longman, 1856.

Pevsner, Sir Nikolaus. *Buildings of England: Worcestershire*. Penguin Books, 1968.

Picton, J. Allanson. *Oliver Cromwell: The Man and His Mission*. New York: Cassell, Petter Galpin, 1882.

Pike, G.H. *Cromwell and His Times*. London: T. Fisher Unwin. 1899.

Power, Eileen. *Medieval People*. London: Methuen, 1924.

Power, Eileen. *The Wool Trade in English Medieval History*. Oxford: Oxford University Press, 1942.

Richardson, A.E. *Old Inns of England*. London: B.T. Batsford Ltd., 1934.

Ridley, M.R. *The New Temple Shakespeare*. London: J.M. Dent & Sons Ltd. 1935. *A Midsummer Night's Dream*; *The Merry Wives of Windsor*, *King Richard II*, *The Tempest*, *The Winter's Tale*, *Henry IV, Part 2*.

Russell, Gordon. *Designer's Trade*. London: George Allen & Unwin, 1968.

Russell, Sydney and Gordon Russell. *The Story of an Old English Hostelry*. Broadway: 1914.

Scott, Eva. *Rupert Prince Palatine*. New York: Putnam's Sons, 1899.

Schoenbaum, Samuel. *Shakespeare's Lives*. Oxford: Clarendon Press, 1970.

Steel, Anthony. *Richard II*. Cambridge: Cambridge University Press, 1941.

Stone, Rev. J.S. "Over the Hills to Broadway." Typescript manuscript in LAA, 1893.

Symonds, Richard. *Diary of the Marches of the Royal Army During the Great Civil War*. Ed., from MS in the British Museum, Charles Edward Long. London: Camden Society, 1859.

Thomson, Gladys. *Life in a Noble Household*, 1641-1700. London: Jonathan Cape, 1937.

Thorn, Frank and Carolyn Thorn, Worcestershire eds. *Domesday Book*. Gen. ed. John Morris. Chichester: Phillimore, 1982.

The Story of St. Eadburgha's, Broadway. Gloucester: The British Publishing Company, n.d.

The Torrington Diaries: Containing the Tours through England and Wales of the Hon. John Byng (later Fifth Viscount Torrington) between the years 1782 and 1794. Ed. C. Bruyn Andrews. Intro, John Beresford. 4 vols. London: Eyre & Spottiswoode, 1934-1938.

Trevelyan, G.M. *English Social History*. 4 vols. London: Longmans, Green, 1934.

Verney, Frances Parthenhope, and Margaret M. Verney, eds. *Memoirs of the Verney Family during the Seventeenth Century*. 2 vols. London: Longmans, Green, 1925.

Victoria History of the County of Worcester, 4 vols. *Victoria County History of the Counties of England*. eds. J.W. Willis-Bund and Arthur Doubleday, Vol I; J.W. Willis-Bund and William Page, Vols II-IV. London: A. Constable, 1900.

Whitfield, Christopher. *Shakespeare's Gloucestershire Contemporaries.* Eton, Windsor: Shakespeare Head Press, 1958.

──────────────. *Robert Dover and the Cotswold Games.* London: Henry Sotheran, 1962.

Watson, Bruce. *Bretforton Village.* Evesham: Mintprint, 1990.

Williams, Penry. *Life in Tudor England.* Gen. ed. Peter Quennell. London: B.T. Batsford; New York: G.P. Putnam's Sons, 1964.

Woodforde, James. *The Diary of a Country Parson.* Ed. James Beresford. London: Oxford University Press, 1926.

DIRECTORIES

Billings, M. *Directory and Gazetteer of the City of Worcester.* Birmingham: M. Billings, 1855.

Cassey's Directory. 1860.

Kelly's Directory. 1896, 1904.

Pigot's Directory. 1825-29.

ARCHIVES

Birmingham Library Services (BLS). Sheldon Miscellanea: Barnard (Rees Price) Collection.

Bodleian Library, Oxford. Phillipps Collection: Catalogue of the Topographical Collections and of the Correspondence and Papers of Sir Thomas Phillipps, Bart., 1792-1872, Given to the Bodleian Library, Oxford, by Lionel and Philip Robinson, 1958.

Evesham Library. E.A.B. Barnard Collection (including Broadway Parish Papers and the Evesham Journal).

Gloucester County Record Office (GCRO). Wills and inventories.

International Genealogical Index (IGI).

Lygon Arms Archives (LAA).

Public Record Office, London (PRO).

Shakespeare Birthplace Trust, Stratford-upon-Avon. Broadway Records.

Society of Antiquaries, London. Prattinton Collection (microfilm copy at WCRO).

Thirteenth/Eighteenth Royal Hussars Archives. Records of 13th Light Dragoons.

Worcester County Record Offices (WCRO). Including Acts of Parliament Relating to the County of Worcester, Broadway Census (1841, 1855), Broadway Papers, Broadway Parish Registers, Deeds (including White Hart Deed, WHD), Inventories, Quarter Sessions Records, Wills.

Index

Abberton, 19, 63
Abbot's Grange, xviii, 136
Adderley, William, 60, 90
Agincourt, battle of, 5
Alfred the Great, King, xiv
Allahakbarries, 137
Anderson, Mary, 137, 147-48
Angel, the inn, 61, 93, 98, 116
Anne, Queen, 101, 104
Armada, the Spanish, 41
Art Colony, in Broadway, 136
Atwood, Giles, 101
Averill, Isaac, 97, 100
Aylesbury, 85, 87

Babington, conspiracy v. Queen Elizabeth I, 33, 39
Badsey, 56
Balfour, A.J., 146
Barrington, Douglas J., 160-61, 165-70
Barrie, James, 137
Bateman, C. E., 145
Bath, 91
Bellue, William, 39-41
Berkeley, Justice, 81
Betson, Thomas, 7, 11, 18
Biscoe, Elisha, 60, 90
Black Death, the (plague), 4
Blenheim, battle of, 98
Boleyn, Anne, 18, 121
Botrey, John, Vicar, 12
Bourton, 3, 109
Bowes-Lyon, Lady Maud, 158
Bowes-Lyon, Elizabeth, 158
Bowker, Effie, 157
Bretforton, xiv, xv$n$, 75, 160
Broadway Court, 74-75, 105
Broadway Parish Register, 1532-1710, 151
Brock hampton, 51
Burford, 35, 71-72
Burne-Jones, Edward, 136
Byng, Lord John, xix
Byshop, Robert, Vicar, 19-20

Calais, 8, 10-11
Cambridge, University of, 48, 86n
Campden House, 74
Catherine of Aragon, Queen, 18-19
Cely family, 5-9, 190
Charles I, King, 64-65, 67-76
Charles II, King, 80, 83, 92,

Chaucer, Geoffrey, xviii-xix, 10
Cheltenham, 127, 136-37, 142
Chettle, Anthony, 49
Chettle, Ursula Sambache, 48, 53
Childswickham, 75, 143
Chipping Campden, 3, 30, 34, 71, 91, 143, 152
Chipping Norton, 35, 85-87, 127
Churchyard wall, 13-15, 20, 59, 98
Cirencester, 34
Civil War, 67-87 *passim*, 79, 91,
Clarendon, Edward Hyde, Earl, 69-75
Clemens, Daniel, 97, 193, 109n
Clothiers, 26-27, 43
Clopton, Hugh, 34
Coaches, carriages, travel, 63, 91-92, 103-04, 116, 127, 130, 136
Cobbett, William, 107
Colonies, American, 59, 98, 136
Combe, John, 45, 46n, 47n,
Combe, Mary, 46
Combe, Thomas, 46
Combe, William, the older, 45
Combe, William, the younger, 46
Compton, Abbot, 25, 28, 191-92
Connygree Lane, 35, 37, 104-05
Constable's Accounts, 100-01
Corbett, 97
Cordell, Robert, 138, 142
Cormell, Ann, 99-100
Cormell, Elizabeth, John, Mary, Sarah, 99-100
Cornwallis, Lord, 98, 108n
Coventry, 80
Coverly, 73, 76
Cromwell, Thomas, 33
Cropredy, Battle of, 72
Cromwell, Oliver, 79-87
Cromwell Room, 110,116, 147
Culloden, battle of, 102

d'Abitot, Urse (The Bear), 3-4, 115, 121
Daston, Anne, 19, 26, 36, 40-45, 47, 50
Daston Anthony, 20-26, 34, 47, 191-92
DeBracy, Joan, 121
Defoe, Daniel, 107
Denney, William, 52
Denning, Constance Elizabeth, 157, 162
Dickins, William, Vicar, 21
Domesday Book, xv
Dover, Robert, 47
Dover's Hill Games, 52-53

Doyle, Conan, 137
Drayton, Michael, 52
Drury, Charles, 127, 129-33
Drury, Charles Richardson, 133-38
Drury, Elizabeth Rimmell, 129
Drury, Henry, 129
Drury, Stuart Lloyd, 137-38
Dumbleton, 51
Dunbar, battle of, 79*n*

Eadburga, Princess, xiv, 17
Eadgar, King, xii, xiv, 173
Edgehill, battle of, 67
Edmund, Abbot of Pershore, 2-3
Edward I, King, xvii
Edward II, King, xvii, xxi
Edward III, King, xvii, xx
Edward VI, King, 39*n*
Edward VII, King, 148
Edward VIII (Prince of Wales), 146
Eggesford, HMS, 165
Elgar, Edward, 147
Elizabeth I, Queen, 22, 30, 33, 39-41, 57, 93*n*,
Ellison, family, 196
Elmley Castle, 22*n*, 40, 93
Essex, Earl, 55, 57
Essex, General, 68, 70-71
Evesham, 34, 49, 62, 71-76, 80-87, 109, 116, 127, 142, 144

Fairs, xvii, 17-19
Faulkes, Robert, 12-14, 45
Fea, Allan, 134
Fires, of Stratford, 49-50
Fish Hill, xvi*n*, 75, 98, 104-105
Fleetwood, General, 80-85
Foldbrith, Abbot of Pershore, xiv
Food and drink, xix, 20-24, 61-62, 90-92, 102, 110-11
Ford, Henry, 146, 148, 167
Freeman, A.V., 158
French wars, 115

George III, King, 98, 101, 108*n*
George IV, Prince of Wales, 101-02
Gervase, Abbott of Pershore, 11
Gin Corner, 165
Gissing, Algernon, 8*n*, 74*n*
Glen, Sir Alexander, 82*n*
Gloucester, 81
Gloucester Cathedral, xvii, xxi*n*
Greene, Thomas, 46*n*

Grevel, William, 3, 152
Griffin, Laura, 134
Griffiths, J.W., Vicar, 98, 118
Grocers Company, 58

Habington, Thomas, 33, 36-37, 57, 104
Hailes Abbey, 34
Hall, John, 49, 51
Handy, Robert, 12-14, 45
Harrison, William, Parson, 23-27, 29
Henry III, King, xvii
Henry IV, King, xxii
Henry V, King, xxii
Henry VI, King, 4
Henry VII, King, 7*n*, 11, 18, 30, 39*n*
Henry VIII, King, 17, 26, 33, 39*n*, 191-92
Hensley, Christopher, 132
Highwaymen, 101, 129
Hissey, James John, 134, 138, 142, 146, 197-98
Hoby, Philip, 22*n*, 191-92
Hodge, Jack, 94, 150
Hodges, Phillip, 89-95
Hodges, Ann, and Luke, 94
Hodges Susanna, 89-95
Hollington, Francis, 159, 169
Holmes, Christopher, 100-01, 109*n*, 115
Holmes, Martha, 100, 109*n*, 115
Hubaud, Ralph, 45-46

Inventories: Thomas White, 21-22; Phillip Hodges, 89-92; Giles Lawrence, 117*n*; Sydney Russell, 182*n*
Ireland, 55, 57
James, Henry, 136
James, John, Col., 86
James I, King, 30
James II, King, 93
Jarrett, Charles, 137, 143
John, King, xvii, 34
Johnson, Samuel, Dr., 112
Jonson, Ben, 52

Kingcombe, 160, 162
Kingcombe Plain, 53
Kipling, Rudyard, 146

Lambert, General, 80-81
Lane, Charles Drury, 138, 142
Langston, Anthony, 73
Latimer, Hugh, Bishop, 25

Index   217

Lawrence, Giles, 117, 118*n*
Leland, John, 23*n*, 33-35
Lenthall, William, 83-84
Livery Companies of London, 56-58 *passim*
London, 35*n*, 41, 43, 57-59, 67, 80, 84, 87, 92, 104, 108, 110, 123, 126, 127, 144
Longton (Langatune), xiii
Lygon, "armiger," 4
Lygon, Edward P., 117-127; Frederick, 118; Henry, 117-127; Hugh, 82*n*; Louisa, 120-127; William, Earl Beauchamp, 117-123; William, 82*n*
"Lygon's Arms," 130
Lygon letters, 194-96

Madresfield Court, 82*n*, 117, 121, 123
Mary I, Queen, 36, 39*n*
Mary, Consort to King George V, 158
Melbourne, William Lamb, 2nd Viscount, 122
Mickelton, 53, 143, 174
Middle Hill, 117-18, 127
Midwinter, William, 3, 6, 7
Millet, Francis, 147
Mill Hay, xviii, 137
Milvain, Margaret, 149
Mitchell, James, 98
Molyneux, Robert, 4
Molyneux, Thomas, 124
Montagu, Lord, of Beaulieu, 145-46
More, Sir Thomas, 25
Morris, John, 99*n*, 116, 137
Moreton-in-Marsh, 72, 161
Morris, William, 136
Morse, Sir Arthur, 155, 166, 167

Napoleon, letters of, 119
Naseby, battle of, 76
Nelson, Horatio, Lord, 102
Newbury, battle of, 68
New Model Army, 75
North Cotswold Hunt, 130, 132, 145
Northleach, 3, 7-8*n*, 34

Oddo, Mercian overlord, xiv
Ogilby, John, cosmographer, 79
Oxford, xvi, 48-49, 67-76 *passim*, 134; University of, 33, 102, 160-61
Palmerston, Henry, John Temple, 122
Parry, Thomas and Walter, 60-61, 89-90, 98

Peel, Sir Robert, 122
Pershore, Abbey of, xiii, xiv, xv, 36
Pershore, xiv*n*, xvi, xvii, 35, 70, 135
Phelps, William Law, 100, 116-117
Philip, Prince, Duke of Edinburgh, 168
Phillipps, Sir Thomas, 117-127 *passim*; Elizabeth, 125; Henrietta Molyneux, 125
Phipps, Anne, 98
Phipps, Francis, 20, 93, 98-100
Phipps, John, Thomasine, 98
Pilgrims Way, 7
Porter, Squire, 101-02
Powick, 82
Prior's Manse, xviii
Purser, John, 97, 100

Quarter Sessions Records, 35, 62, 104
Quiney, Adrian and Thomas, 48, 50

Rees Price, Dr., xiv*n*, 70, 151
Richard I, King, the Lion Heart, xvii, 187-89
Richard II, King, xvii, xxi-xxii, 187-89
Ritchie, Kirk, 170, 173-75
Roads, conditions of, 35, 62-63, 103-05
Roose, Mary, 169
Rosetti, Dante Gabriel, 136
Royal mail, 108, 127
Rupert of the Rhine, Prince, 68-73
Russell, Sydney, 41, 141-152
Russell, Gordon, 141-52, 155-63
Russell, Donald, 142-52, 155-63
Russell, Richard, 142, 157-58, 167-68
Russell, Marian Pepler, 161, 168
Russell Room, the, 155, 166
Russell Workshops Ltd., 158

St. Eadburgha, xiv, 71
St. Eadburgha, Church of, xiv, xv*n*, 41, 45*n*, 48, 60, 137
St. John the Baptist, feast of, xvii, 7, 17-19
Salters Company, 58, 89
Sambache, "armiger," 4
Sambache, Elizabeth White, 22
Sambache, Walter, 22, 55-56
Sambache, William, son-in-law to Thos. White, 22, 23-30 *passim*, 41; Sambache, William, "The Elder," 21, 22, 23-30 *passim*, 41, 48-53 *passim*, 64

Sargent, John Singer, 136
Savage, Richard, Stratford Curator, 151
Savage, Walter and William, 46
Savoy, The, 170, 173-75
Severn, Jane Sambache, 22-24, 41
Severn, river, 81
Shakespeare, Judith, 48, 50
Shakespeare, John and Mary, 44-45
Shakespeare, Susanna, 49
Shakespeare, William, 29, 43-52 *passim*
Shaw, G.B., 146
Sheldon, Baldwin, 36
Sheldon, Ralph, 19, 25
Sheldon, family, 68-74
Snowshill, 51, 94, 150-51
Spencer, arrest of, 27; Spencer Cottage, 193, 194, 198
Spetchley (Spikely), 81-82
Spring Hill Estate, 115-127 *passim*
Stalwarts Club, 169
Stanley, John and Elizabeth, 4
Stanway, 34-35, 149; Stanway House, 149
Stanway, Robert, Abbot of Pershore, 12
Staple, merchants of, 5-12 *passim*, 26, 190
Stone, Rev., 135
Stonor family, 3-9 *passim, 190*
Stoneywell, John, Abbot of Pershore, 25, 191-192
Stow-on-the-Wold, 30, 36-37, 73
Stratford, 34, 49, 80, 142
Strelly, Abraham, 48-49
Strelly, Henry, 43, 48-53 *passim*
Sudeley Castle, 40, 70
Swan, the, xxii, 22, 53, 56, 61, 187
Symonds, Richard, 69-74 *passim*

Tate, John, 6, 9
Taylor, Sarah, 99
Taylor, William, 99*n*
Teme, River, 81
Tewkesbury, 34, 68
Theville, M. Aumont, 147
Torrington, John Byng, Fifth Viscount, xix, 107-113
Tower Close, the, 149, 152
Treavis family, 56-59, 61-65 *passim*
Treavis (Travis, Travers, Traves), John the older, 57-59

Treavis, John the younger, 55-76 *passim*
Treavis, Matthew, 57, 59, 60, 89-90
Treavis, Thomas, 57, 59, 60
Treavis, Ursula, 55-65 *passim,* 85-89 *passim*
Tunbridge Wells, 91
Turner, Jim, 144, 197

Upton-upon-Severn, 81

Verney family, 12*n*, 61
Verney, Sir Edmund, 64-65; Mary, 65; Ralph, 64
Victoria I, Queen, 127, 137-38, 142
Vintners Company, 55, 57-58

Wagner, Ronald, 169
Wagons, 104-05
Waller, Sir William, 69-71
Wars of the Roses, 4
Warwick, city, 80; Earls of, xvi, 115
Washington, General George, 98
Waterloo, battle of, 113, 117, 122
Welche, Walter, 26, 205-206
Welcombe, 45-46
Wellington, Duke of, 117, 122, 123*n*
Wells, Thomas, 63
Westerdale, Christopher, 26, 191-192
Westminster Abbey, xx
Westminster Hall, xxii, 5
White Halle (hall), 13
White hart, symbol, xx, xxi, xxii, 201-203
Whyte of Bradway, 3-14
White, Joan, 18-19, 21, 41
White, Thomas, 7, 9, 12-14, 18-30 *passim*, 59
White Ladies Aston, 68, 81
Wickhamford, 63
Willersey, 143
William I, The Conqueror, 3
William and Mary, King and Queen, 93
Williams, Vaughan, 147
Winchcombe, xv, 143; Jack of, 27-28*n*
Woodforde, Parson, 102, 103
Worcester, 35, 39-40, 70, 72, 79-84 *passim*; Worcester Assizes, 99; Worcester, battle of, 79-84; Worcester Cathedral, 70, 83
World War I, 149-150; World War II, 159-161